THE JUSTIFICATION OF THE LAW

⚬⚬⚬ THE JUSTIFICATION OF THE LAW

CLARENCE MORRIS

University of Pennsylvania Press

Philadelphia

Acknowledgments

John Dewey's seminar at Columbia in 1926 and Roscoe Pound's at Harvard in 1931 introduced me to legal philosophy. Derk Bodde took me in hand—late in my middle age and earlier in his—and guided my study of Chinese legal thought; he was, like Mentor, a patient and willing counselor. To these three I am specially indebted.

A fellowship in 1968 at the Center for Advanced Study in the Behavioral Sciences gave me an opportunity to start work on this book. Four chapters are revisions of earlier work and were written in a quiet "studio" at the Center. Other fellows read first drafts of these chapters and made valuable suggestions. A Fulbright grant took me to Cambridge University in 1969. The hospitality of Clare College and Cambridge Law School afforded an opportunity to re-draft another four chapters.

CLARENCE MORRIS
University of Pennsylvania Law School
Philadelphia
Winter, 1971

Contents

Introductory Schema

This foreword is an overview of the book that follows. Like other small-scale maps, it does not depict the local scenery. It is my hope, however, that it will unify the book by expressly relating its various parts.

To a navigator, a chart may be worth a thousand pictures, but charts are not very attractive to some passengers. This abstract foreword perhaps may serve readers better if read as a conclusion, rather than as an introduction; should it seem ponderous before the book has been read, perhaps you should skip it and give it another chance after reading the main body of the book.

JUSTICE

The crux about which this book revolves is a theory of justice. Justice is not the only concern to one justifying law, but it is by far the most important. Stated in its simplest form, my theory of justice is this: the more that law implements the public's genuine and important aspirations, the more just the legal system becomes.

This view resembles Rousseau's theory of the rectitude of the

1

general will; he believed that governmental action was unjust unless it conformed to the general will. Though Rousseau did not stress the point, his system, like mine, declares no identified and specific rule to be eternally just; the general will of any society (like the public's aspirations) is bound to differ from that of any other society; the general will may also change from time to time.

Rousseau's procedure for discerning the general will calls for assemblies at which the populace discusses and adopts rules for its governance. Legislation by town meeting is not feasible for formulating the policies of complicated, industrial societies. The only practical course for implementing our public aspirations is delegation of the job to public servants—and, to some extent, to nongovernmental elites—who are obliged to seek out the public's genuine aspirations as best they can.

Though some public aspirations are obvious (e.g., for high quality drinking water), some emerging but still inchoate aspirations of first importance are not easily discerned and understood. Polling is illsuited when it evokes only superficial answers. Unstructured evidence of public attitudes is easily misinterpreted. The public's aspirations are not the same as widely held desires for individual gratifications; public aspirations are social, deep-seated, unselfish, and nonexploitative.

The abstract noun *justice* is best understood as denoting a congeries of justices; *justice* should not be thought of as connoting enduring inherent characteristics of just law, such as "fairness," "equality," "the right reason of the Gods," "consonance with natural law," and so forth.

Since just laws are adopted in a body politic at a time and place, each may thereafter become more just or less just than it first was; each may remain timely and just or become obsolete and unjust.

Since just laws implement the public's aspirations, justice can be realized only when there exists a public capable of aspiring. When a legal system responds consciously only to the promptings of a small upper class, many of its laws may be unjust, and those laws that happen to be just are only accidentally so. When the bulk of a people are so undereducated and so overworked that they have neither the ability nor the energy to hope for meliorating social change, they, in fact, are not likely to entertain any public aspirations, and therefore they have no capacity to be ruled by a system of just laws. Justice, so defined, has only begun to emerge in modern times; until the humanized public is greatly expanded our capacity for justice will remain very limited.

Nongovernmental elites sometimes exercise powers much like lawmaking, for example, collective bargainers in the automobile industry. When these powers are used to thwart the public's aspirations, they produce injustice which is as bitter as that flowing from corrupt legislation or wrongheaded judicial decisions. These elites are therefore not always acting "privately." Public toleration of their power implied by their position obliges them to implement some of the public's aspirations.

Much law, of course, is neither unjust nor just. Governmental institutions are ongoing and sometimes must choose between alternatives none of which is responsive to existing public aspirations. Sometimes then the lawmakers take the lead by imposing a norm, at a time when the need for that norm has not yet been perceived by the public. If and when the public develops aspirations in accord with or in conflict with the previously adopted law, that law becomes just or unjust.

❧

Justice cannot be produced by experts who use only science and technology. Once lawmakers discern a public aspiration, but do not know how they should implement it, they may, of course, turn to scientific experts for advice on techniques. When lawmakers suppose they know how a public aspiration should be realized, technologists may be able to warn them against dangerous side effects which should be taken into account.

Three kinds of information justify the law: (1) knowledge of the public's aspirations; (2) acquaintance with possible means for implementation; (3) data on costs, both in dollars and side effects, of alternative ways of proceeding. Science and technology may assist the maker of just laws by presenting data on any of these three factual areas.

The conclusions of pure science, however, do not of themselves call for social action; the scientist, as a citizen, may want to understand and advance the common weal; as a scientist, however, he looks only for scientific truth. Truth is not validated by public acceptance. The public, insofar as it understands the discoveries of science, tends to believe its conclusions. Scientists, nevertheless, do not dismiss discoveries that turn out to be unpopular; scientists austerely and aloofly reject nonscientific demands that call on them to distrust what they know.

If a corps of scientists were to publish, once and for all, complete data on the aspirations of a widely affranchised public, and the costs of alternative means of implementing them, the making of just laws would be relatively easy. The hypothesis is, of course, ridiculous; data on society's aspirations will always be incomplete, and what we know steadily becomes outmoded. Some political theorists have said, however, that lawmakers should advance justice pragmatically—that is, by trying to foresee all the probable consequences of any legal course of action. A pragmatic attitude is, of course, one aspect of adjusting the law. A lawmaker who knows how a proposal and its alternatives will work soon comes to know what alternative he prefers. His personal preference as such, however, cannot determine how a public servant should discharge his stewardship. When he has no suspicion that the public's aspirations differ from his own he has no reason to discriminate between his predilections and his responsibilities. But once he knows that his own preference is idiosyncratic, or that the public holds no aspirations at all on the issue, his own partialities are no guide to justice.

The public's genuine aspirations cannot always be tested by referenda. How the public votes on a proposal, say, to pledge the public credit to finance a stadium, may have little to do with its genuine aspirations; many voters may not seriously consider an issue before they enter the voting booth, and once therein they may act on whim. An opportunity to vote for or against a concrete proposal suppresses all the other alternatives.

Ongoing popular customs should not be equated with the public's aspirations. A custom may outlive both its usefulness and its appeal;

a custom often starts accidentally and persists without being questioned. A new law running counter to an old custom can, of course, conflict with the public's dearly held aspirations and be both unenforceable and unjust. Sometimes, however, witless customs—such as giving children Fourth of July firecrackers—are struck down by statutes, and the resulting new law is more just than the old custom. Were the growth of justice geared entirely to the slow growth of custom, too many injustices would persist.

Some think that the inhabitants of the western world, as it is now structured, are too suppressed to aspire to a sound society and that true justice will emerge only after their liberation. Herbert Marcuse, for one, calls for revolution ousting the reign of corporate capitalism. Modern market economy, he says, has disabled us from entertaining our inborn, natural aspirations. Marcuse characterizes the public's present goals as misoriented and solidified until liberating revolution naturalizes the public's consciousness.

Marcuse prophesies that the people, once liberated, will intuitively sense society's needs; society when freed will become sweetly considerate and will effect mergers of poetry and science, beauty and technology, law and justice. This new society will thrive in a sensuous, aesthetic ethos.

John Stuart Mill, more than a century ago, voiced concern about society's monolithic suppressions of innovative thought, speech, and action. Some fresh diversities, he said, demonstrate to society that it should hold new and sounder aspirations. Mill's case for liberty was, like Marcuse's case for liberation, calculated to release men from the molds of conformity into which law and morals pressed them.

Mill, however, was no revolutionary; he argued for peaceful nonconformity only insofar as dissenters do not transgress important rights of others. Mill's case for tolerance was based on the likelihood that free thought, free speech, and unmolested idiosyncracy would, some of the time, point out how thoughtful reform might produce a more satisfying and, therefore, more just society. Freedom was equated by Mill to scientific experiment; both freedom and scientific experiment sometimes go awry; both can, however, throw useful light on the reasoned way to a happier world.

Marcuse prophesies that intuited, sound values, once liberated, will permeate society; he holds that society is incapable of moving toward true justice until freed by violent revolution. Mill puts his trust solely in man's corrigibility—his capacity to improve society by deliberation and rationality.

Mill and Marcuse are both wrong. Though there have been times past when destructive revolution seemed the only way to loosen the bonds of despotic and repressive government—for example, the Russian and French revolutions—it is hard to believe that society is so intransigently contaminated that only through bloody rebellion can we make the radical advances needed for our common weal. Mill's unremitting stress on rationality as the means for improving man's lot would lead to the rule of philosopher-kings, justified in implementing their aspirations for society, whether or not their aspirations accorded with the public's. Such is not the proper role of the public's servants.

Marcuse overstresses the importance of our present and future emotional sets. We are not now paralyzed; we will not become capable of righting our world solely as a result of heightened aesthetic sensuousness. Aspirations, however, do come from the heart as well as the head; the worth of each man as a man is an article of faith and not a scientific invention. We should learn from Marcuse that every aspiration has an emotional dimension. We should not allow Mill's more congenial—and extremely important—stress on rationality to induce us to believe that the improvement of justice is produced by only factual discovery, spurred on by the free expression in words and deeds of men who by use of their reason have rediscovered suppressed truths.

RATIONALITY

Though reason alone is not sufficient to make a legal system more just, the rational aspects of the justification of the law are important. A discussion of the relation between the norms of rhetoric, deduction, and induction, as they are set out in texts on logic on the one hand, and sound reason in judicial processes on the other, throws light on the norms of justifying the law.

Logic falls short of supplying criteria of sound judicial thought because logic does not concern itself with forensics; that is, logic's norms are applicable to judicial decisions only after both a satisfactory rule of law and an acceptable statement of a proposition of fact are accepted. Logic may not deal with the social considerations bearing on the formation of just legal principles or with the burdens that marshall the proof of facts. That is, the elementary logic books focus principally on the *validity* of implications or inferences—on the conclusions that can be properly drawn once the grounds for reasoning are established. The major problems of judicial thought usually are solved before logically valid operations are begun. Before a judge or juror can use decisive reasoning conforming to the rules of logic he must already have in hand both the proper interpretation of the applicable law and the permissible statement of the facts of the case.

Rhetorical errors are irrational inferences, slyly induced and uncritically accepted. Invalid deductions are non sequiturs. Erroneous inductions erect generalizations on either insufficient or nonsupporting data. When these irrationalities occur in judicial process, the resulting decision is, of course, unjustified.

Typical of the rules of rhetoric is the one that frowns on attacking a man's proof by attacking him, rather than the argument or evidence he puts forward. A jury should not turn against a black prosecuting attorney and, as a result, acquit a guilty white defendant. Sometimes, however, only by pointing out a prosecutor's excess zeal can a defense counsel call attention to the prosecutor's failure to prove guilt beyond a reasonable doubt; this legitimate defense tactic is not calculated to sway the jury by an appeal to irrelevant emotions; the tactic is, on the contrary, calculated to insulate the jury from the prosecutor's irrelevant fire and thereby allow them to make a cool appraisal of the proof before them. The forensic occasion may legitimate a legal argument formally at odds with classical rhetoric.

Given a just common law rule and given proven facts to which that rule properly applies, subsumption of the case under the rule produces, of course, a logical and a just decision. A common law rule, however, grows out of earlier decisions. Synthesizing common law decisions and thereby arriving at a traditional rule is a common practice of judges, lawyers, and text writers. Insofar as all of the cases supporting the rule pose tangible problems in justice and receive identically just treatment, the logical induction solidifying past individual experiences into a general rule serves convenience and tends to advance justice when a new case of the same sort arises and is dealt with in a routine manner.

Common law judges have, for example, long honored many rules of law on landlord and tenant. One of these rules, presumably just, requires those landlords who rent parts of a building to different tenants to use due care in maintaining the common passageways. The decisions for claimants out of which this rule emerged compensated them for injuries caused by slippery floors, collapsing ceilings, dark stairways, and the like. When electric lights came into use, the courts saw no reason to distinguish between an injury caused by a fall on a stairway darkened by neglect to replace a burned-out light bulb and a similar earlier case of neglect to replace a worn-out gas mantle.

Suppose, however, a court is asked to extend this rule and thereby compensate a tenant beaten and raped in a common passageway in consequence of the landlord's neglect to take measures to exclude marauders. If the rule justly applies to this case, the justice does not flow entirely from the meaning of the old rule, and the decision is not just another datum evincing the correctness of the old generality. The analogy between the facts of the old cases and the facts in the new one seems at first glance to suggest that justice may lie in extending the rights established by the old rule to the novel proof in the new case by holding that the just meaning of the old rule covers a kind of injury not heretofore contemplated. This suggestion, even though based on the rationality of the norms of deduction and induction, can be logically valid only if the suggestion is accepted on extralogical, juristic grounds. If the novel injury justly becomes an instance subsumable under the old rule, this result is logically valid only because the upshot is an implementation of the public's aspirations. If the new resulting burden on land-lords might push up the rents of a class of tenants who can least afford to pay an increase, it might be sounder policy to solve the problem some other way.

❧

General rules of law are, of course, sometimes enacted by legisla-tures. It goes without saying that justice, as I define it, emanates from enacted law only insofar as enactments implement the public's aspirations. Statutes that are just when enacted may obsolesce and become unjust unless revised.

Judges, in our system of separation of powers, are obliged to respect and effectuate the intendment of constitutional statutes. Constitutional statutes are not likely to be patently unjust, but if a valid enactment is unjust, the courts are, nevertheless, obliged to apply it whenever it is genuinely applicable, leaving to the legisla-ture the responsibility for such injustices, else the courts usurp the legislature's prerogative. Equally important, courts are bound to respect the limits of the intendment of a statute; they should not extend the ambit of applicability beyond the intendment, else they assume legislation where none truly exists and, as a result, shirk their own responsibilities that inhere in judicial lawmaking.

When a legislature does forward a policy by enactment, the courts have often been emboldened to forward that same policy in other ways. For example, a criminal statute, silent on civil liability, often motivates a court to hold that conduct in violation of that statute harming a private individual is negligent in a civil action for dam-ages. Since this ruling is not an application of the statute, the court uttering it is responsible for its justice.

Most of the enacted law currently in force in the Western world stems from an upsurge of legislation that started in the first years of the nineteenth century, and such law has steadily increased in volume and importance ever since.

Kings, in earlier times, often promulgated ukases, and philoso-phers recognized the virtues of proclaimed law long before the modern legislation burgeoned. The nineteenth-century groundswell of enactments was, however, inspired at least in part by several eighteenth-century philosophers. Their rationales were, in sum, the following:

1.   Enactment of rules of law stabilizes and regularizes property and contract rights and so promotes domestic tranquillity, industry, and commerce.

2.   A legislature enacting an abstract general rule is likely to allot burdens less arbitrarily than a court; a judge applying predetermined enacted law is not likely to give unjust effect to his own irrelevant prejudices.

3.   Legislative lawmaking is likely to be more responsive to popular desires than is judicial lawmaking.

4.   Law stated deliberately as general principle can be more carefully adopted than law declared *ad hoc* while a particular case awaits decision.

5.   Since a court decides only the narrow issues presented by the case before it, a judicial change in the law is often fully effected only after many claims happen to be filed. Legislative changes in the law can be smoother, immediately effective, clearer, and more timely.

6.   Enacted law can be compactly codified, and therefore can be readily available to guide civil and commercial transactions.

Responses to these eighteenth-century precepts are still going on apace; new statutes are enacted; old ones are revised. Each American state has, for example, a penal code, in which the various crimes are expressly defined. These delineations of offenses are usually clear enough to estop trial judges from extemporizing on the ambit of legal guilt. Another example is the enactment by fifty states of the Uniform Commercial Code; as a result of this large-scale codification, the laws of business transactions have become more available, certain, and uniform. The courts are, of course, constantly dealing with problems of statutory interpretation in borderline cases. Statutes will never eliminate all uncertainties; nevertheless, well-drafted enactments do narrow uncertainties in the law.

Modern legislators, however, are seldom motivated by a wish to realize the benefits of legislation promised by the eighteenth-century philosophers. New statutes are usually put forward either to strike down injustice entrenched in old law or to satisfy new needs for justice never before dealt with by law. The common law had, for example, so limited recoveries compensating the victims of work injuries that in every state the legislature has enacted industrial accident laws that are both procedurally and substantively more just than was the common law.

The eighteenth-century proponents of enacted law were concerned with the perfectibility of men in society as they knew it. They thought of good law as law that properly regulated the conduct of the habitants of the state. To them, the laws of good government dealt effectively—and without tyranny—with little else than threats of disorders, that is, war, crime, ouster of property owners, nonperformance of contracts, and so on. The eighteenth-century legal philosophers did not cast government in the role of dynamic developer of society through law. Therefore they did not foresee a more organic development of social justice through law, as evidenced by public school codes, low-cost housing and slum clearance laws, unemployment compensation statutes, and so on.

Of course there is a modern need for the promulgation and application of rules and regulations by specialist-experts. The complexity of the times has given rise to much administrative law, put forward by legislatively authorized expert bodies, and interpreted and enforced largely by arms of those administrative bodies. The eighteenth-century philosophers could not have dreamed of the need for justice produced by implementing the modern expanding aspirations of a more educated and chary public. Though private elites and the judiciary have wider roles in meeting current demands for justice, the main burden of trying to implement the public's aspirations is borne by legislators and administrators.

Judicial lawmaking, nevertheless, will no doubt continue importantly to be looked to for advances in justice, as it has recently, for example, in enlarging the scope of manufacturers' liabilities for harm resulting from dangerous defects in their products.

Europeans, long accustomed to "complete" codes of law, are

likely to be critical of the common law. One of the most respected of the critics was Max Weber, a legally trained patriarch of sociology. He insisted that decisions reached by judicial process in areas not covered by enacted law are irrational. Only systems following the Roman tradition of codified law, said Weber, are rational.

Weber divided rational legal decisions into two classes:

1. A decision is "substantially rational" when it follows from applying a statute that was passed to effectuate ethical, utilitarian, or political goals.
2. A decision is "formally rational" when based on a statute that was produced by a legislature using analytical, systematic, legal reasoning. The traditions of both legislation and judicial decision, Weber believed, inevitably press toward a predominantly legalistic system of deciding legal issues, and therefore a system that is mostly formally rational.

Benjamin Nathan Cardozo also depicted the bulk of common law decisions, even though they are not made by applying enacted rules of law, as highly formalistic; most common law judgments result from purely analytic reasoning leading to foregone conclusions; and this process promotes orderly and impartial judging. Only a small percentage of cases receive more than routine analysis and induce judges to indulge in more creative and less channeled reasoning. The way of dealing with problem cases most congenial to Cardozo he called "the method of sociology," by which he meant filling gaps in a legal system with an eye on widely shared values; he seemed, then, to favor the reduction of the fluidities of the common law in ways that will implement the public's aspirations—a thesis which, of course, I find quite gratifying.

Weber de-dignified the "creative" activites of common law judges by calling them "khadi" decisions, by which he means decisions based on a judge's notions on ethics, politics, or social goals. Weber believed that the hope for social improvement as a result of judge-made law is vain, because legislators and judges will inevitably suppress impulses to reform the law and retreat to formal, abstract legal reasoning; he foresaw that the response to the growth of technology will be an enactment of complicated, formally rational statutes, which will virtually replace the common law in Anglo-American jurisdictions. Formally rational statutes are bound to be legalistically applied.

Weber correctly foresaw the growth of enacted law. American legislators have responded to technology in various ways. Technologists have greatly affected the specificity of rules of law and rules of administrative agencies. Trucks on highways must, for example, not exceed stated dimensions, must carry flares to be set out at specified times and places. Foods and drinks must not be sweetened with cyclamates. Boxcars must have automatic couplers conforming to stated specifications. This sort of particularization has reduced judicial discretion and will continue to reduce it more and more. American legislation has, however, generally purported to bring about social, rather than logical, change; as such it is, in Weber's classification, "substantively" rather than "formally" rational. Judicial application of legislation in contemporary America has tended toward fidelity to the intendment of statutes. This fidelity to ends-in-view, when the statute is substantively rational, usually, then, produces substantially rational decisions. Such fidelity often results from a routine reading of statutes in obviously clear cases. Sometimes, however, more sophistication is called for, and fidelity is not the result of simplistic, logical thought.

Cardozo's "method of sociology" does not involve statutory interpretation, it is a method of deciding common law problem-cases affording, in Cardozo's view, occasions on which judges properly implement the public's aspirations. Of course common law judges had for centuries sporadically done just what Cardozo advocated. His words were descriptive, as well as evocative; since their publication, however, American judges have increasingly seized opportunities to attune the common law to widely shared values. Judges have also more candidly articulated their authority to deal with social factors affecting their decisions; they are nowadays unlikely to mask substantial justice under purely formal reasoning.

Cardozo championed only the *authority* of judges to adapt the common law to the public's aspirations; he did not say that judges were *obliged*, in proper cases, to update the common law's justice.

I do not hold that the common law should be revised whenever a judge feels that he can make it more just. Judicial innovation once made and then repudiated may both be disruptive and bring the courts into disrepute; as a result, some judges may tend to turn away from sound opportunities to innovate. However, a court that benevolently implements its own idiosyncracies, rather than the public's aspirations, is likely to feel it must do an about-face when its personnel changes. And a court that alters common law in hopes of more justice, and thereafter discovers it has paid too great a price in unjust side effects, may or may not know what to do next.

The judge's *obligation*, then, to improve the common law is limited. It is wider than the obligation to act creatively when the common law is silent or ambiguous. Many contemporary American courts have on occasion held that a clearly established common law doctrine is unjust and have altered it. The boundaries of the judicial obligation to improve the common law, however, are not yet well perceived; the ambit of the obligation should be better defined than it has been, so that the obligation will coincide with the occasions on which judges can properly conclude that it is their duty to implement a public aspiration.

Though judicial invention of new justices is narrowly limited, nevertheless, judge-made justice has been significant, and promises to become even more important.

CULTURE

The character or tone of a society affects its values. The ethos in which men live plays a part in determining their aspirations. Lawmaking is a response to felt needs, and legislators and judges are tenants-in-common, along with the rest of their society, in the culture of their time and place. Though logic and the principles of sound legal reasoning are norms applicable to all societies, each local public's aspirations inevitably differ in some details, and therefore justice will also differ somewhat from place to place. One way to appreciate culture's influence on justice is to examine an ethos different from our own.

The law of imperial China was virtually untouched by Western influences until late in the nineteenth century. Chinese law was first codified about two thousand years ago. Copies of the T'ang code (653 A.D.) and the codes that followed after it are all still available. The discussion that follows is largely based on a group of Ch'ing dynasty cases, all of which were decided around 1800 A.D.

Chinese codes were not drafted with an eye to promoting civil liberties or even-handedness, articulating the common man's legal wisdom, or facilitating commerce and industry. Chinese codes were intended mainly to set exactly suitable punishment for each of many narrowly defined crimes.

Human order (thought the ancient Chinese) was imbedded in and a part of nature. Human misconduct, not properly requited by proper punishment, they thought, could cause floods, droughts, and other natural catastrophes. To avoid these disasters, codifiers defined many crimes and affixed a single punishment for each crime defined; since the punishments set were thought to be exactly suitable for every instance of crime, usually each definition was couched in very narrow terms, so that every violation of one statute would be equally reprehensible. As time went on the idea that unpunished crimes might bring on natural catastrophes was almost, though not entirely, forgotten. When the Ch'ing code was drafted in 1740, nevertheless, it followed the ancient style of highly specific definitions of crimes, each calling for a suitable, invariable penalty.

"Reasonable" interpretations of these statutes made by Chinese judges inevitably reflected the attitudes that actuated the Chinese draftsmen who codified the law. When, for example, the terms of a statute called for a small penalty, that statute was obviously not intended to cover a serious crime, and vice versa.

Other strands of the Chinese ethos had impact on drafting and interpreting sections of the code. Chinese attitudes toward status, the importance and structure of the family, filial piety, the basis for distinguishing between various kinds of capital punishments, the significance of the calendar—attitudes quite different from our occidental attitudes—were bound to color the way in which Chinese wrote and read their enacted law.

An outlander who is not acquainted with the Chinese ethos is likely to mislead himself into believing that Chinese magistrates held little respect for enacted law. Westerners who look on Chinese magistrates as whimsical often have themselves misjudged the intendments of the codifiers, intendments which were more readily grasped by the acculturated magistrates.

Perhaps the Chinese system of finely adjusted penalties should be viewed as an example of Weber's "formal rationality"—a system of abstract and technical rules, legalistically applied. In this view, the draftsmen of the Ch'ing code archaistically undertook the redevelopment and elaboration of an ancient agglomeration of taboos and a technical gradation of punishments, and the magistrates, caught up in slavish fidelity to enacted law, did a purely formal job of applying technicalities.

Though Weber's "formal rationality" is probably part of all post-tribal legal systems, nevertheless, the two millennia of Chinese efforts to punish crimes befittingly may not have run counter to a public aspiration of the Chinese; the Chinese purists were, therefore, for their society not so legalistically formal as they seem to us. Insofar as their punishments were, in ancient times, thought to preserve and restore natural harmony, and therefore to prevent or moderate natural calamities, the system must have appealed to the habitants of a subcontinent populated mostly by farmers who lived in dread of floods and drought. In the Han dynasty (206 B.C.–220 A.D.) the aims of the law probably reflected the shared hopes of the thinking public and did not disturb the less reflective common people. A system thought to assign befitting punishments for crimes could continue to be responsive to the public's aspirations even after the motivation that first produced the system had waned. Most people recoil from the imposition of overly severe punishments. Widespread satisfaction with a criminal code thought to impose suitable punishments is not hard to understand.

The culture of farmers differs from the ethos of nomadic shepherds. Farming Chinese thought of themselves, not as nature's masters, but as stationed participants in nature's process of production of rice and millet. Yields were improved by good cultivation, but inevitably fluctuated because nature indulged in vagaries over which tillers had little control.

Flock raisers, too, have good and bad years. They are, however, players of roles more active and less localized than the parts of farmers; they move their flocks out of harm's way; they milk; they control mating, fattening, and so on. Those who in the Psalms celebrated the Lord as their shepherd also read in the first chapter of Genesis that God said unto men, "[R]ule the fish of the sea, the birds of the sky, and all the living things that creep on earth." The Chinese believed that fish, birds, animals, and men were all part of the same natural order; they did not think, however, that beasts and trees could disrupt that order; only men could jangle cosmic harmony. Chinese legal punishments were visited on the human dregs of society to requite their misdeeds and so preserve the natural order. Law came into operation after the fact of wrongdoing; as such, it was a purgative and did not enjoy the prestige of the norms of propriety, which were formulated by the sages, studied by the elite, and generally honored as righteous.

The difference between these two points of view is illustrated by attitudes toward sex-reversals in animals, such as, for example, cocks laying eggs. As late as the fifteenth century, Westerners were indicting, trying, convicting, and punishing these wayward birds for violating the natural law. Natural creatures, thought Westerners, owed duties to God, and man as God's surrogate was obliged to enforce those duties. The Chinese looked on these queer phenomena as portents of greater natural disorder about to happen. The egg-laying cock was an omen, not a miscreant; human misconduct had disturbed the natural order and unless proper steps were taken to requite men's crimes, floods or droughts were on their way.

Modern science and technology depict the regularities of nature, and most Westerners in modern times have relaxed their concern with *normative* natural law and turned to learning about the *existential* laws of nature. Nature is not, in science's view, right or wrong; natural phenomena are just what they are. So in the West prosecution of beasts and trees has stopped and nature no longer owes duties which must be enforced by men; since man is nature's master he has never had any duties toward nature. Nowadays, then, Westerners think of legal relations as one form of human relations; legal duties are owed to men by men.

Comparatively recently some anomalies have developed in Western legal attitudes toward beasts and trees. Now, for example, we legally protect animals against cruelty and species against extinction. Public awareness of catastrophes which pollution can bring is currently swelling, creating attitudes on ecology which resemble the Chinese posture toward nature; many public servants and private elites are searching for ways of implementing the public's new ecological aspirations. Progress toward solutions of our environmental problems can be underpinned by considering men's activities as part of the natural order. Nonhuman aspects of that order should be thought of as at least presumptively valuable in themselves. If, for exmple, we clean up our campsites, not only out of considerateness for future campers, but also because we think of the campsite itself as having a right to be clean, our obligation will be more urgent and better honored. Were this example expanded so that we all tended to hold a general presumption in favor of the natural we would move more unquestioningly and surely toward an ecologically sound world.

SUMMATION

This book deals with three aspects of the justification of the law —justice, reason, and acculturation.

Up to now the world's capacity for creating justice has been small. Justice (defined as the realization of the public's aspirations through law) is not a static external measure that can be known introspectively by those who enact law, decide cases, or design social arrangements. Man's capacity for justice does not flow from divine reason or divine revelation. Men enjoy justice steadily and by design only when they live in a society that affords opportunities to all its habitants to develop their capacity to form aspirations for their society. Even such a society will not enjoy justice unless social goals are shared widely, and unless public servants are ready and able to implement the public's aspirations. Since down through history large numbers of adults have had neither adequate access to learning nor reasonable amounts of repose, attempts to create justice have been too narrowly based. Though in modern Western societies the numbers, education, and repose of the public have greatly increased, we have made only a beginning. Our hope should be for societies much more just than any that have ever existed.

Justice is, of course, arrived at in a process in which one major ingredient is reason. The legal reasoning used to produce justice has its special characteristics. Since legal reasoning is calculated to implement aspirations, and since aspirations involve the heart as well as the head, justice cannot be a product of pure reason untainted with emotional desires and heart-felt satisfactions.

Of course public servants will know neither all the public's aspirations nor how all known public aspirations can be well implemented. And since aspirations and knowledge of the ways of implementing them are always in flux, the justices of one time or place are not necessarily the justices of other times and places. Many of the same public aspirations, however, are held in virtually all societies over long periods of time; some justices, therefore, seem— and practically are—universal and eternal. Beware, nevertheless, of the past. Far more justice is within our grasp in the future.

Our society's justice can be another society's clumsy legalistics, because of their cultural differences. Justice, therefore, is not always exportable. Difficult as it may be to know our own public aspirations, it may be much more difficult to know the values of those whose ethos differs greatly from ours. There should be, however, aspirations for world justice. Some values seem held widely, —for example, the condemnation of genocide. Universal public aspirations are the basis for justices the world over.

Chapter 1

Law, Justice, and the Public's Aspirations*

The twin themes developed in the following pages are these:

1. Absent law, there can be no justice.
2. Justice is "done" (i.e., intentionally produced) only when lawmakers act as the public's agents. When law is imposed upon the public by lawmakers acting as though they were principals it is just only by accident.

1. Law can, of course, be unjust. Justice, however, is realized only through good law. "Just" is an adjective that modifies only the noun "law." This point may be made clearer by two analogies. Literary merit is a quality only of good literature. Often poems are mediocre, dramas are piffling, novels are trash, and so on. There can be no literary merit, however, unless literature is written; only when poets, dramatists, novelists, and other litterateurs produce is literary merit possible. Pulchritude describes

---

* An earlier discussion of this topic by me appeared in *Nomos VI: Justice,* Friedrich and Chapman, eds. (New York: Atherton Press, 1963).

21

some people. Many people are plain, but pulchritude cannot exist on unpopulated, unvisited islands. Literary merit can be thought about, analyzed, and discussed to some extent without focusing on specific literary works; just as pulchritude can be considered with no one person in mind. Similarly some aspects of the nature of justice can be searched for without focusing on particular statutes, single judicial decisions, or specific legal obligations. But were there a society without concrete law, in that society there would likewise be no concrete justice. When the word "justice" is used in other senses, as in "a just employer," the use is metaphorical except when the employer's justice results from obedience to just law. The existence of law is not the only prerequisite of justice. Good literature could not be composed unless there were language, and, similarly, good atomic energy law could not be enunciated before the advent of modern physics. 2. Though imposed law can accidentally be just, it is not intentionally so. A Machiavellian ruler's pretended concern for his subjects or a Confucian emperor's wish to preserve natural harmony may happen to coincide with a realization of some of the public's aspirations. But such felicity is not the object of either Machiavellian or Confucian law—both of which are imposed on a public by its master, rather than effected for the public by its agent. Justice is intentionally done only when the lawmaker intends to serve the public and advances those of its aspirations that are appropriately furthered by lawmaking.

Many human aspirations are not, of course, public aspirations; a man's hopes for his own success in trade, office, or profession are for himself as an individual. Many of the public's desires are not grave enough to be called aspirations. The public wants clean streets—a hoped-for nicety; the public wants safe streets—a serious aspiration.

Conscientious lawmakers do not always understand the public's aspirations, and even when they do they often do not know how to implement them. But the public's aspirations do, in fact exist; even though some are inchoate and hard to formulate.

Few of us could state precisely even the most fully formed and stable public aspirations; nearly all thoughtful people, however, have at least a sketchy notion of their ambit. There are widely held importunate desires not worthy enough to be called public aspirations; they are too selfish, too unreasonable, too much rooted in widespread mental illness. The public's genuine aspirations are deep-seated, reasonable, and nonexploitative. They are nearly always in flux but are relatively stable; change in them is usually deliberate and slow. New public aspirations arise in response either to social change or to development of new human capacities and capabilities. The realization of some known aspirations must await the development of techniques; we often know what we want before we know how to get it. Codification of the public's aspirations is difficult for five reasons: (1) No one is experienced and wise enough to do the job. (2) Some of the public's aspirations are, as yet, uneasy, vague strivings, which can be appreciatively understood and expressed only by prescient experts. (3) Techniques used to investigate the public's aspirations are still crude and often misleading. (4) Membership in the aspiring public expands and changes. (5) Though the public's aspirations are relatively stable, at any one time at least some are significantly in flux.

One more introductory point: We should not say that justice is realized only through law unless we are willing to define law broadly. In this essay I use the word "law" to mean more than statutes and ordinances; it includes both adjudicated decisions of cases and social recognitions of those legal obligations that exist without governmental prompting. I do not, however, really quarrel with others who define law more narrowly; I could use any of their more restrictive definitions; but to do so would probably complicate my kind of discussion of the nature of justice.

LEGISLATION

Legislators can be lazy, mistaken, stupid, capricious, selfish, and tyrannical; both their enactments and their failures to legislate, therefore, can be unjust. Even when they are well qualified and well meaning, they may become unmindful that they are only the

public's agents and not its master; on such occasions they may implement values of their own that differ from the public's aspirations
and, as a result, act unjustly. Capable legislators who conscientiously try to keep to their proper place may be hampered by awk-
ward procedures and lean resources; the best legislators, therefore,
sometimes are thwarted and may default or err.

In spite of all of these impediments to just legislation, several
great legal philosophers locate a font of justice in lawgivers' promulgated rules. All of these savants, of course, know that enacted law
can be unjust law. Aristotle, for example, told us that "conventional
justice" comes into being when a lawgiver announces new rules on
matters previously indifferent.[1] He qualified this, however, by saying that such enactments prescribe law rightly only insofar as the
law has been rightly enacted, and "not so well if it has been made
at random."[2] Hobbes, who sought, for political purposes, to promote unquestioned obedience to a powerful peace-keeping lawmaker, said that the laws of a properly selected ruler cannot be
unjust, but he avoided foolishness by saying that legislation can be
both iniquitous[3] and inept, which comes to much the same thing.[4]
Hume, who sought to promote the stability of property and the
sanctity of contracts by insisting on the strict application of a system of prestated legal rules, nevertheless implied that individual
rules may be poor artifices standing in need of amendment or
repeal.[5] These three, then—and of course others—saw justice not
existing in fact before legislation as justice was "done" by enactments and their aftermaths.

We must not, however, be unmindful that for other great jurists
the font of justice is anterior to enactment. Cicero, in his third book
of *The Laws*, illustrated justice by describing the Roman system of
public law; he believed, nevertheless, that the justice of that, or
any other, system exists in the right reason of the gods.[6] Earthy
Montesquieu, in an untypical mood, said, similarly, "Before laws
were made there were relations of possible justice. To say that there
is nothing just or unjust but what is commanded or forbidden by
positive laws, is the same as saying that before describing a circle
all radii were not equal."[7]

Since legislation should be, and usually is, a deliberative process, it must indeed begin before it ends; since its beginning has crucial antecedents it is never an uncaused spontaneous event. While, of course, good reasoning's eternal qualities have something to do with, for example, the justice of contemporary social security legislation, the justice "done" by that legislation cannot sensibly be said to have existed at the time of the American Revolution. Promulgated legislation, then, can and sometimes does produce justice unrealized until the process of enactment is virtually completed, just as a surgical operation can produce health that did not pre-exist.

But how dependent is the process of producing justice on the process of legislation? British judges not too long ago held—as did American judges in several states—that, even though certain conduct was not prohibited by statute, nevertheless that conduct might be, in appropriate cases, punished as a "common law crime." [8] This would have delighted an ancient Confucian. When Tzu-chan promulgated criminal laws in 536 B.C., Shu-hsing, a critical scholar, said that he should not have flouted the example of the ancient kings, who had always eschewed general rules of law. The vice of rules, Shu said, is that people given exact laws lose their awe of their superiors, bicker over the application of statutory provisions, and become unmanageable. [9] Shu's position is not merely a curious and outmoded primitivism. Now, nearly twenty years after China's Communists came to power, they have yet to promulgate a criminal code. Mao's doctrine of "permanent revolution" seems to imply a need for constant legal flux inconsistent with stable general rules of law. Both Communist Chinese and foreign observers thought only a few years ago that a new criminal code was in the offing. Now it seems likely that no criminal code will be promulgated within the foreseeable future. This, of course, does not mean that in China formulated governmental programs producing social control and institutional patterns are not being administered along predetermined lines. No doubt administrative officials—who receive consultative guidance or approval—are developing some relatively stable policies and procedures for punishing criminals, running the postal service, caring for the aged, banking, and the myriad other governmental activities that cannot be conducted by improvisation. Perhaps, indeed, sometimes these programs are thought of as embody-

ing the substance and procedure of the masses' aspirations which
—in conformity with Marxist predilections—are thought to be
readily known.

Western criminal procedures are considerably different. In more
than a third of the American states the courts no longer have the
power to punish "common law crimes," and legislated penal rules
are the measure of criminal liability.[10] In other states the courts, in
theory, are authorized to convict wrongdoers whose misbehavior is
not interdicted by any penal statute. They are, however, very reluctant to use this power.[11] In recent years only a few petty offenders have been punished for common law crimes.[12] It does occasionally happen; in 1924 without statutory authorization a Pennsylvania Court of Common Pleas punished a woman for being a common scold.[13] (Note the court's appropriately archaistic name.) We
can say on the court's behalf that defense counsel limited his argument to contending that the state's evidence was not credible; that
is, he attacked only the prosecution's proof of facts and did not question the prosecution's theory of law. Since the illegality of murder,
rape, theft, and so on, antedate American penal statutes by centuries,
how can these statutes be said to embody any *new* justice? They
were enacted thousands of years after the conduct that they interdict first became unlawful. They did, however, create new justice.
Even though no American state legislature invented the classic
crimes, their penal statutes developed limitations on the authority
of judges who try and sentence accused persons. No doubt a number of these penal statutes are unjust in some particulars. But new
criminal justice was created when crimes were defined in the formulated texts of statutes with resulting channeling of decisions that
were fluid before those statutes were enacted.

Penal statutes, of course, can be drawn so loosely that they do
not confine the judgment of the courts "applying" them. Obscenity,
conspiracy, and vagrancy laws are likely to be especially vague. No
doubt, from time to time, there have been "interpretations" of
other criminal statutes surprising to both legislators and citizens.[14]
Especially were these unexpected interpretations common in earlier
times. When a nineteenth-century American judge doubted the
wisdom of the policy embodied in a statute he was likely to man-

age a manipulation which would thwart the legislature's purpose.[15] Twentieth-century judges, however, are more likely to respect our system of separation of powers. Nowadays most judges do try to carry out the legislature's intentions.

Many of the public's aspirations for safety and honesty are so traditional and, therefore, so acceptable to legislators that they move with great assurance when they interdict, for example, murder, theft, and arson. The limiting force of legislative definitions of these crimes is, however, a response to another public aspiration—the aspiration for preformulated, deliberate, clear, and promulgated criminal law. This aspiration grows out of the public's fear that, absent preformulation, judges often will be unable or unwilling on the spur of the moment to define crimes dispassionately—a fear that judicial biases may prejudice unattractive defendants or pander to the more favored accused. Even when only petty crimes are prosecuted we recoil from procedures permitting punishment in the absence of a clear criterion legislatively promulgated before the crime was committed. Great departures from this public aspiration are likely to run afoul of our constitutional guarantees.

The public aspiration for dispassionate definition of crime might conceivably be realized in some other way. In a static society a common law of crimes could perhaps become so fully developed and so frozen that, after a period of development, the criteria of guilt would usually be fixed in advance of trial. But no such system of preformulation has, in fact, existed in a modern industrial society. As a practical matter our aspiration for objectivity probably cannot be realized without promulgated statutes defining crimes. If the public aspiration for judicial dispassionateness in criminal law exists—and its existence seems to be undeniable—and if this aspiration cannot, as a practical matter, be realized in our times without statutory definition of crimes, we can draw two conclusions. Penal statutes illustrate: (1) A justice that could not exist without law, and (2) A justice that came into being when legislators, as the public's agents, tried to advance one of the public's aspirations.

The Confucian, Shu-hsing (mentioned earlier), who believed that officials should be the public's masters, also harbored a fear that governing power is embarrassingly weakened by promulgating laws.

Tzu-chan's promulgations, which occasioned Shu's criticism, may have been actuated by a desire on Tzu's part to give his people something *they* wanted; the chances, however, that such was his objective are not great. His promulgations were, more likely, attempts to teach his officials and people what *he* wanted, and therefore only accidentally realized a public aspiration.

The promulgation of criminal laws by legislators is a simple, almost artless example of legislatively produced justice. There are, of course, innumerable topics on which realization of justice is unlikely without legislation—justices that can be neither effectuated by judges and other governmental adjudicators nor developed without governmental procedures. Nonlegislative institutions have struggled for centuries, for example, with economic insecurity, but without legislation modern social security (starting with the workmen's compensation statutes enacted in the first decades of this century and extending to recently enacted Medicare) would have advanced haltingly, if at all. Similarly, the development of (1) just regulation of business and traffic, (2) just military conscription, and (3) just allocation of taxes had to be the product of either legislatures or their rule-making administrative nominees.

Of course many statutes are not creative. Legislators spend much of their time passing routine and transient laws. Only a small part of legislative energies are expended in improving administration of justice. Legislative output of justices falls far short of all the justice needed. Even if legislators tried to solve all justice problems in advance, they could not anticipate the inevitably novel future. Unless courts, administrators, and nongovernmental power-wielders constantly created justice, our lives would be intolerable.

What I have said above discloses that my theory of justice deals with only procedures that may produce justice; I set out no criteria that can be used to tell when those procedures have misfired. Most legislation is of value only for a limited time. Most statutes, even those promoting justice when pasesd, eventually become outmoded and stand in need of revision or repeal. The human race evolves physically, psychologically, and socially; its environment changes constantly. It would be strange, indeed, if its requirements for justice did not also constantly change. No doubt the difference between human life and human death, in some ways, remains constant and the number of food calories needed to sustain life does not vary rapidly or radically. Three-legged trousers may come into style, but they will never serve a practical need. Nevertheless man's world is in flux and new justice problems constantly arise.

JUDICIAL DECISION

Workaday holdings of courts seldom break new ground. Judges who preside over litigation usually follow established procedures and apply traditional rules of law when they hear the cases that come before them. Since new suits are not exact copies of old ones, courts are continually trying cases differing a bit from those decided earlier.

Judges, adapting law to cases, are often like doctors adapting medicine to patients; capable routine medical treatment, since it aims at cure, imperceptibly and in the long run advances the standards of good medical practice. Similarly routine adjudication may, almost unthinkingly, add bits of justice to what has been realized earlier. The law of trespass to land originally condemned wrongdoers who made "unauthorized entries." The typical entrant walked or rode on the surface of someone else's land. Then sometime or other a malefactor perpetrated harm by standing outside of private property and casting a missile over the boundary line. The judge who classified such conduct as an "unauthorized entry" probably gave little thought to the unjust alternative of confining the legal meaning of "entry" to bodily entries. Capable judicial decision, then, since it tends toward justice, thus imperceptibly advances the standards of good judicial practice. Sound policy rather than proper lexicography fills up the gaps.

In stubborn cases the analogy between medical and legal practice breaks down. When a patient does not respond to standard treatment his doctor scrambles for either a sounder diagnosis or a more deft therapy—until his patient responds or the need for treatment ends in death or natural cure. Judges, too, quicken when they are confronted with novel cases; only rarely, however, does their opportunity to decide disappear while the court keeps a case under advisement. When a court, after due deliberation on a case, still is baffled, it is likely to dismiss the suit and leave the litigants where it found them. Judges who reject a claim because they are unable to decide the suit on its merits, of course, create no new justice; they may even discourage later judicial creativity; their dismissal becomes a precedent which may dampen future deliberation on the merits in similar cases.[16] Utter lack of precedents, too, may intimidate; courts, habituated to self-justification by citation, may shy away from unprecedented results. Our judiciary, however, is neither authorized nor obliged to cure all injustices. Its main job in our times is to work only some of the machinery that helps keep society going.[17] This, however, was not always so.

Before the nineteenth century both the British Parliament and the American legislatures rarely concerned themselves with private affairs, and when they did it was usually in response to dissatisfactions of little importance. Only in the last hundred and fifty years have American and English legislatures promulgated systematic and extensive laws on such subjects as crimes, corporations, insurance, and commercial transactions. For the five hundred years before 1800 virtually all of the creative advances in justice in common law countries were made by the courts dealing with litigations. The court's occasional willingness to act boldly over the years implemented many public aspirations that otherwise would have gone unheeded. Justice so created is strikingly illustrated by the seventeenth-century judicial invention of the "rule against perpetuities." The rule limited the period of time during which a transferor of property could prevent that property from being freely re-transferred by those to whom it went; the rule invalidated restraints lasting longer than the lifetimes of the living transferees plus twenty-one years and nine months. The invention of this bar to frozen ownership rests on two grounds: (1) "Perpetuities" are unjust, and (2) Judges are enfranchised to correct this injustice. The reform was no small change [18]—like, for example, that made by the twentieth-century judges who outlawed spite fences.[19] The rule against perpetuities reduced the power of landed proprietors who formerly could and had exercised long-time posthumous control over family assets by rendering subsequent generations powerless to dissipate them. The judges who invented the rule themselves belonged to the propertied class; they must have had to hold their own predilections in check when they favored a public aspiration for a society enjoying economic and social mobility over the squirearchy's less widely held liking for country-home stability.

We who are unused to wide judicial creativity—except in some areas of constitutional law—should find it remarkable that seventeenth-century judges dealt with such a pervasive and complicated social problem and solved it with a rule of such precision. Courts nowadays seldom draw so hard a line—especially when that line could just as well be placed quite differently. Perhaps the times both emboldened those seventeenth-century judges and diverted other governmental forces from concern. Most private law judicial creations of justice seem more accidental, more interstitial, more intuitive, more a product of institutional forces in which lawyers as well as judges play a part.

The developments in ejectment and trover illustrate gradual growths of judicial justices. Ejectment was originally a minor supplement to the various common law actions for regaining possession of land after the owner had been wrongfully ousted. It extended the justice of the "real actions" (available only to the owners of important estates) to tenants who theretofore could bring no action. The new remedy was, perhaps accidentally, not called a "real action," but became a kind of "trespass." The procedures used in trespass cases were fast and simple; those used in the real actions were slow and complicated. Ousted owners of estates that were more important than leaseholds envied the tenants' remedy and invented a way to enjoy its speedy simplicity. An ousted owner would enter into a fake lease with one of his friends. A second friend would pretend to enter and oust this spurious tenant; the "tenant" would then file suit against second friend in ejectment. Second friend would thereafter send a notice of the suit to the occupant, along with a disclaimer of intention to defend the suit. If the occupant ignored the suit he might well find himself having a brush with a sheriff "restoring possession" to the fake tenant. The occupant, to avoid this vexation, would put in an appearance at court and petition for permission to defend the suit. This request would be granted and the ejectment trial would proceed with the real parties in interest as the actual litigants. This hokus pokus was probably invented by lawyers; [20] judges, however, with their eyes on speedier and simpler procedure, readily acquiesced and refused to accept the defendant as a litigant unless he agreed not to challenge the useful flummery. Thereafter farce became fictions and eventually even these fictions were dropped.[21] The enlargement of ejectment was a procedural reform; a faster remedy supplanted slower ones. The injustice of delay is, however, no mere bother. Today we desperately hunt for ways to speed up traffic accident litigation, which has so clogged our urban courts that jury cases are not tried until several years after they are docketed.

Enlargement of the common law remedy of trover produced new substantive justice. This remedy lay originally only against a finder of lost property who refused to deliver over to the true owner. Knowledgeable case readers, however, are not surprised to come on trover claims based on so unlikely a story as that a plaintiff casually misplaced forty tons of coal, found by the defendant, who has refused to redeliver.[22] Lawyers and judges again had connived to turn the facts of loss and finding into a fiction—a fiction which allowed trover actions to proceed against all defendants who, in any way, wrongfully converted another's goods to their own use.[23]

Judges implementing a public aspiration in a new way are often prompted by lawyers urging the novel result; lawyers also sometimes dissuade judges on the verge of impulsive new injustice. In imperial Chinese tribunals there were no lawyers; the practice of law was itself a crime. Chinese magistrates in consequence sometimes overindulged their own cleverness. In an ancient case an orphan asked a famous Chinese judge, Ho Wu, to order his older sister to give him possession of his dead father's sword. The father on his deathbed bequeathed all his property to his married daughter with the proviso that his blade was to be turned over to his son on the boy's fifteenth birthday. When the son reached fifteen the daughter dishonored the proviso. Ho Wu, after investigating the surrounding circumstances, said that the daughter was violent and domineering and her husband was greedy and low-minded. The dead father, continued Ho, was afraid that the daughter would harm his infant son if he left his estate to the child. The father, "in Ho's opinion," did not intend a literal interpretation of his bequest of the sword to be delivered on his son's fifteenth birthday; the bequest symbolized his intention to leave his son the whole estate, and he armed the son at fifteen to encourage him to find ways of taking over his full inheritance. Ho Wu ordered the daughter to turn over the whole estate to her brother.[24]

In imperial times a Chinese father who had a son was, indeed, unlikely to leave all of his assets to his daughter—and more especially so if she were married. Ho Wu did not, however, rule that such a bequest was invalid. Judge Ho implied that had the father intended to leave all of his assets to his daughter, he had a legal power to do so. The judge refused, nevertheless, to treat the ordinary meaning of the father's words as the father's intention because he thought the father had signaled a different message. Suppose Ho Wu, the superior man, had conjectured aright; should, then, Ho Wu, the magistrate, have attached legal force to the decoded cryptogram? What would he have done if this daughter could have been represented by a lawyer who championed the value of accepting the ordinary meaning of all testator's words in the absence of sound objective grounds for believing that he intended some other meaning? Forensics, of course, sometimes mislead courts and head them away from justice. Inquisitorial procedures can, however, sometimes result in pronouncements favoring predelictions of the inquisitors.

It is not easy to demonstrate that the judicial process should be manned by public servants who both should and do recognize that by accepting a seat on the bench they have incurred some duties to implement public aspirations. A judge is not so clearly a representative of a constituency as is a legislator. Those judges who must run for office announce no adherence to specific platforms, make no campaign promises to decide cases for one litigant rather than the other, offer no detailed program of allegiance to a political party's current aims. Candidates for the bench must appear to be neutral to voters since the judge's role is usually performed by administering a system of justices already formulated; theirs is only rarely a primarily creative role. This is not to say that we do not appreciate the influence of our judge's predelictions on their decisions; no one wants to be tried for his life by a "hanging judge"; no one wants his petition for strike injunction to be heard by a judge known as "the workingman's friend." Nevertheless we properly believe that the law's direction (if not its detail) is pre-fixed in most cases, and the judge's job is even-handed application or dispassionate adaptation of existing law to fact of cases. Only occasionally do judges properly innovate widely, and when they do they should not be partisan. Judges not willing to follow legalistic tradition should be guided by the values of the corporate public. This, indeed, is what happened when the torpid procedures of the real actions were supplanted by ejectment's speedier justice and when trover was stretched to cover more kinds of misappropriations of chattels. These two expansions of existing remedies extended justice; that is, they added a mite to the recognition and implementation of pre-existing public aspirations. The judges who extended the historical boundaries of eject- ment and trover were not merely serving elegant jurisprudence by rounding out doctrines to achieve legal symmetry; they were imple- menting public aspirations. Their use of fictions to reach their goal exemplifies the judicial style of the times.

The judicial invention of the rule against perpetuities is also, I believe, an extremely bold example of understanding and imple- menting a public aspiration. No doubt the aspiration for social mobility in seventeenth-century England was, to say the least, incipi- ent and unarticulated; nonetheless, in the eyes of the judges, it existed and deserved to be furthered by the law. These seventeenth-century judges, who announced a full-blown, novel, complicated, and precise rule of implementing an unformulated public aspiration, used a style that makes their product seem to be entirely their own self-inspired invention. The style of the judges who expanded ejectment almost concealed its novel justice. In both instances, however, the judicial creations were technical implementation of the public's and not the court's aspirations. The orthopedist who furnishes skilled therapy to his immobile patient does not invent the patient's desire to walk. Similarly these technically qualified judges, as public servants, did for the public what it could not do for itself. However, the boldness both in style and substance of the innovation of judges who formulated the rule against perpetuities is rare.

In our own times we have seen great changes effected by the United States Supreme Court's reinterpretations of the Constitution.[25] Until recently, however, twentieth-century common law innovation has been inconspicuous.

Judge Learned Hand, writing in 1916, said that earlier common law judges were able to innovate more extensively and more easily than the judges of today because the self-conscious elements in their society were homogeneous and likely to agree on where justice lay.[26] He continues, "All this has changed . . . [new] demands are vocal that before were dumb. . . . If justice be a possible accommodation between the vital and self-conscious interests of society it has taken on a meaning not known before."[27] For many reasons some of the children of parents who in their time contributed little to the development of the public's aspirations are now voicing thoughts on our society's proper goals. As a consequence, values are now more likely to conflict and produce congeries of inconsistent private or group aspirations, rather than the monolithic public aspirations of earlier times. This pluralism should, in theory, reduce the scope of palatable newly pronounced judge-made justice.

Twentieth-century judges have not, however, foregone new implementation of public aspirations. Two examples illustrate.

(1) In the nineteenth century a wheelwright contracted with the British Postmaster General to maintain certain mail coaches. The wheelwright neglected his duty, and as a result a mail coach going at full speed cast a wheel. The coachman was badly hurt; he brought a personal injury suit against the wheelwright. The British Court of Exchequer heard this case in 1842; it held that, since the source of the wheelwright's duty to service the coach was a contract, and since the coachman was not a party to that contract, the wheelwright owed no duty to the coachman.[28] This precedent inspired the formulation of a "privity of contract rule"—a rule that insulated many suppliers of goods and services from liability for injuries to third persons. This rule was so obviously unjust that the courts soon developed a few minor exceptions. Extensive injustice, however, resulted from application of the rule in American cases

for a period of more than seventy years. In 1916—the very year in
which Hand remarked on the obstacles to modern judicial innovation—Cardozo pared down the rule and held the Buick Motor
Company liable for an injury resulting from negligent manufacture
of one of its cars even though that car had been bought from an
independent dealer by a customer with whom the Buick Company
had made no contract.[29] Cardozo's opinion purported only to smooth
out the theory of the earlier exceptions to a logically implied wider
principle—following popular twentieth-century judicial style. Nevertheless it did not take a very sharp legal eye to see that he had sliced
close to the heart of the old rule, and his holding emboldened
judges to whittle away at the rule. The rule now has become history instead of law. Cardozo, it seems to me, bespoke justice where
those not trained in law hardly knew the law had been so unjust.

The advance in justice resulting from Cardozo's slash into the
old privity of contract rule fell short of implementing the contemporary public aspiration for safe consumer goods; the courts
are now engaged in a far-flung expansion of products liability
which seems to be spreading to consumer protections appropriate to
modern housing construction, car rentals, and so on. The contemporary style of judicial creativity tends to be more candid than
ever before. Policy problems are often expressly discussed; analogies are often used for their social force rather than to mask
creativity. This candor often centers on widely held aspirations
that emerge from the welter of diverse values held in our times.

(2) Another judicial creation plows virgin soil—the twentieth-
century common law development of a right to privacy. This innovation was urged on the courts in an imaginative and persuasive
article published in the *Harvard Law Review* in 1896.[30] The article
inspired many state courts to develop new protections against
unscrupulous advertisers, wiretappers, and debt collectors. The
judicial development of this congeries of rights is an impressive new
implementation of public aspirations.

The difficulty that Hand foresaw has not stopped twentieth-
century courts cold. The courts have, however, fallen far short of
seizing all of their opportunities to create justice. Wooden technical-
ity, unwarranted conservatism, and covert partisanship are pervasive

enemies of justice; they occupy many niches in the substance and procedures of our case law. Judicially inflicted injustices may, indeed, outweigh the creativity of judges who implement public aspirations. Cardozo is guilty of easy optimism about our courts' creativity when he says, "Not all the progeny of principles begotten of [judicial] judgment survive . . . to maturity. Those that cannot prove their worth and strength by the test of experience are sacrificed." [31] Traynor seems closer when he says that every time a judge innovates he must reckon with the ancient suspicion that judicial creativeness darkly menaces the stability of the law and, as a result, our real concern should be not with the likelihood of too many judicial innovations, but with their continuing scarcity.[32]

Though judges create justice, they have neither the courage, nor the versatility, nor the resources to create all the justice we need. Judges bespeaking justice are not, however, authorized to consult only their own consciences. When they have done so, and attempted to further their own idiosyncrasies, they have disrupted justice. When they are egocentric and clever they may persuade their bench mates that they can see new justices not visible to a sleeping public, but seldom will their successors follow their novel holdings that are inconsonant with the public's aspirations. Only when judges recognize the limited extent to which they are able to discern and implement public aspirations can they advance justice without undue costs in instability. When, however, they lie torpid in their proper sphere of creativity, the doctrine of *stare decisis* tends to consolidate the evil they do and keep it alive after them.

NONGOVERNMENTAL LEGAL OBLIGATIONS

The sum of all the justices created by public officials cannot, without supplement, produce a just society.

Savigny, a nineteenth-century forerunner of modern sociological jurisprudence, looked on law as issuing from society much as language does—a social product arising and developing in response to folk needs and character. In expounding this theory he makes the following points: Every society generates its own, unique binding customs, embedded in popular faith; since law is not consciously fabricated, law is created only in a metaphorical sense. Folk law cannot be set down in black and white rules because abstract formulations cannot convey the rich meanings of living customs. Only legal officers who are steeped in folk history are properly attuned to serve on those rare occasions when legal customs need clarification. Functionaries ignorant of folk history do not appreciate the folk spirit and will not, therefore, heed folk wisdom; when these cosmopolite jurists promulgate abstract rules, their laws, since they are detached from local custom, do not command popular respect.

Law that each people exudes for itself is, in Savigny's view, good law. Since good law dealing with socially important topics creates justice, he implies, then, that each folk is the corporate author of its own justice. Savigny, however, was no Rousseau. Even though he admired the public's taste, his primary interest was not in popular lawmaking; the heart of his message was a warning against the academic jurists who had turned away from the tangible local scene and wanted to issue an abstract code made up of formulas bearing only remotely on regional conditions, needs, and desires. His main thrust was against systems of codified universal and permanent justice. An abstract, uniform, and complete code, he feared, would turn out to be only a false front which would mask the true nature of the decisions made by officials; behind this grandiose facade magistrates could be foolish and capricious with reduced risk of detection.[33]

There seems to be little likelihood that common law countries will soon desert their ancient pattern and ape the nineteenth-century European civilians who codified their countries' laws. We prize some lengthy and complicated statutes systematizing special areas of the law because they bring expert opinion and careful study to bear on areas of the law needing overhaul. We live in hope that well-qualified governmental officials will hasten to implement some of our unrealized public aspirations.

Nevertheless, Savigny's warning still has value. Since genuine culture [34] is achieved only in communities affording widespread participation in vital social decision-making, folk decisions, in a sense, are indeed part of the stuff of justice. Legislation, systematic or sporadic, is just only when it implements the folk's aspirations; legislation modeled on Roman law abstractions may fail in justice.

Savigny pointed up another important fact, which is that in every community rights and duties often come into being in society; obligations originate without governmental invention or intervention. In some respects, however, Savigny's version of folk lawmaking is very misleading; his folk are monolithic and unconscious; each community, he assumed, has a coagulated character and a pervasive unitary set of local folkways.

Savigny's twentieth-century follower, Ehrlich, built on a more realistic and more useful sociology; he recognized the teeming plurality of lesser group organizations found in all communities. Many of these groups are artfully structured; they are deliberately invented; they are not accidental happenings. Within such groups, men intentionally develop the obligations that will serve their purposes. Like Savigny, however, Ehrlich held the position that the bulk of men's legal duties come into being without and apart from official governmental activity and are performed without thought of —much less, fear of—governmental sanctions:

Man lives in innumerable legal relations and . . . , with few exceptions, he quite voluntarily performs the duties incumbent upon him because of these relations. One performs one's duties as father or son, as husband or wife, does not interfere with one's neighbor's enjoyment of property, pays one's debts, delivers that which one has sold, and renders to one's employer the performance to . . . which one obliged himself. . . . As a rule, the thought of compulsion by courts does not even enter the minds of men. . . . Would an employer sue a servant girl for not tidying the house? [35]

A spectacular example to add to Ehrlich's is the law originating in collective bargaining agreements and its private interpretation and adjudication. A single pact between management and labor in an automobile manufacturing enterprise legislates for more people than most statutes. An interpretation of one of its clauses by an arbitrator can be more significant than the decisions of most litigated cases.

Justice (defined in this paper as the implementation by law of the public's aspirations) is rarely an aim of private activities. In commercial dealings each trader is, of course, bent on protecting his own fortune.[36] When traders expect to deal with each other again, each has a special incentive to deal fairly with his vis-á-vis. Concern for the welfare of those with whom one trades can and often does transcend self-interest; few people habitually and continuously overreach. Nevertheless, protection against injustice often warrants governmental intervention into private transactions; witness our pure food laws, antitrust laws, standard insurance policy laws, and so on; remember the supervisory functions of the Securities and Exchange Commission and the Federal Trade Commission.

Rarely, however, are private business and professional activities calculated to advance the interests of those not immediately involved. In most routine dealings there is in fact no occasion to think about strangers to the transaction.[37] Some private transactions, nevertheless, do profoundly affect the public and decisions made in commerce and industry may, therefore, tend to thwart or promote the public's aspirations. When a collective bargain is struck in, for example, the steel industry, should the bargainers be concerned with inflation? Should they try to arrive at a contract that will not necessitate a rise in the price of steel? Should the public be represented at the bargaining table? Answers to these questions are not assayed here, but the fact that such questions raise problems which are important to the public demonstrates that some nongovernmental processes produce justice and injustice.

In a 1961 Delaware Supreme Court case an unprecedented question was raised. Does a hospital have a duty to take care of strangers *in extremis* who ask for treatment at the hospital's emergency ward? The court held that these unfortunates cannot be turned away with legal impunity.[38] The significant aspect of this suit was that the case was unprecedented; neither the lawyers who argued it nor the judge who decided it could, in 1961, find a single American decision in point. No doubt American institutional medicine had long before decided that those who applied at hospitals for emergency treatment were entitled to it. This right varies in small details from one hospital to another, and at the hospital sued the right was aberrantly constricted. Those who control the inner order of hospitals had, however, acted to implement a public aspiration long before the Delaware court in 1961 vindicated that right. Though the Delaware court seems to have perfected the right, this justice exists as effectively and valuably in Pennsylvania, where the state government has done nothing to implement it, as in Delaware where the Supreme Court has acted. The threat of legal liability in Delaware has, as a practical matter, added little or nothing to the functioning justice implemented by hospital routines.

Institutional medicine has faced and solved another interesting problem. Trained nursing is a service in short supply; not only are there fewer nurses than wanted; some nurses work only when they feel like it, others are unwilling to work on holidays and weekends. Well-to-do patients are, to some extent, more able to get nursing care than less affluent patients who may be more in need of it. The public aspires, I suppose, to the best use of this service that can be devised. Legislatures and courts have done nothing about the problem. Medical and nursing associations, which have a large measure of control, have not used their disciplinary powers to tackle, much less to solve, the problem. Nevertheless, the medical goal of adequate treatment for all (a tacit general recognition of medicine's responsibility to implement public aspiration) has inspired a solution advancing justice. Now, in most large hospitals, patients desperately in need of constant, vigilant nursing are put into "intensive care" where both (1) adequate nursing for the desperately ill is no longer hindered by lack of affluence and (2) the shortage in nursing rarely deprives those who urgently need nursing from getting it. In this instance, the inner order of private association has responded to provide some important implementation of a public aspiration that has not been implemented at all by legislation or judicial decision. Once private institutional medicine invents intensive care, government may reinforce its invention. The National Institutes of Health can refuse support to hospitals who do not organize intensive care units. A court may hold that a hospital not offering intensive care is guilty of malpractice. Government could have done little with the problem, however, had private medicine not taken the lead.

Unless, then, the inner order of some nongovernmental associations implements some of our developing public aspirations, our society will become increasingly unjust. I do not mean, of course, that all inner orders of private associations should constantly respond to public aspirations. Private power, however, is sometimes not utterly private; it sometimes is tolerated by the public only because those who wield it are both willing and able to advance important public aspirations. When this expectation is disappointed the vacuum is likely to be filled by government. When such disappointments become common and intolerable the resulting injustices may attract support for totalitarianism.

THREE INTERLOCKING COMPONENTS IN THE PROCESS OF PRODUCING JUSTICE

New justice emerges from an admixture of foresight, good will, and fidelity to the public's aspirations. Without using foresight a lawmaker cannot know that a proposal for new justice will work; he does not know what he is doing. Unless his foresight is affected by good will, it may focus only on technical efficiencies or selfish gratifications and not come to grips with the proposal's public utility. Though a lawmaker uses foresight and is actuated by good will, he will nevertheless ignore an element essential to the ongoing function of updating, preserving, and extending justice if he imposes laws on the public without considering its aspirations.

The inspirational aura of this statement about the core of preserving and extending justice is overly dramatic in respect to day-to-day developments of law departing only slightly from established ways. Usually the foresight needed is only common sense; the good will called for is only common honesty; the fidelity to public aspiration required is only reasonable deference to public opinion. When more radical departures from the past are proposed, large doses of all three components may still be inadequate.

The essential most likely to be slighted is deference to the public's aspirations. Some legal philosophers have become preoccupied with foresight, and ignored the lawmaker's obligation of fidelity to the public's aspirations. John Stuart Mill (one of my idols) left this element out of the process of developing justice. After discussing justice as an aspect of man's apprehension of his community of interest with the society in which he lives,[39] Mill cited several instances of reasoned disagreements on where justice lies. One of his illustrations, for example, involves a dispute on the theory of just wages. He asked:

In a cooperative industrial association is it just or not that talent or skill should give title to superior remuneration? On the negative side of the question it is argued, that whoever does the best he can, deserves equally well, and ought not in justice to be put in a position of inferiority for no fault of his own. . . . On the contrary side it is contended that society receives more from the more efficient labourer; that his services being more useful, society owes him a larger return for them. . . . Justice has in this case two sides to it . . . *social utility alone can decide the preference.*[40]

Here, it seems to me, Mill's method for "deciding the preference" is mistaken. The lawmaker who does use his foresight to determine what theory of wages will produce the most pleasure and least pain, cannot, of course, be accused of lack of good will; the utilitarian posture is that everyone's pleasures and pains are important; the lawmaker who favors himself or his friends at the expense of the public is no utilitarian. Mill's particular brand of utilitarianism is specially a philosophy of good will because he makes the case for equality and freedom as enhancing pleasures and avoiding pains. Public aspirations are, however, unimportant to Mill's lawmaker except insofar as the public's stupidity may lead it to oppose measures that, according to its lawmakers' foresight, would in fact increase human happiness. This scientism turns the attention of lawmakers to the facts of happiness and away from the public participation, through its representatives, in decision-making meliorating the public's own fate.

Even apart from the intrinsic desirability of lawmaking that seeks to implement public aspirations, there are two forces that tend to direct lawmaking into this channel. (1) Laws that run counter to public aspirations, and therefore do not seem just to the public, are often enacted in vain. Laws purporting to advance pruderies widely rejected are likely to be widely disregarded; breaches of such laws are only sporadically prosecuted. Speed traps are for tourists who are caught but once; home folks usually ignore them with impunity. This point, of course, can be overstressed. Unjust licensing laws may effectively exclude deserving and qualified men from trades and professions. Unjust taxes may be collected from people unready to rebel. (2) Legislators acting singly are helpless. Those who want to espouse legislation of extremely wide and complicated import usually attract few allies. It is almost inconceivable that either of Mill's two alternative approaches to just wages would be acted on by a modern legislature. His two alternatives sound like the sides of an academic debating exercise, staged to display extemporaneous forensic skill. They are not like legislative proposals. Since neither alternative is, or is likely to become, consonant with the shared values of our pluralistic society, neither is likely to have potent appeal to a legislator who must attract support to enact law. Some aspects of just wages have, of course, been dealt with by law— for example, minimum wage laws and laws prohibiting wage discriminations against women and racial minorities. These new laws were enacted because they were thought to implement live public aspirations. Pointed and pointing public aspirations are, then, not only criteria of justice, but also energizers of lawmaking.

Lawmaking cannot always be laid on the table until the relevant public aspirations are known. Tax bills must be enacted before legislative sessions adjourn. Once lawsuits are heard they must soon be decided. When the public's aspirations are not known and time is of the essence for the lawmaker, he should often turn against novel solutions and favor traditional ones; old practices usually are more likely to accord with public aspirations than novel changes cleverly invented by self-confident individuals. However, a representative who must act quickly for his principal without knowing what the principal wants need not always stick close to standard practices. A representative who considers what he would want if he were the principal may come closer to his principal's wishes than one who ignores his own predilections; after all, the principal who appointed him may have preferred him over other candidates because of confidence in his judgment. Appointments based on confidence occur in public as well as private enterprise; in following their own judgment agents may indeed be true to their trust.

It is important, however, that lawmakers do not think of themselves as principals; they should play neither god nor philosopher-king. They serve the cause of justice steadily by working at implementing, not their own, but the public's aspirations. Their work can be creative because, and only insofar as, the public develops and evinces aspirations which they imaginatively understand and implement. When these aspirations are inchoate, great talent is needed for responsible formulation. Many unrealized public aspirations are, however, well known; sound ways of implementing them are already at hand. More just consumer credit legislation is now in the hopper; more just personal injury law has already been formulated and applied by some judges; it awaits application and emulation by others. More just safety practices have been tested and expounded in private institutions; they only await organizational approval to become new just obligations as standard clauses in private transactions affected with a public interest.

Many human aspirations are in no sense the corporate public's aspirations. Aspirations to experience and create beauty and to find and know truth are not, however, always private hopes totally unconnected with justice. The public does aspire to democratic distribution of opportunities to develop talent and to widespread convenient access to works of art. Legislatures, courts, and private power-wielders in implementing these aspirations can, of course, produce new justice for us. Often, nevertheless, the greatest works of art and most significant discoveries of science are the accomplishments of principals, not agents. An artist who is not allowed to act as a principal will have to pander to others; a scientist not given the role of a principal may be nudged off course by the counsels of prejudice or ignorance, which may absorb his energies and distort the truth he would otherwise learn. I do not mean that those who beautify artifacts are always entitled to indulge their idiosyncrasies and that those employed in applied science are licensed to wander off the job. Even the independent artist and the pure scientist are, in some measure, products of society; they may properly hope to speak to and be understood by significant and sizable audiences; they are, however, not obliged to serve their audiences as agents; they work in their own right and ought first to satisfy themselves. The creator of justice, however, is more closely channeled to public function; he is not only a product of society, he is an agent of society whose work products properly implement his own aspirations only insofar as he can identify them with the public's. In no other way can justice be intentionally created.

Of course both public and private wishes sometimes accidentally come true; some injustices accidentally lapse. The cotton picking machine liquidated tenant cotton farming in the Deep South, and its injustices were incidentally washed away. The hope for a more just future, however, is not likely to be furthered much by accident. Automation, including the cotton picker, can advance many public aspirations; it will, at least at its onset, thwart many others.

My theory of justice involves no search for the substance of universal and eternal justice; it is a theory of the sources of justice and the procedures by which raw materials of justice are made into the product. In my theory there can be no justice without a public; there could at most be kindness to a people kept in bondage. Only in a society in which numbers of people are allowed to contribute to the formulation of significant social designs is there a public whose apirations can set the criteria for creation of justice. When such a public exists it usually does not include all people who have potentials for contributing to the formulation of social designs. Insofar as the existing public aspires to incorporate into itself those excluded ones, and insofar as that aspiration goes unimplemented, the resulting exclusion exemplifies injustice. If, however, the limited and existing public has no such aspiration, then the source of criteria of justice is narrowed, and, as a result, the potential for justice itself is undesirably limited. In some verbal sense this is not included in my definition of justice, and a puristical logic may foreclose the possibility of calling it an injustice. But a polity which dwarfs its capacity for justice by snobbery must, it seems to me, be called unjust.

My kind of justice, then, can have no substance apart from society. It hardly exists at all in primitive societies; it may have little play in despotic societies. It will expand as the genuine public expands; it meliorates as the public's aspirations grow and are creatively implemented by the public's servants. Its stagnation is disserving and stultifying; its decline is social tragedy.

Chapter 2

The Austerity of the True
and the Sociality
of the Just*

In both medieval and modern times some legal philosophers have maintained that the methods used to discover justice significantly resemble the methods used to find scientific truth. An example appears in the writings of St. Thomas Aquinas. He compares speculative reason with practical reason. For St. Thomas the speculative reason encompassed, among other things, the sciences of his day. Law is one branch of the practical reason. St. Thomas said:

'[T]he same procedure takes place in the practical and in the speculative reason: for each proceeds from principles to conclusion . . . [J]ust as, in the speculative reason, from naturally known indemonstrable principles, we draw the conclusions of the various sciences, the knowledge of which is acquired by the efforts of reason, so too it is from the precepts of the natural law, as from general and indemonstrable principles, that the human reason needs to proceed to the more particular determination of certain matters. These particular determinations, devised by human reason are called human laws, provided the other essential conditions of law be observed . . .[1]

* I discussed some of the materials in the first half of this chapter in an article entitled "Justice and Scientific Method," 60 *Columbia Law Review* 936 (1960).

47

Seven centuries later some philosophers also drew parallels between making scientific discovery and formulating just laws. John Dewey's convinced and articulate disciple-in-law, Walter Wheeler Cook, wrote in 1941 "[T]he same logic of inquiry used in physics and chemistry will yield useful results if applied in all fields in which intelligent inquiry can be carried on . . .[2] The logic of inquiry developed by scientists is applicable in the work of lawyers, judges, law teachers and legal investigators."[3]

Dewey himself maintained that values should not and could not exist apart from the concrete conditions in which they functioned. An aim or end, he contended, really exists only after fact-study has transmuted a vague hankering into potential accomplishment by adaptive effort. Men who dreamed of flying could aim to do so only after they studied the flight of birds and learned practical ways of adapting to human flight what they discovered about the way birds fly. Dewey wrote:

[E]nds arise and function within action. They are not, as current theories too often imply, things lying beyond activity at which the latter is directed. . . . In general, the identification of the end prominent in conscious desire and effort with *the* end is part of the technique of avoiding a reasonable survey of consequences. . . . Thus the doctrine of the isolated, complete or fixed end limits intelligent examination, encourages insincerity, and puts a pseudo-stamp of moral justification upon success at any price.[4]

These words from Dewey are not simply the universally accepted statement that the safe and sound implementation of values involves careful consideration of the facts. Dewey, it seems, maintains that the process of developing aims resembles the growth of scientific knowledge, in that pure justice, like disembodied truth, produces either no action or unjust action; practically just programs are devised when, and only when, a more just future is envisioned in existential detail; from a preview of the congeries of all reasonably foreseeable consequences of alternative proposals, the paths to improvements in justice emerge, more or less automatically.

Though the resemblance between St. Thomas' and Dewey's accounts of the discovery of justice is slight, both men, in accordance with the lights of their times, assign the role of discoverer of justice to experts capable of exercising sound investigatory reason.

Other philosophers disagree; they reject the theory that justice can be found by competent and unselfish professionals who then turn their carefully reasoned personal evaluations into law. Radical Rousseau and conservative Savigny looked on justice as necessarily a product of society itself.

For Rousseau justices had no existence until the whole citizenry met, in advance of the time when occasions for applying law might arise, to formulate and announce the "general will." "When among the happiest people in the world," wrote Rousseau, "bands of peasants are seen regulating affairs of state under an oak, and always acting wisely, can we help scorning the ingenious methods of other nations, which make themselves illustrious and wretched with so much art and mystery?" [5]

Savigny's justices grew up in society with less formality than Rousseau's; in his view, just laws are not proposed to and voted on by the people; they develop as one aspect of the customary behavior of the populace. Savigny maintained that the way in which legal customs are generated is much like the way popular language evolves; both law and language adapt themselves so that common needs are met. The process of law's unfolding is, he said, slow and stable; experts can discover the customary law as historical fact and apply it to cases, but they should only rarely tamper with it. Law so developed, contended Savigny, draws its wisdom from "internal silently operating powers, [and not from] the arbitrary will of a law-giver." [6] If experts are allowed to refashion the law, Savigny forewarned, they will divorce law from everyday life and rob it of "the moral energies of the nation, by which alone it can attain a satisfactory state." [7]

Rousseau's *The Social Contract* was published when he was fifty. He attained his first recognition as a social philosopher years earlier when he won the Dijon Academy's essay contest. The Academy had assigned the topic, "Has Restoration of the Sciences Contributed to Purify or Corrupt Manners?" Rousseau's entry was probably the only one that (in the "age of enlightenment") disparaged science. Apart from some companionless, bucolic botanizing, he had none of the scientific curiosity that absorbed much of the spare time of many of his intellectual contemporaries. It is not surprising, therefore, that Rousseau did not take scientific method as the model for the process of formulating just laws.

Savigny's motivations probably stemmed from his interest in history and his consequent dislike for the unhistorical Napoleonic Codes. He maintained that a jurist did his work properly only when he was versed in the history of local legal customs and formulated his decisions in conformity to the palpable and heartfelt cultural predilections of local society.

Modern science and its methods have long since moved beyond the grasp of those uninitiated in its techniques. Even though justice in democracies is generally thought of as responding to the common conscience, nevertheless neither Rousseau's nor Savigny's jurisprudence has proved prophetic. Most of our developments of justice nowadays result from legislation fashioned by small bodies of elected lawmakers. No one would argue now, as Hobbes once did, that common sense was the only proper qualification for those who formulate law and that training in the common law and its methods was stultifying.[8] The question remains, however, whether or not advances in justice should be the products of inquiry into consequences prosecuted by lawmakers, who in the course of their tenure become somewhat expert, and who are enfranchised, for the time being, to protect the public weal and advance the common good as they think best. Such an austere enterprise turns lawmaking away, of course, from the Rousseauean-Savignyesque requirement that the commonalty actively participate in lawmaking and thereby assure the justice of new law.

We all know that elected officials, who may seek re-election, pay some attention to public opinion. Ehrlich contended, nevertheless, that a creative lawmaker always puts something of his unique self into his law. Writing in 1913, he said, "Though justice is based on social trends, it requires the personal activity of an individual to make it effective. In this it is most like art." The artist, too, as we know him today (1913) does not produce his work of art from his inner self; he can but give shape to that which society furnishes him with. "[J]ustice owes to society only its rough content, but it owes its individual form to the artist in justice who created it." [9]

If Ehrlich's simile is apt, the materials of just laws come in part from society, and those who work these materials establish the worth of their product only if their law elicits some quantum of public approval. An artistic fashioning of new law—like the writing of a poem or the painting of a picture—does not take its form from a norm that was pre-existing in the local culture; a new law, however, will not have much popular appeal unless the populace believes it to be a suitable way of treating the ill it is meant to remedy. A beautiful work of art and a just law, then, both must to some extent draw on their creators' society and prove congenial to its culture. This social dimension of justice does not foreclose the possibility of merit in a demand made by a singular individual for legal implementation of what he alone regards as just, a demand made long before the demandant attracts substantial popular agreement with his position. However, he who seeks a change in law without hope that his aspiration will become a public aspiration either is lobbying for a special interest or is pampering his singularity —and, impliedly, retracting his humanity.

Scientific discoveries, of course, stand in no need of validation by popular understanding and acceptance. Though some scientists may be actuated, in part, by desire for public acclaim, the scientific soundness of their work, nevertheless, lies ultimately in the judgment of other scientists, and not in public approval. In this regard the methods of discovering scientific truth and framing just laws are poles apart.

One aspect of modern science should, however, be the envy of lawmakers, that is, science's prodigious ability to produce hypotheses. The vitality of modern science lies not alone in its objectivity and open-mindedness; human minds can lie torpid even when they are open; sweet reasonableness can be more sweet than reasonable. In contrast to the mysterious fecundity of science, the modification of law is rarely considered until lawmakers are faced with disturbing exigencies. Law does change constantly, but much legal adaptive growth is interstitial, small scale, and slow. In our times the improvement of justice is puny when compared with the brawny growth of science.

The enterprise, Science, becomes a less coarse, more corrected, more detailed body of knowledge as times goes on. And this is true even though contributors to scientific advance differ widely in their aspirations, methods, and their views on the acceptability of virtually all new scientific theories. Perhaps the unifying element in scientific advance is that verification develops consensus.[10]

Maritain drew an anology between the consensus of scientists and the concordance of the civilized world on some concrete programs for human betterment. Worldwide agreement on practical programs of welfare, he proposed, should be forwarded by an international formulation of the rights of man with a view to developing their concrete implementation through a study of their actual consequences.[11] He warned that this program will not resolve abstract disputes; he wrote that theoretical moral differences will flourish even after practical rules of conduct are accepted widely. He concluded, nevertheless, that moral progress can be made from the sociologic point of view whenever practical proposals for advancing the common good are tried and turn out to be both workable and worthy.[12]

The record of strivings for justice and how they have worked has, over the years, grown longer, more accurate, and more significant. The chronicles of efforts to develop justice are, nevertheless, sketchy. Wide-scale attempts to advance social justice have never been tried except in revolutionary times. These times, however, rarely favor cool appraisal of results.

The elders of any society are likely to regard with suspicion and apprehension most proposals for improving law. Aristotle, for example, said in his later years:

[C]hanges in other arts and sciences have certainly been beneficial . . . And, if politics be an art, change must be necessary in this as in any other art. The need for improvement is shown by the fact that old customs are exceedingly simple and barbarous . . . Hence, we infer that sometimes . . . laws may be changed; but great caution would seem to be required. For the habit of changing the laws lightly is an evil, and, when the advantage is small, some errors both of lawgivers and rulers had better be left; the citizen will not gain so much by the change as he will lose by the habit of disobedience . . .[13]

Today the public's respect for law depends little on law's oracular qualities; respect is not likely to be undermined by amendatory legislation. Nevertheless, every sponsor of a bill altering existing law must unhorse the presumption favoring things as they are. That presumption is grounded on the probability that law revision is likely to entail disquieting side effects; amendments sometimes disappoint reasonable expectations that were rooted in the erstwhile law. Revision may also produce contrary holdings in identical cases, divulging at least one instance of injustice. Science, on the other hand, neither has any obligation to avoid dashed hopes of those who relied on corrected scientific errors nor any duty to apologize for inconsistencies between previously undetected false-hood and newly discovered truth.

Hobbes did not subscribe to Aristotle's sufferance of imperfect laws. Judges are obliged, Hobbes maintained, to overrule all un-sound precedents. Hobbes—though he had a lively interest in science—was not inspired to advocate free-running improvement in the law by science's progress. The source of justice, Hobbes held, is the ruler's (Leviathan's) commands; judges, the ruler's surrogates, are obliged to assume that Leviathan prefers to have current dis-putes well decided (in the absence of Leviathan's orders to the contrary); as a result judges are obliged to decide cases on their merits and owe no respect for the erstwhile errors of their pre-decessors.[14]

Hobbes was unschooled in law and had little understanding of the English legal system. Cardozo, a luminary in twentieth-century American jurisprudence, decided some landmark cases in which he advanced justice by making changes in the common law. In his extolled essay, *The Nature of the Judicial Process* (written in 1920), he expounded the authority and responsibility of our courts to de-velop a more just common law. He did not, however, urge as Hobbes did, that each case should be decided on its own merits and with-out regard for earlier decisions:

I think adherence to precedent should be the rule and not the exception . . . The labor of judges would be increased almost to the breaking point if every past decision could be reopened in every case . . . But

I am ready to concede that the rule of adherence to precedent . . . ought to be . . . relaxed. I think that when a rule, after it has been duly tested by experience, has been found to be inconsistent with the sense of justice or with the social welfare, there should be less hesitation in frank avowal and full abandonment . . . There should be greater readiness to abandon an untenable position when the rule to be discarded may not reasonably be supposed to have determined the conduct of the litigants . . .[15]

He constricted judicial creativity this way. "We [judges] must keep within those interstitial limits which precedent and custom and the long and silent and almost indefinable practice of other judges through the centuries of the common law have set to judge-made innovations." [16] The judicial tradition limiting the proper occasions for innovation was not for Cardozo the sole force tying judges to the past. He said:

Given a mass of particulars, a congeries of judgments on related topics, the principle that unifies and rationalizes them has a tendency, and a legitimate one, to project and extend itself to new cases . . . It has the primacy that comes from natural and logical succession . . . Adherence to precedent must . . . be the rule rather than the exception if litigants are to have faith in the even-handed administration of justice . . . The judge who moulds the law by [this] method . . . is keeping the law true in its response to a deep-seated and imperious sentiment . . . In default of other tests [formal legal reasoning] must remain the organon of courts if chance and favor are to be excluded, and the affairs of men are to be governed with the serene and impartial uniformity which is of the essence of the idea of the law.[17]

Roentgen discovered X rays while doing an experiment on a totally different subject. He used quartz, for its strength, to make a light bulb that was to be subjected to forces stronger than those that an ordinary bulb could withstand. Fate lodged a pair of scissors on a photographic plate in a drawer in his laboratory table. X rays (which can pass through quartz but not through glass) penetrated the heavy tabletop and took a picture of the scissors. Roentgen, who was both alert and discerning, turned this chance happening into an important scientific discovery.

Suppose, however, that Roentgen had said to himself, "To conjecture that light rays can penetrate a solid tabletop and take a picture is to reject the traditional theory of photography. Since the history of photography, the custom of photographers, and the public's attitude toward picture-taking suggests no such hypothesis, I had better forget the whole business." These words, ridiculous if they came from a working scientist, paraphrase Cardozo's admired analysis of the judicial process.

A statement appropriate to experimental science also can be bizarre if paraphrased in the course of writing a judicial opinion. Take, for example, an unprecedented 1931 case decided by Cardozo's court and in which he wrote the opinion.[18] The facts were these: A dishonest merchant, after falsifying his records, engaged a public accountant to audit his books. The accountant would have discovered the tampering alteration of records had he used due care; however, he was negligent and therefore failed to spot the swindler's spurious entries. Consequently, the accountant's certified audit added up to affluence, when it should have disclosed bankruptcy. A creditor had been shown this audit by the swindler, and as a result, sold him goods on credit; the creditor was unable to collect the purchase price of the wares, and sued the accountant for damages. The court refused to entertain this claim. If public accountants were required to answer to creditors who rely on honest, but negligently made, audits, said Cardozo, auditing would be so risky a venture that financially responsible accountants would refuse to make independent audits.

Suppose, however, Cardozo had instead written this: "I doubt the wisdom of predicating liability of auditors to misled creditors on mere negligence. If we held that they must answer for mere negligence to creditors who did not hire them we might, we surmise, deter all the financially responsible public accountants from undertaking to make independent audits, leaving only novices, wastrels, and third-raters to perform this service. Certain it is that independent audits are much needed in our commercial world. There is, however, no way in which we can know that our surmise is sound without making a crucial experiment; perhaps our fears (that auditors' liability to creditors for negligence will destroy an essential service) are unfounded. For the next several years, therefore, accountants whose negligence misleads the creditors of those whose books are audited will be required to answer for resultant losses. We will, of course, take appropriate steps to observe the results of this experiment, and if our hypothesis proves correct, we will change the law accordingly." This imaginary opinion fantastically assumes that judges are empowered to experiment to test the truth of their theories on social dynamics. Judges do occasionally take some chances without mentioning their expectation that the court will retreat from their mistakes, but when they run these risks they are not conducting experiments to discover the truth; instead they are deciding in ignorance and in hope, as best they can.

Legislators, perhaps, feel themselves empowered to experiment a bit more; they may be forced to adopt untried measures to solve the unique problems of their times. Chief Justice Traynor said:

There are no precedents for much of the law that must be formulated today to regulate multi-minded, multi-handed human beings. The main preoccupation of such law must be with the future. Its main formulation belongs appropriately to legislators, who are freer than judges to write on a clean slate . . . and to erase and rewrite in response to community needs.[19]

However, when legislators enact laws and afterward become dissatisfied with them and, therefore, repeal or amend them, their posture bears little resemblance to the attitude of laboratory scientists. Only when legislators are in the throes of crisis are they likely to be frankly experimental. Such, for example, was the unusual case when the Congress, during the dark days of the great depression, adopted a municipal bankruptcy law and evidenced unsureness by including a clause providing that the law was to remain in force for a period of five years.[20] This lack of total commitment was not, however, based on the notion that the Congress was empowered to pass laws in order to discover fiscal truth. The experiment of permitting municipal bankruptcy was undertaken because it promised to advance the common good. The difference between liberals who supported that measure and conservatives who opposed it is that the liberals believed more firmly than the conservatives that the promise to advance the common good would be fulfilled.

There can be, however, neither a left nor a right wing in scientific method. Imaginative scientists think up vital experiments oftener than their more prosaic brothers—which may evoke praise or envy, but not methodological opposition. Cautious scientists evaluate experimental evidence more skeptically than their rash brothers— which may evoke efforts toward more convincing proof, but not promotions of "grass roots" support to effectuate the scientific validity of the theory advanced. Corporate science is likely to withhold judgment on the truth of untried hypotheses; it judges their scientific validity only after they have been put to some test. Experimenters do, of course, know the style of the criticisms that are likely to be voiced by other members of their disciplines and this knowledge affects their methods and procedures. If, however, an experimenter thinks that the way to an important discovery involves a use of unorthodox procedures, he is likely to adopt those procedures on the theory that once he establishes his theory, its truth will speak for itself to his brothers. In other words, an experimenter's own personal judgment on the worth of the procedures he uses to test his hypothesis has force that drives him on. By contrast a legislator who is convinced that he has a meritorious proposal to make, may, nevertheless, hesitate to put it forward if it promises to evoke acrimony from his colleagues or other critics. He may, therefore, make no move at all toward a legal goal that he himself greatly prizes. A legislator cannot ask critics to keep still until his proposal has been checked in action; only after he convinces his colleagues— and, sometimes, the public as well—that his proposal is very promising can the test be made. The qualified scientist, on the other hand, need answer to no one for staging experiments that he believes are worth making—unless, of course, his methods transgress a nonscientific legal or moral norm (as do atomic explosions that subject people to radiational injuries, and medical experiments on human subjects that are illicit or inhumane). These limitations on experimenters are, however, not scientific; they are dictates of prudence impinging on science.

Ehrlich, as quoted earlier, said, in effect, that lawmakers, like artists, inevitably put something of themselves into the law they make. There is a rarely challenged belief that great works of art are unique and, therefore, not susceptible to reduplication. This belief has never attached to scientific truths; they are validated only when their demonstration can be duplicated by others than their original discoverer; a scientist who claims a discovery made during an experiment that no one else can repeat is suspect; an experimentalist's idiosyncrasies may make him a trail blazer, but the trail he blazes must be one that other qualified scientists can retrace.

Ehrlich exaggerated the personal impress of lawmakers. Many litigated cases are routine and can be decided only one way. Statutes like traffic laws and poison-labeling laws tend to become uniform, impersonal, and institutional. Even when a democratic solon pioneers by drafting and sponsoring *tour de force* legislation dealing justly with a newly emerged social problem, he may not, with propriety, overrate his own predilections. Theorists differ on the dimensions of a legislator's obligation to be faithful to the public's wishes. Maritain would give legislators considerable elbow room; he characterized them as servants of the people, but, nevertheless, he did not fully trust the public to be perceptive and steadfast. He hoped, therefore, for legislators who will be headstrong servants when their own consciences recoil from public clamors.[21] Tumult and outcry may or may not betoken the public's genuine aspirations; the populace is sometimes carried away by its passing fancies and exciting whims which for the nonce may conflict with deeply held and widely shared values. Only genuine aspirations are the measure of justice; they alone should constrict the authority of the legislative incumbents. The public's fleeting caprices are neither a measure of justice nor instructions to their representatives; they should be resisted. Furthermore, a solon who knows that his own conscience speaks quaintly should not, as the public's servant, embody his eccentric views in legislation. Sometimes the public's genuine aspirations are difficult to identify, formulate, or implement. The democratic legislator is, nevertheless, obliged to try to recognize and realize the public's deep-rooted shared values.

Scientists, on the other hand, have neither constituencies nor obligations to bring to heel their personal scientific hopes or doubts, simply because they are personal and do not attract widespread support. Nonscientific factors do, of course, channel many scientific investigations; industrial employers of scientists may not give them free rein; scientists in universities may not be given the funds or the equipment that they must have to prosecute dearly held projects. Governmental and foundation grants for scientific projects may be unjustly withheld from areas in which the realization of the public's aspirations depends on scientific developments. Some scientific innovators have been able, however, to make momentous advances because they were free, as scientists, to harbor warranted suspicions about scientific beliefs that had theretofore been regarded as impregnable. Large and lonely imaginations such as Copernicus' and Einstein's were needed to correct respected Ptolemaic and Newtonian inadequacies.

The public's aspirations do not, of course, spring spontaneously into the minds of the citizenry at the same moment. Men ahead of their times urge law reforms and at first seem to make little headway; later on these proposals catch on and become widely wanted. The first objections to slavery bore no fruit for thousands of years. When John Stuart Mill made common cause with the suffragettes, very few males had shown enthusiasm for woman suffrage. Perhaps, however, Mill was speaking for an inchoate public aspiration to give women full political rights—a subliminal value, already widely shared, though rudimentary. Mill's stand attracted male allies, as humane causes often do. Not many decades later the justice of woman suffrage became the law of much of the Western world.

Maritain called strident and importunate forerunners of justice "prophetic shock minorities." Times change, wrote Maritain, but governments make few accommodations; office holders enjoy and nurture routine; consequently the body-politic's health calls for occasional disrupters like the fathers of the French Revolution, Tom Paine, and Thomas Jefferson.[22] Maritain also includes John Brown in his list of prophetic shock minorities. John Brown, now revered, was deplored as much too extreme in his own day even by most of the determined foes of slavery. Another Brown, our contemporary, Rap, may, too, look better in retrospect. (Of course, not many shock minorities are prophetic; most of them are sterile and noisy cranks, freaks, and faultfinders.)

Science has been enlivened by one-man breakthroughs shaking

up a smug discipline that theretofore coasted for decades. I have heard it said that physicists in the early years of the twentieth century thought of their science as virtually complete. What surprises they were to have when seminal advances destroyed their placidity! Scientific innovators may, while seeking scientific truth, happen to become pacesetters able to step up the rate or significance of discovery in their disciplines; they are not, however, agitators whose end-in-view is the destruction of complacency. Break-through scientists operate austerely in the sense that they work at satisfying themselves by discovering where scientific truth lies; they need not persuade other scientists (much less the public) that their ends are desirable. The social effects of modern science have been profound; the discoveries of science in themselves, however, contain no substantial component of sociality.

Two views of justice were contrasted at this chapter's outset: (1) the growth of justice resembles the discovery of scientific truth, and (2) the development of justice lies in the unfolding of commonality's intuition and is a product of cultural evolution. Both of these views are partially unsound. Criticism of the first has been the main topic of this paper; it is too austere, too unsocial, too disengaged from the public's aspirations.

However, the second, too, is inadequate—especially as expounded by Rousseau and Savigny. In their systems, the assumption that justice flows automatically from law generated by society is too anti-intellectual; Rousseau and Savigny divorce lawmaking from the skills and techniques of recognizing and implementing the public's aspirations. Those two philosophers were, nevertheless, right in their insistence that the proper understanding and realization of justice must be basically humanistic, and that any theory of justice not responsive to the public's aspirations entrusts men's fate, at best, to benevolent masters and, at worst, to malevolent dictators.

The development of living justices in the modern world is realized through the establishment of new just, living law (widely defined). Some new just law is generated, unplanned, in society, and without any formalization of new rules; heightened public conscience can result in general recognition that old prejudices were baseless and unjustly dispossessed some people of their dignity and opportunities; these reversals of conscience can bring about a remolding of patterns of behavior. For the most part, however, justice develops as the result of new doctrines promulgated by judges, legislators, administrators, and the unofficial elites that control the "inner orders" of our important institutional associations.

Our times are specially charged with vocal disaffection and alienation. Demonstrations and confrontations are not novelties in America, but their recent bulk is unusual. The ages of the participants in our recent mass protests vary; young people, however, predominate.

Donald MacRae, writing in 1967 on the subculture of college students, set forth some factors that may contribute to the outbreak of disorderly student protests. He maintained: (1) students in universities are not so predominantly upper class as they once were, and consequently are less channeled by tradition, (2) modern students are more likely than their predecessors to view the world as essentially contingent, and, as a result, they deem present social relations arbitrarily arrived at and, therefore, subject to changes to their liking, (3) the models of revolt have proliferated with the de-Stalinization of the politics of the left, and consequently a wider spectrum in the styles of rebellion affords choices that readily suit nearly every stamp of restive youth, (4) traditional knowledge and high culture have been devalued so that all data seem either relative or trivial; students turn readily, as a result, to arcane doctrines.[23] These factors (or at least some of them) may converge and, along with other special causes, stimulate violent assertions of student dissatisfaction; they then voice disapproval of their education and governance in particular, and of the ways of "the establishment" in general.

Fifty years earlier, Learned Hand said that the common law courts made innovations more easily when society's self-conscious elements were homogeneous and likely to agree on where justice lay. In his 1916 article, Hand noted that new demands were then being made by elements in society that theretofore had been silent. "If," he said, "justice be a possible accommodation between the vital and self-conscious interests in society it has taken on a meaning not known before."[24]

Lively participation of diverse constituents of the populace in the formulation of public policies need not result in dire conflict on all topics; nearly all of both the old and the young, for example, probably subscribed to the recently recognized need for governmental regulations of automobile design to promote safety. On the other hand, widespread disagreement characterizes the public's values on some topics, such as obscenity and nudity. If this discord is real and not only apparent, justice, as I define it, must await greater unity; the best that can be hoped for in the meantime is beneficent and wise law, so salutary that it will, in the long run, become cherished widely enough to transform it from imposition into justice.

Many of our contemporary protestors are "shock minorities." Perhaps some of them are "prophetic shock minorities" who will eventually rally the public and its servants to some of the public's genuine, but muted, aspirations. The older and better-established members of society, fearing the disruptions of change, sometimes muffle their own inclinations to concur in public aspirations urgently needing novel implementation. Protestors may embolden them to give vent to their genuine, but slumbering, views. "Prophetic shock minorities" are, of course, sometimes so far ahead of their times that they espouse values which the contemporary public will not share.

MacRae's analysis implies two directions of future development:

1. The causal factors in student protest are likely to operate, after some time, in a much wider segment of society than they now do, to the point that the values which students hold now may eventually become public aspirations. The variety of classes from which college students spring will not diminish. College students will continue to look on the world as contingent and malleable. The spectrum of choices in styles of revolt is more likely to expand than to contract. Traditional knowledge and high culture, now devalued by students, are not likely to be rehabilitated soon. As oncoming generations of students in ever larger numbers are subjected to MaeRae's congeries of influences, their value systems may differ little from the value systems that their parents developed going through the universities. The extraordinary width of the present generation gap may already be narrowing; the generation gap may, consequently, become relatively small in, say, three or four generations. All of MacRae's protest-producing factors favor

change; once they have exerted force for years, the premium now placed on stability may subside, clearing the way for public aspirations which can be implemented with new laws greatly advancing justice.

2. MacRae's factors are, nevertheless, freighted with contrariety which may thwart the development of shared values and prevent the development of aspirations held widely enough to be public. The educated are likely to be members of the self-conscious elements of the public. If university graduates in oncoming generations are more representative of all classes, less inhibited in their belief in the wide possibilities of reordering the world, more divided by alternative styles of revolt, and less respectful toward traditional learning and culture, they may, indeed, balk at sharing affirmative values to the point that new public aspirations evolve. The most cherished hopes for a better society may be voiced as a bedlam of conflicting demands incapable of supporting just reform. Some evolution of justice there still will be, because some evolution of public aspirations is virtually inevitable; we will, for example, aspire to better land use, wiser conservation, and so on. The most dearly held aspirations, however, will win out in the future only *if* the public develops support for them. Dare we extrapolate from the history of man's sociality which, over the ages, has been uniform enough for the gradual realization of an impressive total of new justices?

In Chapter One I have said that only when large numbers of people are allowed to contribute to society's formulation of new social designs and movements is there a public whose aspirations can set the criteria for just law. Absent an aspiring public, there can be no justice. A small elite whose law imposes that elite's values on society, whether that elite is upper class and old or revolutionary and young, implements its own aspirations and creates just law only by accident. Even though there is a self-conscious public whose shared values count with lawmakers, that public may, however, arbitrarily exclude some habitants from participating in the formulation of the public's aspirations. Insofar as the existing public aspires to incorporate into itself habitants arbitrarily excluded, the exclusion is an injustice which public servants are impliedly charged with remedying. When, however, a limited and existing public has no such aspiration, this debasement, too, is unjust, for no society can arbitrarily exclude habitants from participating in the formulation of the public aspirations and at the same time be just.[25]

The voice of the outsider should not be stilled even though it is not now persuasive and may not be convincing in the long run. The outsider need not be afforded an opportunity for interminable jangle and din, but all denizens deserve at least a reasonable opportunity to speak in their own way and be heard, and, sometimes, an opportunity that is more than reasonable. The protester guilty of civil disobedience today may in the long run turn out to be a public benefactor.

On the other hand, proponents of separatism, balkanization, and private aspirations as prime measures of public policy are potential destroyers of, rather than possible contributors to, the public's aspirations. If a disaffected outsider intends to destroy the aspiring public, rather than change or improve the public's aspiration, his goal is a fragmented humanity incapable of the sociality essential to justice.

Individual men and women, of course, are the constituent parts of the public; the "common weal" is a collective norm standing for widespread, interlocking personal satisfactions. Most people want, however, not only to further their own immediate interests, but also to live in a society in which others enjoy privacy, liberty, dignity, security, education, culture, opportunity, companionship, and love. Austere scientists have, of course, contributed to the realization of some of these ends, and their past contributions are, we are told, only a beginning in the technology of meliorating human existence. The public servant whose laws are made with this technology in mind may not, however, look to it alone. The humane worth of science—as distinguished from the truth of scientific theories—depends on a just distribution of personal satisfactions. Since justice results from the implementation of the public's aspirations, the lawmaker's art succeeds in enhancing justice only when his law, well fashioned in other respects, is also a product of sociality.

Chapter 3

On Liberation and Liberty: Marcuse's and Mill's Essays Compared*

The parts of this chapter are three. The first abridges Marcuse's essay on our coming liberation as the result of an impending revolution; the second sums up Mill's essay on the desirability of extensive individual liberty; the third compares and discusses the first two.

I †

In *An Essay on Liberation*,[1] published in 1969, Marcuse charges that the elders of our society (especially the Establishment) are presently suppressing or thwarting all suggestions for radical change. Until, therefore, rebellious young whites and militant ghetto blacks can mount a revolution unseating the Establishment, our society will remain in thralldom to corporate capitalism. A quest for a zestful

* This chapter was printed first in 118 *University of Pennsylvania Law Review* 735 (1970) and is reprinted by permission.
† The following ideas are Marcuse's and not mine. I have reordered them, presented them out of context and condensed them, often paraphrasing rather than quoting, for clarity. When Marcuse's exact words are used, they are in quotation marks.

life, lived without hurting others, is a hopeless search in our society as it is now structured; men who accept the currently taught aspirations and seek to enjoy generally desired satisfactions injure themselves; corporate capitalism's dependents, by their fealty, perpetuate their own servitude. Thus most young rebels today refuse to school themselves to take conventional places in our obscene society. They hold the following objections:

1. Society forces many people into jobs that keep them at stupid, inhuman, and unnecessary work.
2. Society's booming business is often done on the backs of ghetto dwellers or by exploiting domestic or foreign colonials.
3. Society is infested with violence, but expects the injured to suffer their hurts without murmuring.
4. Society maintains its structure (including its allotments of power) by practicing waste, wreaking destruction, and distending human needs and desired satisfactions.[2]

The mass media are under the thumb of corporate capitalism and have stifled the case for radical change. Telecasting, broadcasting, and the press have dulled most people's emotions and have addicted their audiences to compulsive buying of mediocre wares. The media have convinced the masses that they should defer to capitalism's domination and defend the system that enslaves them.[3]

Every society has a second nature; this second nature consists of the hopes and responses that have been (and continue to be) introjected into the people's biology. A society's morality, therefore, is a system of organic norms of behavior. Once people are so conditioned, their acts are controlled by these introjections into their physical beings; they are receptive to and react to only certain stimuli, ignoring or repelling other excitants (which might affect differently conditioned people). In our consumer-oriented economy, men are libidinally and aggressively driven to acquire commodities; they resent any threat to reduce their access to the merchandise market. Until revolt reshapes the second nature of our society, significant improvement in social conditions is unlikely.[4]

Once the revolution dethrones corporate capitalism, the new

society's goal will extend far beyond a collectivistic eradication of poverty. The revolution will aim at *qualitative* social change. The old ways of producing commodities will be scrapped and replaced by a system of production designed to meet freshly perceived, genuine, human needs. Reconstituted society will be characterized by solidarity, and, as a result, social goals will be harmonized with individual desires. An understanding respect for every individual's hopes will, perforce, eliminate exploitation.[5] The guarantee that the revolution is genuinely humane will be attested by the appearance of two qualities in the new second nature of the citizenry: a percipient tenderness, and an instinctive recognition of and revulsion from falsehoods and evils.[6] The new culture will be rooted in sensuousness and will create for itself an aesthetic environment. Parks and gardens will replace highways and parking lots, and areas of withdrawal will be sanctuaries from massive fun and tawdry relaxation.[7]

The development of more and better accoutrements of life will decelerate or stop; society will settle down to enjoy its hard-won technical and scientific progress, and will become satisfied with a reduced supply of equipment and wares. High-pressure selling will disappear. De-emphasis of the market will, unfortunately, retard the development of machines that relieve men from dull, time-serving tasks, but this minor setback is the price that must be paid for liberation from the despotic rule of merchandisers.[8]

When men are liberated, their newly won biological sensitivity will enable them to convert the techniques of production into arts; the differences between the quality of scientific thought and poetry will then vanish; all intellectual activities will merge into an over-riding aesthetic ethos.[9] Society itself will become a sensuous work of art, and its liberated members will evolve an environment in which making a living will no longer have ugly or aggressive aspects.[10] Liberated men's incentives for work will be instinctual, because the human animal has a desire to unify and enhance his life, and his liberation releases libidinal energy for work when he lives in genuine freedom. "The social expression of the liberated work instinct is *cooperation*, which, grounded in solidarity, directs the organization of the realm of necessity and the development of the realm of freedom." [11]

Marcuse holds out no hope that revolution can be averted by parliamentary procedures. Corporate capitalism has indoctrinated most of us so thoroughly that reforms made legally can be only piffling gestures—never significant advances toward a truly free society.[12] The contaminated masses cling like barnacles to the market economy. "[I]t makes sense to say that the [contemporary] general will is always wrong. . . ." [13] (Shades of Rousseau's remonstrating ghost!)

The radicals of today are not yet able to launch a revolution. A profound and unmanageable economic crisis will, however, inevitably disrupt the capitalistic system. Then society's moral fiber will weaken. The symptoms of general demoralization will be a spread of discontent, an increase of mental illness and growth of unwillingness to work, indifference, inefficiency, and negligence. At that point in time the new forms of organizations that are needed to wage the struggle for liberation will emerge.[14] The rebels are not yet very well organized; they are not yet in rapport with labor, the middle classes, or the masses. At the right time, nevertheless, they will radicalize the industrial working class [15] and become the catalysts of revolution.[16]

Nowadays many workers are much more highly educated than the laborers who formerly bore the brunt of exploitation. Contemporary workers are, one by one, becoming members of a scientific intelligentsia, competent to operate automated production machinery. As technology develops, industry needs more and more employees who have college educations. Current campus protests and confrontations, therefore, are especially provoking to the captains of corporate capitalism, whose reaction is, naturally, violent vituperation.[17] The students, however, are not yet a vanguard; there is, for the time being, no main body of rebels behind them and willing to follow their lead. The student movement is nevertheless "the ferment of hope. . . . [I]t testifies to the alternative— the real need [for] and the real possibility of a free society." [18]

Thus spoke Marcuse.

II *

Mill's influential, classic essay, *On Liberty,* which was first published in 1859 [19] starts with a discussion of the great powers wielded by bygone monarchs. Tolerance of their might was based on the belief that strong government is needed to repel foreign aggressors and suppress domestic disorders. Rulers with so much legitimate power were likely, however, to take advantage of their position and become tyrants. Earlier publicists, therefore, were likely to direct their concern for liberty to the prevention of the tyranny of monarchs.[20] A time came when more democratic governments were in the offing and populaces came to believe that public officials would soon hold their places only so long as the public was satisfied with their services. An accepted corollary of this view was that officials whose powers were so limited would not have the opportunity to enthrall the public.[21] The notion that government when it can readily be ousted is unlikely to become tyrannical was a misbelief, founded on pre-democratic imaginings. After popular government became a reality, such phrases as "self-government" and "the power of the people over themselves" lost some of their allure. The people who came to exercise power were not always the same as those over whom it was exercised; self-government turned out to be the government of each by all the rest. "The will of the people, moreover, practically means the will of the most numerous . . . *part* of the people. . . . '[T]he tyranny of the majority' is now generally included among the evils against which society requires to be on its guard." [22]

Society has sanctions other than law for tyrannizing over dissidents. "Society can and does execute its own mandates: . . . it practices a social tyranny more formidable than many kinds of political oppression, since . . . it leaves fewer means of escape, penetrating much more deeply into the details of life, and enslaving the soul itself." [23]

---

* As in the preceding section of this essay, I have resorted to paraphrase. When Mill's exact words are used, they appear in quotation marks. The ideas that follow are, however, Mill's and not mine. All citations are to the edition published by E. P. Dutton in 1951, Everyman's Library, No. 482A.

Mill does not argue for unlimited permissiveness. Legal and moral coercion aimed at the control of deviance is properly exercised over a member of civilized society when it is used to prevent him from harming others. Obnoxious conduct is permissible, but only when it does not infringe on "the interests of . . . another; or rather certain interests, which, either by express legal provision, or by tacit understanding, ought to be considered as rights. . . ." [24]

Since speech rarely violates the rights of others, the privilege of free speech is accordingly broad, and is not lost even though the speaker is unmannerly and argues heatedly. Speech creating a clear and present danger of riot, however, exceeds this privilege. An assertion "that corn-dealers are starvers of the poor . . . ought to be unmolested when simply circulated through the press, but may justly incur punishment when delivered orally to an excited mob assembled before the house of a corn-dealer. . . ." [25]

Utterance of half-truths advances the public interest. Enlightenment expands when new verity, embedded in error, is sifted out and burnished by being considered and discussed. [26] Even the utterance of arrant mistakes can be socially valuable; men confronted with falsity develop a "clearer perception and livelier impression of truth, produced by its collision with error." [27]

Informal social forces suppressing unpopular views are more deplorable than legal penalties exacted for dissidence. When the public stifles opinions held by men with inquiring minds, fearless thinkers with logical intellects are muted and the influence of conformers is enhanced. [28] Freedom of discussion is not limited, however, to its power to advance the development of masterminds; the part discussion plays in the mental maturation of ordinary men is of even greater value. [29]

Experiments in new and different ways of living should be prized. "[F]ree scope should be given to varieties of character, short of injury to others; and . . . the worth of different modes of life should be proved practically, when any one thinks fit to try them." [30] We not only should tolerate the piquancy of attractive loners, but we also should enact no laws forbidding vices and foibles like gambling, incontinence, idleness, or uncleanliness. "If, for example, a man, through intemperance or extravagance, becomes unable to pay his debts, or, having undertaken the moral responsibility of a family, becomes . . . incapable of supporting or educating them, he is deservedly reprobated . . . but it is for the breach of duty to his family or creditors, not for the [intemperance or] extravagance. . . . No person ought to be punished simply for being drunk; but a soldier or a policeman should be punished for being drunk on duty." [31] In essence, when obnoxious conduct does not immediately violate the rights of others it should be endured for the sake of the greater good of human freedom.

III

Mill, like Marcuse, harbored little hope that the public could easily be convinced that it ought to tolerate dissent. "Wherever there is an ascendant class," says Mill, "a large portion of the morality of the country emanates from its class interests. . . ." [32] Spontaneity is hardly recognized as having any intrinsic worth, or deserving any regard on its own account. The masses, who are satisfied with the status quo, have little patience with individualists who disdain established ways, and even social reformers usually belittle spontaneity, fearing it may threaten their pet reforms. [33] "[S]ociety," Mill concludes, "has now fairly got the better of individuality. . . ." [34] "At present individuals are lost in the crowd. . . . Their thinking is done for them by men much like themselves, addressing them or speaking in their name . . . through the newspapers." [35] Marcuse updates and intensifies these views.

Mill also seems to have anticipated Marcuse's awareness that men have never lived up to their capacity for sensitivity and taste. Mill looks on the measurement of a man's worth as properly made not only by looking at his deeds but also by taking into account the manner of man he is. "Human nature is not a machine to be built after a model, and set to do exactly the work prescribed for it, [it is like a] tree, which requires to grow and develop itself on all sides, according to the tendency of the inward forces which make it a living thing." [36]

Unlike Marcuse, Mill did not believe that promoting men's liberty releases a considerateness for others lying repressed in human breasts. Mill had little foreknowledge of modern psychiatry; not surprisingly, he did not consider the effect of suppressions on man's libido. He was a bit of a snob. "[T]here are but few persons, in comparison with the whole of mankind, whose experiments, if adopted by others, would be likely to be any improvement on established practice. But these few are the salt of the earth; without them, human life would become a stagnant pool." [37] There is no counterpart of this "salt of the earth" theory in Marcuse's writing; he does not believe that sensitivity will spread as a result of following a few fine examples. Instead, Marcuse says, the people of the world, once liberated, will each naturally become tender and full-souled on his own. When the new sensuous culture follows on liberation, people intuitively will recognize and shun stupidity, falsity, and evil. Production plans will become so well attuned to the life instincts that men's libidos will supply the impetus for doing the world's work. The liberation of genuine human nature will set in motion man's natural desire to create a society that will be the greatest work of art of the coming aesthetic ethos.

Some other students of psychiatry are less confident than Marcuse about man's innate tenderness. Dr. Robert Waelder (who himself sat at the feet of Freud) wrote in 1966:

All morality is a restriction and modification of inborn strivings. If man were . . . good by nature, no morality would be needed. . . . In our days . . . men are expected [by reformers] to be concerned only about the good of all and not about their own personal interests. Aggression in the service of . . . self-aggrandizement including . . . one man considering himself as better than another . . . is completely condemned.[38]

Dr. Waelder also points to scientific research on group behavior of both chickens and baboons which reveals that these animals live socially stratified lives and often act brutally to each other. Dr. Waelder continues:

The moralists of today try to purge man of all selfishness and personal aggressiveness; they refuse to believe that, in most cases, self-concern and a measure of aggressiveness cannot be completely suppressed except at enormous cost in terms of other human values. . . . [A]n egalitarian society needs an authority which has the power to enforce equality and which sees to it that nobody gets out of line.[39]

Marcuse's prophecy that men will become nonaggressive and tender when liberated from corporate capitalism seems at odds with Waelder's theory.

Mill would probably have been standoffish about both Marcuse's and Waelder's opinions on the wellsprings of men's conduct. Mill put his trust in man's ability to improve his lot by deliberation; through constant resort to his rational faculties, man could and would, bit by bit, improve society. "[T]he source of everything respectable in man either as an intellectual or as a moral being [is] that his errors are corrigible. He is capable of rectifying his mistakes, by discussion and experience." [40]

We surely should accept Mill's opinion that various forms of deliberation on untoward experience may lead to the correction of mistakes of fact. Rethinking has improved sciences (like physics) and crafts (like carpentry). The whole truth about the good life, however, exists *as fact* for Mill; once that truth is discerned (accurately and fully) and explained (clearly and widely), all men with good sense will understand it and live by it.

To discover to the world something which deeply concerns it . . . to prove to it that it had been mistaken on some vital point of temporal or spiritual interest, is as important a service as a human being can render to his fellow creatures. . . . History teems with instances of truth put down by persecution. If not suppressed for ever, it may be thrown back for centuries. . . . The real advantage which truth has consists in this, that when an opinion is true, it may be extinguished once, twice, or many times, but in the course of the ages there will generally be found persons to rediscover it, until some one of its reappearances falls on a time when from favourable circumstances it escapes persecution until it has made such head as to withstand all subsequent attempts to suppress it.[41]

The instances of suppression of truth that Mill had in mind were such outrages as the Spanish Inquisition's short-lived, sixteenth-century suppression of Copernican astronomy.[42] Science's discoveries were not, however, seriously threatened with censorship in Mill's own day. His Victorian world was, of course, afflicted with prudery and posturing, against which he inveighed. The blights that cried out for reform when he was writing *On Liberty* were, however, dire poverty, paucity of education, child labor, industrial accidents, and poor sanitation. True, knowledge of the facts bearing on these evils was then sparse, but lack of public concern resulted as much from inertia as from suppression. In mid-nineteenth century, Mill and his fellow liberals were interested in a few worthy causes, such as women's suffrage, but by and large they did little to understand (much less develop) the aspirations of the general public. They did not deplore that many people were hardly citizens; that is, many people hardly counted. Too few of the elite concerned themselves with social betterment, and those who did, including Mill, wanted to give the masses what was deemed good for them rather than to clarify and implement widely shared values of their society.

Most of the elders of modern western societies have tended to regard proposals for wide social change with suspicion and apprehension. Nevertheless, the human condition has been, in various ways, irreversibly meliorated in the past dozen decades. The legitimated procedures of social change have produced some advances which accord with the unformulated, but known, general will. Perhaps our legitimated procedures can be used effectively in the future to down great lurking evils (like overpopulation and pollution) which are now at odds with the public's aspirations. Society's permitted, lawful methods of change have, however, often been found wanting. Determined and selfish autocracies in France and Russia were unseated only after bloody revolutions, and the United States was unable to outlaw slavery without a civil war.

Marcuse believes that we need revolution now; that social perversions introjected into our biology by corporate capitalism cannot be cleared away by using legitimate methods of law reform; that parliamentary change moves at a futile, snail's pace. He may be right.

Mill's defense of liberty is calculated to advance justice insofar as (and only insofar as) dissidents' protests and examples awake or change and invigorate the public's aspirations. Modern-day protests and confrontations have stimulated some re-examinations of our law and mores. At times they also have evoked deeply felt divisiveness—a condition which, by definition, disrupts the wide sharing of values and, at least for the nonce, prevents the solidification of new and better public aspirations. Unless and until values are widely shared, there is no base on which to rest justice. Perhaps, however, time, births, and deaths will turn some of our ferments into new solid values, shared widely enough to be the whole public's, rather than a lesser group's, aspirations. This does not, of course, mean that all dissidents have their fingers on, or even near to, the pulse of the future.

The one injustice that can persist (even when the public does not aspire to its correction) is exclusion of groups of adults from participation in the processes of formulating the public's aspirations. Mill's call for free speech and uninhibited verve falls short of full enfranchisement of the dispossessed; he does not press on to advocate education of the uneducated and advantaging the disadvantaged; he does not urge that they be given the liberty to become fully active citizens. Free speech is a snide gift to present to the unarticulate; the right to hear is rarely serviceable to the benighted. Tolerance toward eccentricity is of little value to those who must so live and work that they have little energy or opportunity for non-chemically induced verve. In sum, Mill's liberties, valuable though they are, were not adequate to dislodge the suppressions of his time, much less ours.

Marcuse, on the other hand, is concerned with liberation which will unyoke each man's pent-up ability to understand his natural desires and to harmonize each individual's hopes with mankind's genuine social goals. After liberation the entire public, according to Marcuse, will enjoy all the individual freedoms that anyone can, in justice, claim; liberated society will afford everyone liberty consistent with social perfection. The solidarity that will result from Marcuse's new individual liberty is instinctual; it will flow from the hearts of men released from the unnatural repressions of corporate capitalism.

Marcuse puts no trust in the rational faculties of either the pre-revolutionary public or those public servants who officiate steadfastly. He writes off the possibility that our society as a whole already has, to some extent, genuine aspirations for individual freedom which have been at least partly understood and attained. This rejection of Mill's case for rationality seems unwarranted. Rational discourse can, in some sectors, advance civilization; public discussion looking toward ways for overcoming shortcomings is of value. Cool development of facts is often enough. Public disclosure of the effects on dental health and the dollar costs of water fluoridation was, for example, persuasive enough for social action. Other social problems refuse to remain so factual, and are met only when our hearts as well as our heads are moved. The economic, social, and educational problems of liberating the ghetto blacks are, for example, problems of will as well as of way.

Marcuse's essay celebrates the potential of all of humanity. He is right in looking with disfavor on some of the tastes and many of the goals of contemporary society; some social reorientations could release more of our better natures. Clarified intuition of the unchallengeable worth of humans and the right of every man to count is of first importance. Adequate respect for the humanity of man will be only theoretical, however, unless and until society consists of an all-inclusive public capable of maturing widely shared values and served by men capable of discovering and implementing the public's aspirations. Revolution, at most, can redirect the slow processes of amelioration. Perhaps Mill's case for a continuously developing right of discourse, plus Marcuse's inspiration for enlivened intuition of man's worth, will inspire needed protests and confrontations that will dissolve unwarranted complacency. Liberation from complacency, however, does not win through when everyone fights to be the first to hear and accede to new prophets' proclamations. Liberty to remember what we have learned, to consider where we should go, to refine the best of proposals, and to dissent from unworthy programs may slow down social changes; these liberties, nevertheless, may contribute much to advancing and protecting the common good. New whims may happen to be better than old conceits. The novelty and excitement of new whims, however, do not guarantee that they are nascent, genuine public aspirations.

Chapter 4

Law and Logic

This chapter is on the logic of law—that is, on the way logic bears on the work of lawyers and judges. For thousands of years logicians have studied the formal aspects of valid thought; they have concerned themselves with the formal principles that govern the validity of sound reason. Many distinguished lawyers and judges have become masters of their craft without studying logic—just as many gifted painters have become masters of their art without studying aesthetics. Nevertheless elementary logic is a sensible point of departure for arriving at some understanding of legal processes. The level of treatment that follows is nontechnical; it stays within the grasp of those who have studied neither logic nor law.

A collection of examples illustrating abstract logical principles in concrete legal settings would not do for us; so limited a joinder of logic and law would not penetrate legal problem-solving processes. We must, therefore, start out with a sketch of legal thought, and then reach out to logic for further enlightenment.

Legal work often is not problematic; lawyers and judges expend much of their energies in routine activity. In the busywork of routine, problems sometimes escape notice and then, of course, go unsolved except by accident. Lawyers know they should be acute, and the best of them become good at reacting nimbly to inklings of legal significance.

Legal problems, when they do occur, have a way of conglomerating. What, at first glance, seems legally simple often turns out to be proliferating and complex. It it not unusual for a single legal issue to mushroom into a patch of problems. A lawyer, for example, is consulted by a client who, when a customer in Publican's Tavern, fell down a stairway and injured himself. Even the least experienced of lawyers would immediately wonder whether this client was, at the time of his accident, taking care enough to escape the defense of contributory negligence. While investigating the facts on the contributory negligence point the lawyer might discover, in turn, each of the following significant possibilities. (1) Shortly before the accident one Tom Toper playfully smashed the light bulb illuminating the head of the stairway. (2) Tom at the time may have been an employee of Publican. (3) Tom worked on the day shift and he may have broken the light after that shift ended. (4) Tom, at the bartender's request, may have given up his leisure to help out for a few minutes. This kind of complexity calls for subanalyses and their organization. The lawyer moves among this constellation of possibilities to, he hopes, an integrated plan of action. He may have to move back and forth between subanalyses and integration to satisfy himself.

Problem-solving lawyers and judges constantly consult "authorities"—statutes, case law, scholarly commentaries. If the authorities are clear and decisive, and a problem still persists, the locus of the problem is in the facts. Sometimes, however, the authorities only appear to be authoritative; they may be unsound and may be subject to attack. A lawyer must know when to be skeptical about authority. His problem orients him to the acceptability of authority; his problem can both inspire re-examination of some authorities and dampen skepticism about others. Suppose in the stairway case the claimant's lawyer discovers that Publican's Tavern is operated by Publican, Inc., and that the corporation carries adequate liability insurance. He will not advance his client's claim by challenging the authorities declaiming that stockholders are not responsible for the misdeeds of their corporation. If, however, the company was not insured and bankrupt, an attack on the usual authority (preferably by using still other authority) may be his only hope.

Authority has a special significance for a lawyer. He can and often must be critical of esteemed legal scholarship. A lawyer, however, not only makes his own decisions, he also must work with a foreglimpse at what judges will do. While judges vary in their deference to authority, none of them is likely to make a show of flaunting it. Few judges scorn judicial opinions, textbooks, learned scholars' restatements of the law, and the like. A lawyer who can cast his documents and arguments so that they mesh with authority may succeed, when equivalent but less orthodox formulations might fail. In other words, a lawyer is well advised to make a noise like a lawyer.

The application of old authority to new problems may or may not come easily, but in one sense it is never automatic. Specific legal problems are always unique; someone must decide whether or not some aspects of a new occurrence removes it from the ambit of a preformulated theory; whenever a problem is not routine, the facts of the new instance had better be skeptically scrutinized.

"Authority" is ambiguous; thus far it has been used to refer to respected theorizing; the common law tradition of following precedents gives judges a position of power extending beyond esteem for their wisdom. An *opinion* written by a clumsy judicial theorist may, insofar as it covers matters not before him, have little influence on the law, but the *decision* of the court for whom he writes will not be overruled lightly. Similarly a bill passed by the legislature has power not dimmed by lack of esteem for the legislator who introduced it—power resting on the constitutional franchise of the legislature.

Law is a linguistical art. Practically nothing done by a problem-solving lawyer or judge can be divorced from words. Legal training and experience are hoarded in verbal symbols, which assign durable meaning to fleeting events. Words gather together likenesses and block apart differences. Language useful in one context, however, may be obstructive in another; words may hamper thought when they either cloak significant differences or scatter significant likenesses. The lawyer's ability to use symbols, nevertheless, expands his storage capacity for remembering significant legal ideas and experiences. Lawyers do not, of course, depend on memory alone for solving new problems—except when lack of time precludes research. The use of lawbooks, however, is of a piece with their legal past; those who look to lawbooks for solutions of legal problems seldom find what they seek unless they are versed in the legal system. Laymen who drop into a law library to look something up are usually more likely to be dumbfounded than informed; their disappointment does not result merely from ineptitude in finding the right volumes; it stems from their artless grasp of law. A reader of reported cases, statutes, and textbooks misunderstands what they say unless he can read them in their legal context.

RHETORICAL FALLACIES

"Rhetoric" is an old-fashioned word. In medieval colleges it was taught as one of the seven liberal arts. In more ancient times rhetoric was sometimes taught as skill in the sly craft of misleading argumentation. At its best rhetoric combined applied logic with good style and persuasiveness. When so taught it identified unsound reasoning and exposed it. Many fallacies were given names, some of which are still in use in the analysis of argumentation. A few of these fallacies are discussed in some elementary logic books. We can use some of them to carry us over a good bridge from legal process to more formal logic.

1. Argumentum ad hominem. (Argument directed to the man.) This fallacy is exemplified on a wholesale scale by the refusal of Texas lawyers and judges to cite or rely on cases decided by a group of hated judges—those who served on the Supreme Court of Texas during the "Reconstruction" period which followed the Civil War. This rejection was excused by the claim that the Reconstruction judges were incompetent. Some of them were; others were probably as competent as the mine run of those who came before and after them. The irrelevant fact that a group of judges were personally distasteful blanked out scores of precedents, some of which were no doubt sound. Fortunately this anathema did not reach to the acceptance of the contraries of the reconstruction decisions.

A stale saying advises defense lawyers to try the prosecuting attorney whenever they have no case. That the prosecuting attorney beats his mother has no bearing on whether or not an accused bank teller embezzled his employer's funds. Jurors who are set at odds with the prosecuting attorney pay grudging attention to his proofs and arguments and, as a result, may acquit an accused even though he has been proved guilty beyond a reasonable doubt. Defense counsel who glaringly interject a prejudicially irrelevant attack on prosecuting attorneys act improperly and are dealt with accordingly.

There is, however, a kind of case in which personal attack on the prosecuting attorney is both legitimate and desirable. When, during a criminal trial of a doubtful case, the prosecuting attorney's demeanor betrays an excess of zeal, the defense counsel can properly impugn his good faith. Defense counsel serves his guiltless clients best when he establishes their innocence; such a defense not only keeps the accused out of jail, it also vindicates him. Defense counsel must, however, often settle for less; he goes into many trials with no hope of establishing his client's innocence; he only expects to protect his client from conviction on evidence insufficient to establish his client's guilt beyond a reasonable doubt. A prosecuting attorney may disregard his own obligation to be objective and may overzealously persist in pressing a charge on marginal evidence. If the victim of his zeal is ill-favored, or has an unpopular religious affiliation or ethnic identity, jurors may tend to suppress reasonable doubt of guilt. During such a trial an alert defense counsel who detects the prosecuting attorney's rancor in his demeanor may legitimately point out the indicia of this animus to the jury. The risk that such a personal attack on the prosecuting attorney may divert the jurors from proper evaluation of the prosecutor's case is more than offset by the likelihood that the disclosure will put the jurors on their mettle to resolve the issue of reasonable doubt dispassionately. The attack on the prosecuting attorney's person does not, illogically, switch the jury's attention away from the true issue; on the contrary it, logically, centers their attention on the true issue, that is, the adequacy of the state's proof.

A hundred years ago, there were common law courts that refused to allow felons, after conviction, ever again to testify; their testimony was thought too unreliable to be heard. Bad men, however, can and often do tell the truth. The old view has long since been repudiated. Nowadays courts hear the testimony of convicts for what it is worth; opposing counsel are, however, permitted to "impeach" these witnesses by proving their previous convictions. Impeachment does not try the witness, rather the case between the litigants. Logicians can afford to say that a bad man's testimony *may be* true, and stop there. When, however, a tribunal is asked to believe a witness and act on what he says, the tribunal must ask itself whether he *is* telling the truth.

There are, nevertheless, practical limits to impeachment. If opposing counsel were allowed to impeach by trying to show that a witness had, in an unrelated law suit, committed perjury but had escaped detection, the court could, indeed, find itself detouring disturbingly from the issues before it, and prolonging and complicating litigation. The limits on "collateral" impeachments are, therefore, drastic, necessary juridical economies. The proof of a previous conviction of a witness is quick and simple; it and a few other simple impeachments are permitted.

Not all previous convictions cast doubt on a witness' credibility. A conscientious objector convicted of violating conscription laws may be equally conscientious in other respects and, therefore, more worthy of belief than most witnesses. To show his conviction would prejudice some jurors against him and tend, illogically, to produce disbelief—an honest-to-goodness case of *argumentum ad hominem*. Other examples can readily be thought of. The impeachment rule permitting these illogicalities can be defended only on the grounds that it rarely works prejudicially and that administrative convenience requires the courts to take a little bad with a lot of good— especially since the fallacy can be explained to the jurors.

One form of *argumentum ad hominem* is an insistence that the person to whom a proposition is stated must accept it as true because of his affiliations. It would have been illogical to say to Bishop Pike that he must accept a proposition as true, because the Bible says it is so. He may have had a religious obligation to abide by certain articles of faith, but he had no logical obligation to do so. A judge, as a man, has no logical obligation to believe the bare assertion that a particular tavern in a residential neighborhood constitutes an unreasonable land use. If a zoning law makes the tavern's location illegal, a judge asked to enjoin the tavern's operation has a legal obligation to issue an injunction. Suppose, however, that although the tavern violates no zoning ordinance, the neighbors, nevertheless, sue to close it down, because it attracts a disorderly patronage, who strike terror into the hearts of nearby residents. A lawyer representing the tavern keeper would shudder at finding the case docketed before a lady judge who is a past president of the Women's Christian Temperance Union. He would not, however, argue *ad hominem* if he told her that she was obliged to reach a legally sound result without regard to where her own moral convictions lay, and therefore that she was obliged, as a public servant, to reflect the community's values (rather than her own) in deciding this issue.

Logic enjoins all thinkers seeking truth to abjure their affiliations as irrelevant. When, however, a judge undertakes to serve the public, justice dictates that he implement the public's aspirations and refrain from implementing views of his own at odds with the public's widely shared values. The judge in our tavern case might, of course, heed this argument and still come up with a holding that happens to accord with her own views.

2. **Accident.** Since the lawyer, St. Thomas Aquinas said,

cannot have in view every single case, he shapes the law by what happens most frequently . . . Wherefore if a case arise wherein the observance of that law would be hurtful to the general welfare, it should not be observed. For instance, suppose that in a besieged city it be established law that the gates are to be kept closed . . . If it were to happen that the enemy are in pursuit of certain citizens who are defenders of the city, it would be a great loss to the city if the gates were not opened to them: and so in that case the gates ought to be opened, contrary to the letter of the law, in order to maintain the commonweal, which the lawgiver had in view.

St. Thomas is talking about the foolishness of being misled when the words of a promulgated rule are read out of context and happen "by accident" to seem literally applicable to a case. Though a certain federal judge did not use the rhetorical term "accident," he illustrated avoidance of the fallacy strikingly in this case: The Congress had enacted a law governing railroads' liabilities to train crewmen who are injured while at work. One clause of the statute barred claims brought to the courts more than two years after the date of the injury. The judge put the case of a railroad that locked up an injured crewman and, to prevent him from filing his suit on time, kept him incommunicado for two years. The words of the enacted rule only "by accident" covered this work injury case. Congress did not intend them to be applicable to such a case as this.

Some illustrations of accident are no more than bad puns. A shopworn illustration involves a Bologna law that provided criminal punishment for "whoever draws blood in the streets." It is said that a Bologna judge held this law inapplicable to a surgeon with Good Samaritan inclinations who came upon a stricken stroller and treated him by bleeding him on the spot. The story is probably fiction; even a stupid policeman would not be guilty of this silly pun, misidentifying therapy with swordplay.

Language used in legal documents to prescribe for future contingencies is uttered by people who intend to say what they mean. To this end legislators, parties to contracts, and makers of deeds and wills all use words that, at the time, seem clear to them in the belief that these words will communicate their intentions to others when, at a later time, a dispute occurs. By and large utterers intend the ordinary meanings of words; improbable meanings are not likely to have occurred to a legislature passing a firearms control bill or to a farmer signing a lease for pasture lands. Courts should initially approach the wording of enactments and documents with respect. Wild surmises of unlikely meanings should never unhorse those common meanings which seem to be the reasonable sense of the language used. Courts become interested in interpretations departing from language's common meaning only after a sensible suggestion is advanced to support the hypothesis that the wording used misspoke intention. Even when reasonable doubt is soundly raised, words are still presumed to have been used in their ordinary sense; the presumption falls only after a showing that an alternative meaning is not only tenable but is the more likely one.

The climax of Shakespeare's *The Merchant of Venice* is reached in the courtroom scene. Shylock, the moneylender, has sued Antonio to enforce the clause in the loan contract by which Antonio agreed that a default shall cost him "a pound of his flesh." Shylock has poised his sharpened knife ready to slice into Antonio's breast when Portia (Antonio's beautiful fiancée disguised as a male lawyer) interjects the argument that since Shylock is entitled to a pound of flesh, he must cut an exact pound—not a bit more or less, and since he is entitled only to flesh, he is not entitled to a drop of blood. This argument dramatically seems to save the day. The judge, however, must have known that the vice in Shylock's claim lay in the iniquity of his bargain, and not in poor draftsmanship. The case would surely have gone the same way had the clause read "one pound, more or less, of flesh, with the necessary blood-letting appurtenant thereto." The judge who purported to sustain Portia's outrageous paltering must have had secret reasons for giving the right judgment on the wrong grounds. Perhaps he had epicene tastes inducing a willingness to approve harmless error when committed by a delicately handsome young lawyer.

Judges can be too quick or too slow to find "accident." In either case, they are likely to thwart the intentions of those who enact laws or execute legal documents. A judge quick to find accident hankers after unwarranted self-assertion; he wants to ignore expressed intentions and require, in their place, what he thinks best. A judge too slow to find accident enjoys ducking responsibility; he wants to live by the security of the dictionary and hold men to words, instead of seeking out their genuine intentions.

There are, of course, times when, as a matter of policy, ambiguities should go one way rather than another. We believe that criminal law should be clearly promulgated in advance of trial; as a result, we tend to construe criminal statutes strictly—that is, resolving serious ambiguity in favor of the accused. And we believe that consumers ought to be favored over large corporations using skilled draftsmen to prepare such documents as insurance policies—

ambiguities in these documents should be interpreted in favor of the consumer.

3. Misidentification. The fallacy of misidentification preys on superficial resemblances; it is committed when a precedent is misidentified, so that it is made to cover a new case not within its reach. Suppose a court decides against John Jones, a burglar who sues for personal injuries incurred when he fell down a defectively guarded elevator shaft while robbing X company's premises. Later nine-year-old Tommy Smith sues for personal injuries incurred when he was playing on an unlocked turn-table on Y railroad's unfenced premises in a residential neighborhood. If railroad counsel cites the Jones case as a precedent barring recovery he commits misidentification.

Whether or not a resemblance is significant or superficial is not always easily determined. Consider this succession of three cases: (1) Mr. Merchant puts a sign in his store window. The sign informs large numbers of passersby that Mr. Quincy Fourflusher owes Merchant $182.00 for goods sold on credit, and payment is six months past due. A court, in which Fourflusher sues Merchant for violating his right to privacy, gives Fourflusher a judgment. (2) A customer of another merchant sues a newspaper for violating his right to privacy by publishing a paid advertisement containing the same sort of message. Announcement in a newspaper is, for this kind of case, clearly the legal equivalent of the announcement in the store window. In the newspaper case, however, the debtor is not suing the creditor who placed the ad in the paper; he is suing the disinterested newspaper who merely supplied a means of announcement. If the creditor (with a right to be paid) commits a wrong by his distasteful collection tactics, a newspaper (with no interest in the debt) is all the more in the wrong when for pelf it does the same sort of dirty work. The extension of the holding in (1) to (2), then, is not a misidentification—though it is a typical step in the growth of the law which becomes a little more textured every time an old precedent is applied to a new case. (3) Buffalo Bill buys a gun on credit from gunsmith Colt. He, too, turns out to be a slow payer, and Colt decides to use a debt-collection tactic exactly the same as that used by Merchant in (1); to that end he orders a sign from T. S. Painter and puts it in his window. A few days later Colt dies. Buffalo Bill's lawyer advises a suit against Painter. Bill agrees. His lawyer argues to the court that Painter's acts in (3) are the legal equivalent of the newspaper's acts in (2). Is or isn't this argument misidentification? The answer to that question is not easy. Courts have the obligation to decide cases even-handedly. When cases resemble each other the court meets this obligation only if it either treats resembling cases in the same way or points out significant differences. Problems as hard as this one make good lawyers and good judges worth their hire.

4. Entrapping Questions. The hackneyed example of an entrapping question is "Have you stopped beating your wife?" Since everybody old enough to have a wife knows the duplicity of this gag, it can no longer entrap. Some double questions do, however, have psychological power to extract self-betrayal from the unwary. An intermeddler, for example, had tampered with delicate machinery and denied his deed. His questioner suddenly asked, "What would you say if I told you I saw you do it?" To his dismay the intermeddler heard himself reply, "You couldn't have; you weren't there when I did it."

The entrapper's strategy is to load his question with duality so that a quick and simple answer is pregnant with a miscalculated admission. Trial judges allow cross-examiners to use this trick, and lawyers occasionally find it useful. Of course, the entrapped witness, whose tongue has slipped, is entitled, with friendly help, to explain. Sometimes he has blabbed and his explanation is unpersuasive. At other times his explanation is entirely convincing, and the cross-examiner's strategy boomerangs, leaving him in the posture of a crafty enemy of the truth.

DEDUCTIVE LOGIC

We turn now to a discussion of more formal logic's relationship to legal reasoning.

A reasoner carries out a deduction whenever he asserts that one or more given propositions imply an additional proposition. The standard example is this: given the two propositions "All men are mortal" and "Socrates is a man," the proposition "Socrates is mortal" is implied. Classical Aristotelian logic subdivides deduction into a great number of different classes; modern logic ignores many classical fine-spun distinctions, but, by adding new operations, it too has developed a complicated range. Our elementary interests will be best served if discussion of deductions is confined to the application of rules of law to facts of cases—concerning ourselves with only a few of logic's subdistinctions.

Since the processes of formal logic work only with propositions, raw facts, as such, cannot function in formal logic. When raw facts are sorted out and stated as the facts-of-a-case, their propositional form gains them admittance into both the theater of logic (where related propositions discover their kinships) and the theater of law (where relevant legal doctrines and meaningful facts-of-cases can interact to a finale). The lawyer can do little with undescribed events. He depicts events so that they display their legal significance—he extracts from a complicated, interlaced, infinitely detailed texture-of-happenings finite, important aspects, and then describes them in terms that match relevant rules, selected from a massive system of laws.

The lawyer's facts, then, are never bare crude existences. The lawyer's past experience and his accumulation of ideas play important roles when he sets himself to discover the significant fact-of-a-case. The meanings that color the facts of law cases are only partly legal; an automobile moving at one hundred miles per hour has a core of meaning for lawyers, drag racers, and safety engineers— though each will, of course, use the core differently. Since law is about life, even the more technical and esoteric terms have to be capable of touching the real world, "easements," for example, have to do with one man's right to make some use of the property occupied by another, and "emblements" are a special form of easement; the man who has an emblement nearly always knows that he has it and uses it. Rules of law, too, are ways of *looking at,* as well as ways of dealing with, what goes on. They do not dart down from out of this world and attach themselves to existences, like eagles capturing hares. Functionally, then, legal processes, moving from events to decisions, categorize those events legally, so that as a result they fit into legal categories involving the legally appropriate disposition of what happened. At the moment the process starts, the problem-solver is looking for the path from events to legal results; for him, events, propositions of facts, rules of law, and decisions are not four unrelated and different things that will come together from unrelated spheres, like four travelers who happen to meet at an inn.

The process of applying law to facts cannot be *fully* described, then, as deduction. What has happened, after the legal process is over, can be formally indicated by organizing the rule of law used (as a major premise), the facts found (as a minor premise), and the decision made (as a conclusion implied by those two premises). In this syllogistic version the premises are taken as given and the dynamic activity that went into shaping them is suppressed. The principles of logic, then, hold out validating models toward which legal processes push. I do not mean, of course, that these validating models of logic have nothing to do with the stages that precede the juncture at which they can be put to formal use; an end-in-view always has something to do with the processes that push toward it.

IMMEDIATE INFERENCE

The proposition "All Share-companies are Partnerships" implies the falsity of the proposition "Some Share-companies are not Partnerships." This is a fleshed-out example of what the classical logicians called "immediate inference"—a process that draws implications immediately from a single proposition—rather than from two or more premises. Of course logicians are not interested in Share-companies or Partnerships, as such, but in subjects and predicates, which they symbolize as Ss and Ps. One kind of immediate inference deals with the implications that persist in propositions that take four forms: "All S is P," "No S is P," "Some S is P," and "Some S is not P." The logicians have formulated several principles governing this sort of immediate inference, three of which will now be discussed.

Rule 1. Given the truth of "All S is P," then if S-es exist, the truth of "Some S is P" follows.

The existential requirement has several logical significances, one of which bears on law. It is logically possible to say, "All who desecrate the flag of the State of Nevada are guilty of felony," even though no one ever has or will do so. Some laws are passed with the hope that a class of lawbreakers will remain empty.

Rule 1 also emphasizes a special requirement of law—even-handedness. Given "all men arrested by the police are entitled to prompt arraignment" implies that none—no matter how shabby, recalcitrant, or guilty—shall be deprived of this right.

"All S" in the proposition "All S is P" is obviously a *class* of S-es. The logician uses "Some S" in "Some S is P" also to describe a *class*, even when this class has only one member. This usage may, at first glance, seem to be a crotchety convention; it is not, however—in many contexts, including legal ones, it illuminates an important aspect of reasoning. A Kansas statute provides in effect, "All vehicles traveling at night must carry taillights." The Kansas Supreme Court held that a night-riding horseman violated this statute. The decision of the court, if proper, was based on its view that this violator was a *typical* night-riding horseman; the court's decision would have been improper if it had applied this statute especially to this particular rider as uniquely violating the statute because he was a black man, mounted on a black horse, and night-riding in the dark of the moon. Whenever a rule of law is identified with the facts of a case, the subsumption should be made, not on the ground that the unique case, as such, is an instance of the rule, but on the ground that the case falls into a category properly included in the wider class governed by the rule. If the taillight statute covers horseback riders, it does so regardless of their race, the color of their horses, or the time of the month. The point can be made in more formal terms by saying that a law requiring that ALL vehicles carry taillights, applies to all VEHICLES. Its ambit depends on the court's development of a reasoned definition of "vehicle," and not on the court's whimsical stowage of a single case in a legal bin at the court's own sweet will. If a horse ridden on the highway is a legal vehicle, it is not because his name is Tom, but because he belongs, as a horse-ridden-on-the-highway, to a sub*class* of legal vehicles.

In more abstract terms, "All S" says something about "Some S" only if S in "Some S" has class characteristics that make it properly described as an area of S-es. Overparticularization of cases subsumed under a rule is not wrong in the sense that those cases cannot fall under the rule; if horses ridden on the highway are vehicles, they are so *in spite of* the ethnic identification of the rider. The important point is, however, they are not vehicles *because of* the ethnic identification of the rider, and a court that gives that fact legal force has lost its way and misinterpreted the rule.

The legal process of proceeding from "all vehicles traveling at night must carry taillights" to "night-ridden horses must carry taillights" is less abstract than the process of proceeding from "All S is P" to "Some S is P." The logician assumes that the meaning of S in the less general proposition falls within the meaning of S in the more general one; lacking that assumption the logician is unwilling to do anything at all. When law is to be applied to facts, the hypothesis that the case is governed by the rule must occur to someone and then be, on legal grounds, substantiated. A highway patrolman who never dreams that night-riding equestrians may be covered by the taillight statute will not charge them with violation, whether or not he has had a course in logic.

Rule 2. Given the truth of "Some S is not P," the falsity of "All S is P" follows.

The obvious way of attacking the sanctity of any proposition is to show that it errs in some respect. A lawyer who wants a court to relieve his client from the burdens of a general rule usually will not accomplish much by demonstrating that the rule works badly in cases significantly differing from his client's case. Some general rules purport to cover a wide variety of cases; a decision holding the rule unsound for one kind of case does not, in itself, destroy the rule for all cases. A lawyer who, for example, can cite a case holding a gambling contract unenforceable does not advance the defense of a client who is sued in contract for nonpayment for groceries bought on credit.

Only total unconstitutionality, legislative repeal, or a long course of judicial repudiation in a variety of cases, wholly destroys those rules of law that apply to widely differing kinds of cases.

As a matter of fact, some theoretical inaccuracies in legal rules

have no practical significance at all. Personal property is, for example, abandoned according to an orthodox rule of law only when
the former owner intends to abandon it and reveals that intention
by an unequivocal act. In an obscure opinion, a bucolic judge
assumes this case: A horseman's mount drops ordure on a public
bridle path—an occurrence which, at the time, the rider does not
notice, much less think about. A scavenger appropriates this manure for fertilizer. The horseman discovers the facts and then
claims that his property has been misappropriated. The orthodox
rule supports the horseman's claim; since he did not intend to
abandon, he has not, according to the rule, abandoned this property.
The judge, nevertheless, is of the view that there is an abandonment
in this case. His opinion, even though it conflicts with the orthodox
rule, seems correct. The rule can be recast in such a way that it
squares with both earlier decisions and this newly imagined case.
The new version could read something like this: Property is abandoned whenever it is found in such circumstances that the finder is
justified in believing that the former owner no longer cares what
happens to it. The change, however, refines only theory; it will not
affect practice which stands in no need of improvement. People
do not go to law over worthless trash. The appropriator of objects
of worth can reasonably believe that they are no longer wanted
(the new test) only when the old owner has intended to abandon
them and has acted so as to reveal his intention unequivocally (the
old test). In law suits, then, the orthodox test works just as well as
the theoretically sounder test and no practical good would come out
of correction. Courts rarely move toward purities that are exclusively academical. Logicians give us no principles telling us when a
defect in a rule evinced by an inconsistent case is of practical
moment. Logic does, however, put us on notice of the folly of
believing the nonsense about the exception proving the rule.

It is, of course, true that a common law rule may be riddled by
a long succession of exceptions, and finally fade slowly into oblivion.
In the late nineteenth century, for example, most common law
courts refused to entertain claims for money damages for illnesses
induced without physical contact but by emotional upset. Given a
heart attack ensuing from the charge of a mismanaged bull, the

courts compensated the victim for cardiac damage only when the bull smashed into the victim; no compensation for the cardiac damage went to a victim nimble enough to jump aside. The traditional reasons for this distinction became unconvincing. This distinction, however, was so deeply entrenched in the authorities that courts, unready to repudiate it, made exceptions favoring some of those injured through wrongful emotional upset. The exceptions were grounded on unstated policies irreconcilable with those that had been used to justify the rule. Emboldened by exceptions exposing the rule's general unsoundness, most courts have repudiated the original rule.

Unwarranted novel exceptions to a sound orthodox rule are, however, not worth arguing for. This is not the same as saying that when facts of a case seem to be instances of a clear, clearly applicable, and sound orthodox rule there is no escape from that rule's prescribed results. A householder, let us say, sells his split-level through an intermediary who pockets both part of the purchase price and a broker's fee from the buyer. Thereafter a local military post is closed and the value of the house falls precipitately. The buyer discovers, for the first time, that the intermediary made more out of the transaction than his broker's fee. The buyer sues to rescind the sale and alleges that the case is governed by the double-agent rule (to the effect that when an agent acts for both parties to a transaction without the knowledge of one of them, the ignorant party is entitled to a rescission). This rule is well established and just. If, however, the seller can show that the intermediary was not the seller's agent, the double-agency rule will by its terms be inapplicable. Such a showing of course cannot be honestly made if there was in fact a double agency. Suppose that seller's lawyer finds out, however, that the middleman approached the seller and paid for an option to buy the house at a stipulated price; then, without knowledge or connivance of the seller, the intermediary exercised his option rights for the buyer. Proof of these facts takes the case out of the ambit of the rule. In spite of the force of first impressions that an impregnable rule is applicable to this case, careful, legally oriented research categorized the facts as "not-S: (not double agency) and the rule "All S is P" (all double-agency contracts are voidable) blows by.

Rule 3. Given the truth of "Some S is P," "All S is P" may or may not be true.

This rule warns against hasty generalization. A layman may, for example, hear about a court decision holding an unwritten contract unenforceable and erroneously assume that all unwritten contracts are unenforceable. Of course it is a pretty good idea to get important contracts down in writing—whether or not the courts will enforce them without the writing. His error may, however, turn this layman away from opportunities to clinch desirable and enforceable contracts.

"Hasty generalization" closely resembles "misidentification" discussed as a rhetorical fallacy. The formalization in our Rule 3 does have an additional important overtone; the rule expressly identifies indeterminacy. Sometimes action in the face of indeterminacy is unwise. That a fungus might have been an edible mushroom is little comfort when after it is eaten it turns out to be poisonous. We can, however, live sensibly with indeterminacy; there are few occasions on which fungus is the only comestible with which to sustain life.

A lawyer is preparing to try a slander suit. His client is a male photographer whose business rival has publicly charged him with unchastity. In earlier slander suits based on oral imputations of unchastity, female claimants have succeeded without proving "special damages." If the lawyer needs to prove special damages in this case he can meet the requirement by proving that the slander caused one customer, Mrs. X, to cancel an appointment. The court has never determined whether or not a male claimant in this sort of case needs special damage proof. There is a likelihood that the special damage proof involving Mrs. X may engender ill will. Lawyer and client are now faced with a dilemma. Should the risk of not proving special damages be run or are the client's best interests served by making the proof? Rule 3 does not tell the lawyer what to do. It does, however, warn that it is time to choose.

SYLLOGISMS

One of many classes of syllogisms is specially apt for this discussion. It is a variety of what logicians call the "hypothetical syllogism." Its major premise is a compound of two propositions, symbolized as P and Q. P comes first and is called the "antecedent." Q comes second and is called the 'consequent." The major premise of this sort of syllogism deals with those situations in which P, the antecedent, never exists unless Q, the consequent, also exists. If a mortal blow is given (antecedent) then death follows (consequent). Whenever it can be asserted that the antecedent (mortal blow) does in fact exist then it can be implied that the consequent (death follows) also exists. A rule of law stating that if certain facts occur (antecedent) then certain legal effects attach (consequent) exemplifies this hypothetical form. When those facts described in the antecedent of the rule (the-facts-of-a case) exist, then it can be concluded that the legal effects in the consequent of the rule also attach. If a husband is a habitual drunkard (antecedent) then his wife has grounds for divorce (consequent):

> Mary's husband is a habitual drunkard (assertion of the existence of a case of the antecedent).
> Mary has grounds for divorce (attachment of legal effect of consequent).

The logician's analysis applies, of course, only when the existence postulated in the minor premise is genuinely identified with the antecedent in the major premise. Recall the Bologna street-fighting law discussed in connection with the rhetorical fallacy of "accident" —that is, "If a man draws blood in the streets, then he shall be punished." A surgeon's therapeutic bleeding is not a genuine case of the antecedent; the antecedent refers to violence that, of course, does not exist in an instance of succor.

Any body of rules that on one occasion gives two diametrically opposed answers to a single problem is irrational. The law in action never does that; when a dispute has been litigated to judgment the court never orders the defendant both to pay the plaintiff $10,000 and to pay him nothing at all. Legal theory, however, may seem to give two equally good and diametrically opposed answers; often a claimant seemingly makes an impregnable case by invoking one rule of law and the defense seemingly makes an equally good one by invoking another rule. A warmhearted uncle says to his favorite nephew, "I promise you that on next Christmas morning my Swiss chiming watch will be in your stocking; I shall be very careful in keeping it for you until then." The uncle dies in November; Christmas comes and goes; the uncle's executor refuses to deliver over the watch and is sued. The executor argues, "If an undertaking is merely a promise to make a personal gift in the future, it is unenforceable. This undertaking is merely a promise to make a personal gift in the future. Therefore it is unenforceable." The nephew argues, "If words constitute a declaration of a trust, the trust is enforceable. These words are a declaration of a trust. Therefore the trust is enforceable." The court that entertains this suit must and will come up with one answer or the other. Only after the court decides will the parties know which lawyer did affirm an antecedent, and which failed to.

The difficulty in this watch case illustrates a profound difference between logical and legal processes. The logician making an assumption that "If P, then Q" says nothing about existence. He also assumes that an assertion of P is an assertion that the antecedent in fact exists. This assumption of existence takes P out of the sky and brings it into the world. As a result, Q, which always follows P, too, comes out of the sky.

We already know that when a lawyer states propositions of fact as the facts-of-a-case, he does not exclusively describe. A judge wrestling with whether or not an antecedent "exists" may be deciding the central question of law in a case, rather than a simple question of fact, which can be answered by anyone with a talent for historical accuracy. In a remote marshy area inhabited only by ducks and suitable for nothing else Mr. Hunter buys a strip of land adjoining a strip owned by Mr. Haven. Hunter builds a duck blind; he sits in the blind as daylight wanes; just as dark comes on he sees a bird in the sky, says to himself, "a mallard," and fires. His shot travels high over the surface of Haven's land, misses the barely visible bird and falls into the open sea beyond. Haven, who loathes Nimrods, charges Hunter with trespassing. The court "disposes" of the question in these words. "If an unauthorized entry is made on private property the entrant commits a trespass. Hunter is guilty of such an unauthorized entry, and therefore is liable to Haven."

The antecedent of the judge's major premise is not just an abstract receptacle that either stays empty or is the socket into which a fact is screwed. "Unauthorized entry" is a legal concept. A burglar slips into this concept so easily that we hardly notice the nonfactual aspect of his entry. Hunter's placement in the category is a little harder. An astronaut flying high in the air column over private land stays out. A pleasure-bound Sunday aeronaut may skirt the edge of it, in law as well as in fact.

The words "unauthorized entry" were first used as ordinary English words with a clear, nontechnical, factual meaning. The core of the words is factually expressive; this core is surrounded by a vaguer border, clarified case by case. Since some new borderline case is always possible, the legal definition will always be, at least theoretically, incomplete. If Haven v. Hunter is a new case, the court that classified Hunter's act as an unauthorized entry did something quite different from what Hunter did when he classified the duck at which he shot as a mallard.

Since whether or not the consequent's legal effects attach to Hunter's act is determined by *holding* that the antecedent exists, the court's *holding* centers on its decision to affirm the antecedent. In some cases the facts-of-the-case are "found" in order to produce those legal effects that the court believes it should reach.

Given "If P, then Q" and proof of the nonexistence of the antecedent P, the consequent Q may or may not exist. If habitual drunkenness is a ground for divorce, and Mary's husband is not a habitual drunkard, she may or may not have other grounds for divorce. This principle of logic is violated in the following case.

The defendant owned a factory and allowed a large gate abutting the public sidewalk to hang dangerously on loosened hinges. He sold the plant; minutes after title passed to the buyer the dilapidated gate fell on a passerby, who brought a damage suit against the former owner. The court reasoned: If an owner of premises abutting a public way ignores disrepair unreasonably endangering passersby, he is liable for resulting injuries. This defendant was not, at the time of the accident, an owner of the premises whose disrepair resulted in injury to a passerby. Therefore this defendant is not liable.

The law of the court's major premise in this gate case opinion is irrelevant; the rule says nothing about former owners. The court's illogical opinion may or may not be unjust. If the pedestrian has no claim against the new owner (which may well be the case, since the new owner had no opportunity to repair before the injury) the result seems unjust. Suppose that the court decided as it did on the unstated theory that liability ought to follow ownership because the seller's liability insurance usually lapses as soon as title passes and the buyer's usually attaches at the same moment. The unstated rationale may be based on mistaken views of insurance law and practice. It also fails to alert the injured man of the court's willingness to favor him if he sues the buyer. Since the court had an obligation to write a meaningful opinion its bad logic is miserable misperformance.

A defense lawyer who thwarts a claimant from asserting the existence of an antecedent may seem to be taking an illogical stance, like that of the court in the gate case. In a divorce suit, the defendant who establishes that he is not a habitual drunkard does not establish that his wife has no other ground for divorce. This is, however, a subtle misrepresentation of his logical posture. He is not using the rule that makes habitual drunkenness a ground of divorce, he is undercutting the plaintiff's use of that rule. By legal convention, in a divorce case the plaintiff has the burden of establishing a ground for divorce. When, in our assumed case, the defendant disproves that he is a habitual drunkard, the wife must come forward with proof of another ground, or fail.

The forensic nature of legal reasoning is hard for the layman to grasp; another example may be helpful.

A yacht owner contracts to sell his yacht to a bank. The vice president of the bank signs for the bank, takes delivery of the yacht and flees in it, with embezzled assets and his pretty secretary, to Brazil. The unpaid yacht seller sues the bank for the purchase price. One orthodox rule provides, in effect, "If a corporation gives its officer actual authority to make a contract then that officer has power to bind the corporation." The bank cannot first deny this antecedent (by showing it gave the V.P. no actual authority) and then claim it has established the nonexistence of the consequent (no power in the V.P. to bind the bank). If the bank had clothed its vice president with apparent authority, while withholding actual authority, he also would have had power to bind the bank. By legal convention, however, the seller in this case (and not the bank) has the burden to prove the officer's power to bind the bank. If the seller pins all of his hopes on establishing actual authority (and makes no case on apparent authority) the bank need not concern itself about apparent authority. In this way time is conserved and law suits move in an orderly fashion. In all litigation, burden of proof conventions determine which litigant must raise each issue and initially offer proof on that issue. Many issues are assigned to defendants rather than claimants; the defendant, for example, has the issue of truth in a libel suit.

Sometimes a rule of law is intended to state the one and only way to reach a particular legal result. In a jurisdiction in which adultery is the only ground for divorce it is legally sound to argue either that Mary's husband has committed adultery, therefore Mary has grounds for divorce, or that Ann's husband has not committed adultery, therefore Ann has no grounds for divorce. The logician's hypothetical form (If P, then Q) is an inadequate statement of such a law. Another form of proposition, called material equivalence, does the job. When P and Q are materially equivalent, two kinds of implications are possible: (1) If either P or Q exists, the other must exist. (2) If either P or Q does not exist, the other cannot exist. When a legislature describes arson and attaches a penalty to it the courts are told not only how arson may be committed but they are (inferentially, if not expressly) instructed also to use no other definition of arson.

Many statutes are not so clear and courts can have trouble in deciding whether their meaning is hypothetical or materially equivalent. In state X it has long been the common law that railroads have no duty to motorists to erect highway warning or grade crossings signs, other than the traditional stationary wooden crossbuck. The legislature enacts a statute providing that all motorists who travel on those roads that are designated by state or federal route numbers are entitled to be warned of railroad grade crossings by electric bell and light signals, erected and maintained by the railroads. What effect does this statute have on the rights of motorists traveling on unnumbered roads and streets? The legislature may have added a clause expressly dealing with this question. Suppose it has not; what does the statute, in its context, mean about crossings on unnumbered roads? There are two possible answers. (1) Courts trying damage suits arising out of accidents occurring at unnumbered road crossings must hold that the railroad was not obliged to give a motorist an electrified warning. (This assigns a meaning like the logician's material equivalence.) (2) The legislature has given the court no instruction one way or another on this kind of case, and the common law court is free to make the appropriate common law decision in this changing world. (This assigns a meaning like the logician's hypothetical proposition.) The art of resolving this ambiguity is a difficult one; suffice it to say that it goes beyond the topic of this essay. We can note in passing, however, that legal substance is not automatically determined in such cases by the formal characteristics of the propositions used. Only through respect for the substance of legislative intention can the democratic practice of separation of powers be honored.

SOURCES OF COMMON LAW RULES

When our courts were enfranchised, judges were neither expressly nor impliedly authorized to set about developing a theoretical body of substantive law rules unattached to the decisions of specific cases; judges are employed only to hear and decide cases, and their decisions, rather than the grounds on which they are reached, are their main end products. Most appellate courts are required or expected to justify their decisions in reasoned opinions, which do give some guidance in both life and law.

In common law cases, courts nearly always purport to rely on what was said or done in earlier cases. The doctrine of precedents favors deeds over words; judges, on their own say-so, fairly often reject unpalatable and unacted-on theories set out in earlier judicial opinions; they label such theories "dicta" and feel no further need to apologize for not adopting them. Precedents are not cast away so casually; when a court expressly overrules one of its own earlier holdings, its judges deem themselves obliged to advance a deliberate justification which sets forth and authenticates an urgent and deep-seated need for change.

Each judicial decision disposes of unique facts. Disposition is rational, however, only when made with a theory in mind, and tradition calls on most appellate courts (and a few trial courts) to issue opinions supporting their decisions. When a court hears a new specific case similar to cases already decided, it can use earlier cases as precedents only after the differences between them and the case at bar are adjudged insignificant. Sometimes, of course, this judgment of identity is immediate and so compelling that it is hardly noticeable.

A judge comparing an old case with one on his docket may develop a new appreciation of the old case. Even though he decides to use the old case as a precedent, details that seemed important when the precedent was originally set may now appear negligible, and details that seemed to have no consequence may now become vital. In other words when a precedent is studied to help decide a case-at-hand some new understanding may come, not only to the case-at-hand, but also to the precedent. Therefore, when precedents are "followed," past as well as present law may take on new meaning.

Occasionally precedents are overlooked. Once in a while a gifted judge synthesizes a whole line of precedents. Academic legal scholarship sometimes mediates between old precedents and new applications. By and large the processes sketched in this paragraph generate two kinds of products: (1) A galaxy of decided cases most of which can be reconciled with each other. (2) An overlay of theories, less consistent. In common law, theoretical inconsistencies result from two facts: (1) Theories grow, contract, and change over an extended period of time during which new thought-provoking details of cases come into view. (2) Theories are announced and reiterated by judges, whose skills in theorizing on cases vary more than their capacity for just decision.

We expect that judges, like scientists, will deal carefully and objectively with their data. The scientist, however, is interested in particulars primarily for their bearing on theory, while the judge is interested in theory primarily for its bearing on particulars. A judge needs sound theory so that he can proceed to well-grounded decisions, explained in reasonable opinions; sound theory is essential, but it is not his end-in-view. Judicial theory can be entirely adequate for a case-at-hand without being broad enough to cover the field; the most capable judges often strengthen their opinions by expressly refusing to opine on related questions not up for immediate decision.

INDUCTIVE LOGIC AND COMMON LAW

Inductive logic deals with those principles of sound reasoning that are applicable to the process of developing theory through investigating facts. Its two classic expositors were Francis Bacon and John Stuart Mill, both of whom were thinking primarily of science. Mill's formulated "methods of induction" were once the mainstay of inductive logic in elementary logic textbooks. Modern logicians, acquainted with sophisticated history and philosophy of science, give these "methods" a reduced position.

Mill calls his first rule of inductive logic, "the method of agreement." The method works this way: An investigator notes a recurring phenomenon; he investigates all of the antecedents of several instances of that phenomenon; when one and only one identical antecedent is discovered in each instance investigated, the investigator has probably found the cause of the phenomenon.

Edward Jenner, an eighteenth-century physician, noted, for example, that milkmaids rarely came down with smallpox; he found that nearly all milkmaids contracted a mild disorder called cowpox, which made them immune to smallpox germs. He went on to perfect a vaccine.

Dr. Jenner's discovery seems as first glance to exemplify the value of Mill's method of agreement. Mill sets the search for one common antecedent, and this is what Dr. Jenner found. Mill, however, also requires discovery of the *only* common antecedent. Since the milkmaids were all human beings following a common calling in England, there were dozens of other common antecedents, that is, they all had exceptional finger strength, manure-tainted shoes, morning and evening work hours; they all sat on three-legged stools, etc., etc., etc. Dr. Jenner would not have found the causal relation between cowpox and immunity had he not developed a sensible hypothesis; without it all he could have done for those who wanted to avoid smallpox would have been to advise them to milk cows. The scientist, like the lawyer, can do little with raw facts before he fastens on to the beginning of a theory with which facts can function.

What does the method of agreement have to do with legal processes? Mr. Espy, we shall say, found a watch on the public highway. Mr. Hood saw him pick it up and, surmising that Espy was a mere finder, rather than the true owner, Hood snatched the watch. Espy now sues Hood for violating his possession. Espy files a statement of these facts; Hood admits the statement's accuracy but denies that these facts make a case against him, and asks Judge Wisdom to dismiss the suit. Where shall Judge Wisdom get the law to try these facts?

With the help of each party's lawyers and his own clerk, Judge Wisdom marshalls all of the similar cases in his state—in hopes of finding suitable theory—a process not unlike Dr. Jenner's investigation of milkmaids. There are a dozen cases, all consistent with articulating the law in the proposition, "A finder has a better right to lost property than anyone other than the true owner." If Judge Wisdom feels comfortable with these precedents, and if Hood's counsel has come up with no way of casting serious doubt on the "established rule," the decision will surely go for Espy, and Judge Wisdom's opinion explaining his holding will be short and tidy.

"It is revolting," said Justice Holmes, "to have no better reason for a rule of law than that it was so laid down in the time of Henry IV. It is still more revolting if the grounds upon which it was laid down have vanished long since, and the rule simply persists from blind imitation of the past." Judge Wisdom, we will suppose, is a gifted judge; he does not swear blind allegiance to the past, though he judiciously appreciates our heritage of legal knowledge. He is deliberate, and though he is almost convinced by the precedents, he says to Espy's lawyer, "The precedents do support your view, but after all this watch does not belong to your client, Espy; he is merely a volunteer who chose to pick up something he knew was not his own; he is not really out anything. Why should this court interfere in this case?" Espy's lawyer responds that if the law holds that found property is fair game for all who grab it, the law will incite violence; a dismissal in this case will encourage Hood and those like him to do battle over found property whenever they hear of it, and will encourage those in Espy's position to prepare to defend their possession by force; the practical result of a holding for Hood would be increased violence in the streets. This convinces Judge Wisdom, and he holds for Espy.

Since Judge Wisdom has dug deeper than the materials in the "authorities" cited to him, he decides to write an elaborated opinion going beyond the holdings and a simple statement of the common law rule found in the older precedents. He, like Dr. Jenner, has found a more adequate explanation of uniformity. Judge Wisdom's opinion includes a discussion of policy along the lines of Espy's lawyer's comments. The formal structure of his policy statement is to this effect:

> If the courts allowed interlopers to violate the possession of finders, then the courts would encourage breaches of the peace.
> The courts should not encourage breaches of the peace.
> Therefore the courts should not allow interlopers to violate the possession of finders.

This deduction is valid; if its premises are granted, the conclusion must follow. But are the premises warranted assertions?

The major premise is only a guess about the way people would act if the law gave no protection to the possession of finders. Behavioral scientists have made no studies throwing direct light on the truth of this guess; it could be wrong. The general run of people may habitually concede that a finder is entitled to possession and may continue to do so without regard to what the civil courts do. People like Hood may continue to contest finds violently regardless of what courts do. Judge Wisdom's major premise seems shaky. In practical affairs, however, the possibility that an unpleasant event may occur is reason enough for taking inexpensive steps that may prevent it. Hood is one person who preyed on a finder; the precedents show that this kind of depredation has happened once in a while in the past. Common sense seems to be more on Judge Wisdom's side than against him; courts that hold that such plunderers may not keep the fruits of their aggression may discourage similar acts in the future. No affirmative value results from those acts, so the possibility that the major premise is correct justifies its acceptance at so low a cost.

Judge Wisdom could expand his opinion by saying that unless the possession of finders is protected, they will be unwilling to advertise their finds for fear of attracting plunderers; this secretiveness will undesirably hamper the return of lost property to its true owners. This argument, too, is based on shaky assumptions, but it adds cumulative strength to the opinion.

Do these policy considerations help "settle" the law for other cases in the way that Dr. Jenner's discovery settled the cause of the immunity? Obviously Judge Wisdom's policy considerations are equally applicable to watches found in a public park instead of on a highway, to found rings as well as found watches, and so on.

Mr. Backwater, we shall say, owns a country retreat on which he quietly enjoys a secluded life. A report that an unidentified fisherman has lost a laden wallet on Backwater's land spreads through the community. The once peaceful retreat swarms with searchers. Backwater futilely warns them off; they stay until Underwood finds the wallet. Backwater demands the wallet. Underwood refuses to turn it over to him. Backwater brings suit.

Judge Wisdom notes that this case is the first case in which property was found by a trespasser on private land. He remembers the legal doctrine, "No one should profit from his own wrong" but realizes that it has never been uttered in a case like this one. Thinking in a more practical vein, he reasons that if he protected Underwood's possession of the wallet, he would encourage invasion of private property and stir up strife between land occupants and fortune hunters; if trespassing self-seekers know they cannot keep the fruits of their search, the temptation to trespass is blunted. Furthermore, the true owner probably will look for his property where he lost it, and a land occupant is more likely to restore it to him than is a self-seeking finder. The judge decides, then, that the policies implemented by protecting the possession of the watch-finder are best served by refusing to protect the possession of the wallet finder.

Judge Wisdom's reasoning in the wallet case, like that in his earlier opinion, is not based on a rock bottom of scientific fact. Some of his bench mates might be unconvinced and want to stand by the traditional rule that protects the possession of all finders—either out of an excess of conservatism or a desire to keep the simple, easily administered rule intact, even though it works some injustice.

Judge Wisdom carries a majority of the court with him, and is asked to write the court's opinion. Since he respects fundamental legal ideas, he starts his opinion with the principle, "No man should profit from his own wrong." Since he is ingenious as well as just, he points out that earlier cases protected the *possession* of finders, but that in this case, since Backwater possessed the land he also possessed the wallet lying on it, and Underwood violated Backwater's possession, rather than the other way around. Since he is candid as well as ingenious, he then points out that the policies stated in the watch case would not be advanced by allowing Underwood to keep the wallet; he goes on to tell why he believes justice will be advanced by giving the wallet to Backwater.

When Judge Wisdom heard the watch case, he looked back at precedents and saw a uniformity. He knew, of course, that this was not a product of nature—that it resulted from conscious-acceptance-of-precedent, which sometimes is no more estimable than a children's game of follow-the-leader. Nevertheless, when he articulated a policy explanation he had reason to believe that his views, like Jenner's, were a discovery—a discovery of the sound reason that tacitly inspired the first precedents and held later ones in line. Should this be bad history, however, Wisdom's insight is no less valuable; if early law was only accidentally sound, that should make no difference to Wisdom and his contemporaries. Judge Wisdom has based his holding on reason, and once he has stated his reasons for the holding in the watch case, he knows what to do when those reasons fail in the wallet case. Without the kind of imagination that leads to what counts, neither law nor science moves forward. Both law and science depend on more than mechanical modes of action.

There is strength in systems of ideas. A general science of immunology has produced knowledge about disease prevention much wider than Dr. Jenner's. But system *qua* system is of little value. No doubt some indexes of immunology are alphabetical; surely they have only limited value. Since law does and should serve the public's aspirations, one dimension of useful legal systemization is expanded by the examination of policies behind rules. Articulation of policy meaningfully relates finder cases to the law of assault and battery and the law of land occupancy. In such a system important corrections of factual assumptions can have wider spheres of meliorative influence. "A body of law," says Holmes, "is more rational and more civilized when every rule it contains is referred articulately and definitely to an end which it subserves, and when the grounds for desiring that end are stated or ready to be stated in words."

Behavioral science furnishes some factual underpinning for policy analyses in few areas of law. Legislation is increasingly premised on qualified social study. Courts are less likely to have reliable social data. The danger for the future of socially sound legal thought lies in a willingness to remain satisfied with meager behavioral science knowledge. Examination of social phenomena is difficult; techniques are underdeveloped; problems are complicated; and guessing is easier than digging.

VAGUE CONCEPTS IN RULES OF LAW

A string of nonsense syllables may train the voice; nonsense syllables are not likely, however, to play an important part in reflective thought. Nevertheless both in logic and in law, premises embodying indefinite terms play important roles. The rule of law, "All contracts against public policy are unenforceable" is not so abstract as the logician's, "All S is P." "Unenforceability" has a palpable meaning, well understood by lawyers—that is, it characterizes those promises the nonperformance of which the courts condone. "Contracts against public policy" denotes many varieties of contracts some of which are readily identified—for example, contracts to commit murder, to make illegal sales of drugs, to sell babies. The orbit of the conception, however, goes beyond violations of the criminal law; "unenforceability" includes an open area dotted with precedents, but, since new patterns of questionable dealings constantly arise, there is plenty of room for new dots. For some unprecedented cases, then, "contracts against public policy" does not have, before decision, a fixed meaning.

Consider this case. The city of Venus enfranchises the Venus Transit Company to operate a bus system. V.T.C. buys a policy of liability insurance from the Nebo Co. A clause in the policy promises that Nebo will hold V.T.C. and its employees safe from liability for misconduct of V.T.C.'s employees. Mr. Grandmal, an epileptic, is a lone, late-night passenger on a V.T.C. bus. He suffers a seizure. Mr. Fulsome, the driver, to get rid of Grandmal, carries him off the bus and lays him on the ground. Before other assistance comes, Grandmal's feet are frozen. On proof of these facts an outraged jury brings in a verdict against V.T.C. and the driver compensating Grandmal for all of his injuries and adding, as the law permits, a $10,000 award of punitive damages. V.T.C. and the driver call on Nebo to shoulder the entire verdict. Nebo admits that it has contracted to pay punitive damage verdicts, but takes the position that the contract to do so is against public policy. The parties go to court with this dispute.

Law has been defined as "what the courts in fact will do." The applicable rule in this case tells the court what to do about a contract against public policy; the rule does not, however, tell the court how to classify this undertaking which insures against liability for punitive damages. If the prediction definition of law is insisted on, we must conclude that the rule, in this case, is not law. Something is wrong with that conclusion. The rule does play a part in the decision of this kind of case. The rule does all of these things: (1) It identifies the problem sufficiently to give it placement in the legal scheme of things—that is, it points toward the analogous precedents, the helpful sections of treatises on contracts, etc. (2) It indicates the general direction of solution—that is, it aims the processes toward policy considerations that should affect a reasoned disposition of the case on the merits. (3) It enfranchises the court to decide the problem—that is, it tells the court that it is not obliged to refer this case to the legislature or the insurance commission. (4) It obliges the court to condemn the contract or give a compelling reason for not doing so—that is, other similar precedents in which the court refused to enforce contracts against public policy must be followed or distinguished from this case. A rule that affects an issue so profoundly is, in fact, a living part of the judicial process. Of course, it is good to remember that the decision the court reaches does not roll automatically from the rule in this case.

It is dangerous to overdo the leeways in the law. In aeronautics a "leeway" is the extent to which an aircraft is blown off its normal course by crosswinds unless the proper correction is made; in aeronautics, then, leeways complicate but do not destroy the art of navigation; planes nearly always get to their destinations. In law the art of dealing with leeways is not so exact and impersonal. The inexactness of that art does not, however, justify the conclusion that law is a convenient false front to comfort the public and gives license to representatives of the establishment to do what they please. Legal processes are seldom intentionally subverted by judges of high courts; these judges, for the most part, deal with leeways in the common law tradition; their art, within its proper limits, should and often has importantly implemented the public's aspirations.

Chapter 5

Enacted Law: Eighteenth-Century Hopes and Twentieth-Century Accomplishments*

PART ONE: THE EIGHTEENTH-CENTURY PHILOSOPHERS

The political theories of Hume, Montesquieu, Rousseau, Kant, and Bentham differed widely. In one respect, however, each of them championed one analogous requirement for just government; they each concluded that unless general rules are formulated and then applied to concrete cases justice is imperiled. Indeed, all but Kant agreed that the governing principles should be laid down before a concrete problem has arisen. Though Kant was not exactly of this view, his position (as I shall explain later) did not differ greatly from it. Thus, long before modern legislative practices and procedures were developed, these thinkers were stressing the value of, and need for, enacted law. In Twentieth-century America legislation is formidable and commands new respect. A look back at the eighteenth-century reasons for espousing promulgated rules of law seems appropriate now.

---

* A similar discussion of mine appears under the title "Four Eighteenth-Century Theories of Justice," 14 *Vanderbilt Law Review* 101 (1960).

I   Hume   David Hume published his *A Treatise of Human Nature*, part III, in 1739.[1] Two seventeenth-century philosophies were, at that time, points of departure for political discussion. They were: (1) Hobbes' apology for government by a strong sovereign legitimately entitled to rule almost without limit in whatever way he thinks best. (2) Locke's theologically based assumptions that man enjoys God-given natural law which helps him, in large measure, to know what he ought to do. Hume rejected both of these views.

In consonance with the current interest in science, Hume turned his back on natural law as a heaven-sent basis for justice. He, instead, dealt in ordinary factual terms with morality and justice; that is, he tried to assume a scientific posture and describe the material aspects of the good and the just. For him, man's discoveries resulting from his powers disclose only "what is" and do not reveal "what ought to be." Man discovers truth, according to Hume, by logic or observation, that is, by deducing conclusions from established premises or by taking note of externals happening in his presence. Human preferences and actions, however, are neither true nor false.[2] The process of characterizing conduct as praiseworthy was, to Hume, like the appreciation of beauty, and, therefore, quite different from the discovery of truth. A warm reception for some act is always, according to Hume, rooted in pleasure (immediately sensed) and not in knowledge (newly discovered). The diversity and uncertainty of acclaim is proof that appreciation of the good is not an inborn talent of men.[3] Therefore since children come into the world with no natural sense of justice they thereafter acquire an artificial one by becoming absorbed into the society in which they live.[4] This product of culture would not appear if society were made up of utterly unselfish men or of men whose every desire was instantly gratified by the bounty of nature. In the real world, however, wants always exceed satisfactions; men, therefore, have learned to serve themselves best by inventing law and teaching their young to respect it. This process stabilizes the ownership of property and facilitates the orderly transfer of property by its owners. Such a system nurtures the production of goods and wares; its development of a system of legally binding contracts makes wider commerce possible. Systems of this sort, according to Hume, have been adopted by all advanced societies.

Hume's case for promoting the peaceful arts through respect for law differs widely from Hobbes' case for promoting that result by conferring almost unlimited power on a sovereign. Hobbes' prescription for preventing disorder and assuring civil peace was the establishment of a sovereign powerful enough to terrorize his subjects into quietude.[5] Hume admired tranquillity no less than Hobbes. Nearly a century had elapsed, however, between the publication of Hobbes' *Leviathan* and Hume's *A Treatise of Human Nature*. Both works were written in France by residents of Great Britain. Hobbes fled to France to save his skin endangered at home by the violence of civil war. Hume left an orderly and peaceful Great Britain, to rusticate in a quiet French college town. He lived cheaply and undisturbed. The even tenor of Hume's times and life probably entered into his prescription for tranquillity—that is, stability, resulting from the inflexible administration of established rules of law.

Stability, Hume thought, is seriously threatened when judges are allowed to consider the special merits of particular cases; even the most conscientious and objective judge when not moored to inflexible rules will fail to maintain stability without which civil peace cannot persist.[6] The inflexible rules guarding justice cannot, of course, be any old rules; they must be good instruments for the governance of the particular society involved. Legal rules are clumsy tools unless they bring wisdom to bear on the problems occurring in the society which they regulate.[7] When conditions change and the change outmodes enacted law, Hume was, no doubt, in favor of revision. But he was dead against allowing judges to make exceptions for atypical cases; their sympathies, he feared, might upset the system and destroy the certainty on which peace, prosperity, and economic integration must be bottomed.

II Montesquieu Montesquieu was over fifty when twenty-nine-year-old Hume's publisher brought out Part III of *A Treatise on Human Understanding*. Eight years later Montesquieu's lively, disorderly *The Spirit of the Law* was published. I do not know whether Montesquieu read Hume's widely circulated work. Montesquieu, however, like Hume, advocated legislative enactment of law before judges decide concrete cases. *The Spirit of the Law* hardly touches on Hume's main concerns, that is, the stability of private property and the protection and growth of private forces capable of producing prosperity. Hume was a private law man; Montesquieu was a public law man, a constitutionalist. Montesquieu was a champion of liberty and a foe of tyranny. All officials given power, said Montesquieu, are likely to abuse it; governments must have great power, but each official should be given limited power and should have only a confined ambit of authority. Compartmentalizing governmental powers reduces, he thought, both the temptation and the ability of office holders to become tyrants. A law-giver only enacting general rules cannot control citizens' lives so arbitrarily as he could if he also were allowed to apply his rules to concrete cases. A judge who must decide cases in consonance with enacted law has fewer opportunities to humor his whims than does the judge who is permitted both to formulate his own rules and to apply them.[8] Montesquieu, then, like Hume, believed that justice was served best when rules were laid down before concrete cases arose. Their motives, however, differed. Hume was against allowing judges to individuate cases from the undifferentiated class of cases covered by a rule of law because, he thought, their decisions were likely to unsettle property and commerce and destroy civil order. Montesquieu was against such individuation because, he thought, judges unconstrained by rules and given power to decide cases were likely to become martinets and oppress those they judged.

III Rousseau In *The Social Contract*, Rousseau, also, disapproved of judicial processes running free of the constraint of enacted law. He, too, made a case for deciding litigations by applying rules adopted in advance. He shared both Hume's fear that unconfined judicial power might favor the litigant who arouses the judge's irrelevant sympathies, and Montesquieu's dread of domineering judges encouraged to tyrannize by authority not restricted to the application of enacted law.

Rousseau had spent his youth as an inept and impoverished wanderer. He first attracted attention by writing a prize essay on the theme that civilization degraded mankind. When he published *The Social Contract* in 1762, he was truculently accepting only so much of a rich patron's bounty as he needed to live frugally. Rousseau saw the Western world as a congeries of systems arrogating power over the many to the few. Monarchical governments not only subverted liberty; they disregarded the wisdom of the natural man and were thereby impoverished.

Rousseau held out hope for a better life in states affording all of their habitants full participation in policy making. He advocated a dispersal of power much greater than that championed by Montesquieu. Rousseau's system empowered all parties to the social contract to have a hand in enacting law; he proposed that every citizen participate in the process of formulating the general rules to be used for deciding cases that at the time of enactment were not at issue but which might arise sometime in the future. When every citizen was so entitled to take a direct part in enacting abstract law all would govern themselves unselfishly. This Rousseau called government in accordance with the "general will." [9] Public servants could be given the office of applying the general will so formulated to those cases that thereafter arose, producing, as a result, just decisions.[10] Rousseau proposed his system of enacted law not only for Hume's reason—to avoid the instability that might flow from erratic decisions of judges unchecked by binding rules—but also for the purpose of getting the rules right in the first place. The general will captures the earthy, instructive wisdom of averaged group opinion, soberly formulated; the general will, so compounded, is infallible because the corporate whole of the state's countrymen is sure to respond wisely to questions of general policy raised at a time when no concrete case is in contention. Rousseau was not for the delegation of the legislative power to a lawmaking body where the countrymen's chosen representatives would make law; he was for legislation enacted directly by all of the countrymen themselves. The state should originate, he thought, in a social contract that bound each citizen to subordinate his person, his power, and his property to the general will. The sovereign in Rousseau's state is none other than all the citizenry enacting the general will into law. Since this sovereign is the voice of all the country's habitants, it cannot forward special interests adverse to the realization of the common good. In such a system no one is invested with power over his fellows. Montesquieu feared that officeholders' power tended to corrupt them and thus subvert liberty. Rousseau meets this problem—at the legislative level—by having no officeholders.

One of Rousseau's main goals was, of course, to promote and protect liberty. Equally important to Rousseau, however, was the dignification of the common man, which could be accomplished by affording him a working role in the most crucial function of government, that is, the enactment of law. He doubted, however, that his system would work well except in small arcadian states. He did not question the capacity of the common man to play his role in such a realm. He says, "When among the happiest people in the world, bands of peasants are seen regulating affairs of state under an oak and always acting wisely, can we help scorning the ingenious methods of other nations which make themselves illustrious and wretched with so much art and mystery?" [11]

IV Kant While all three of the philosophers discussed above were "inner directed" (to borrow Riesman's overworked but expressive phrase) none of them was so solitary, self-contained, and introspective as Immanuel Kant. Never during his eighty years did he venture beyond sixty miles from his birthplace.

Kant's prodigious skill with abstractions, perhaps, influenced him to believe in all men's ability to control their actions by using "pure practical reason." A priori thought, Kant believed, was the only route to knowledge of justice. A seeker for justices not only need not, but indeed should not, draw on his past experience; he has only one proper guide—his free will. He cannot act in accordance with his free will unless he steels himself against his emotions and holds himself aloof from the advancement of his own or other people's happiness. An act that is freely willed will of necessity be recognized as just by all men who exercise free will; this is so because free will always accords with pure practical reason.[12]

Kant stated two closely related principles that guide pure practical reason.

1. The Categorical Imperative. "Act according to a maxim that can be adopted as a universal law." [13] Some say that this injunction is a form of the Golden Rule. The comparison, however, underemphasizes the categorical imperative's stress on reason. The golden rule instructs us to act only with warm considerateness; the categorical imperative enjoins us to act only after cold consideration.

2. The Universal Principle of Right. An action is right only when it can co-exist with each and every man's free will according to universal law.[14] If we keep Kant's conception of the free will in mind when considering this principle, it, too, is seen as a criterion to be used only by the coldly rational seeker for justice who keeps his emotions under control and abjures concern for his or anyone else's happiness.

The three philosophers already discussed all advocated systems of government in which law is enacted to control or guide judges; they dealt with statecraft. Kant focuses, at least at the outset of his legal philosophy, on the single just man, rather than on the procedures of just government ruling a body politic. The stuff of pure practical reason is free will. Free will brings all those who exercise it to identical conclusions; it is not, however, corporate will. Each individual man is capable of exercising his free will.

Because men have reasoning capacity they merit respect; they should never allow themselves to be mere means to a lawgiver's ends.[15] One should exile himself from society whenever he can avoid wrongdoing only by withdrawal.[16] Even though Kant thus has required each man to conclude whether, in particular circumstances, he is being treated justly, Kant did not divorce these concrete decisions from general rules; the categorical imperative and the universal principle of right both enjoin the victim of injustice to apply an abstract and rational maxim to his case.

If Kant did not require preformulation of general policy before a particular case arose, he nevertheless called for the formulation of a just general policy as an essential part of the process of reaching the right concrete decision. The process so approved is consonant with thoughtful, objective, judge-made law; it does not call invariably for the constriction of judicial processes by legislatively enacted rules. Another of Kant's postures, however, reduces his implied toleration of a judicial process that makes concrete decisions without the guidance of enacted law. He requires man to enter society to avoid wronging others. This obligation of men to enter society, as Kant saw it, is little affected by Hume's and Rousseau's cases for enacted law. Hume's system was based on utility; and utility is not a permissible consideration in the exercise of pure practical reason. Rousseau's system was based on the value of the views of

common men averaged in conclave with little regard to how the
voters reached their genuinely held views; he did not require these
voters to look away from utility and to check their emotions.
Kant, however, propounds a demonstration showing, to his satisfaction, that man has an obligation to "enter society to avoid
wronging others." His a priori reasoning runs this way: society
unregulated by right implies violence; society and violence are,
however, contradictory concepts; hence reason demands that com-
patriots form a union regulated by compulsory laws; if these laws
are derived by pure reasoning from the idea of juridical union
under public laws, men will live with each other in peace.[17] The
reign of law, rather than the reign of men, is in Kant's opinion meta-
physically sublime and may lead to the highest political good.[18]

We see Kant, then, as an admirer of enacted law that is the
product of pure reason. He does not, however, completely rule
out decisions of judges unconstrained by enacted law. When judges
decide cases covered by no statutes, their decisions can be just.
A judge hearing such a case should not, however, reach his decision before framing or finding a suitable maxim. Unless that maxim
can be adopted as universal law the decision may be unjust. He in-
sists that all cases be decided in consonance with reasoned general
policy; even though he favors a system in which legislative policy is
formulated in advance of the hearing of cases, he does not unquali-
fiedly demand such formulation for all cases. He is not like
Hume—who was concerned with the utility of stability—nor like
Montesquieu—who was afraid that great power would produce
tyranny—nor like Rousseau—who was intent on giving the corporate body of citizens a leading role in government. He urges the
enunciation of general rules ("maxims," "laws") as a means of perfect-
ing free will in action so that men can live according to the universal principle of right.

V Bentham Bentham was learned in the law. He listened to
Blackstone's lectures at Oxford (and was a bit bored). He often
enjoyed playing the truant and going up to London to watch the
courts in action at Westminster. After he took his Oxford degree
he studied for the bar at an Inn of Court. He never, however,
asked to be called to the bar and instead embarked on a career

of writing political theory and jurisprudence. One of his conclusions was that the law should be legislatively codified.[19]

The English courts of Bentham's day dealt with large areas of "common law" which were little affected by any enactments. Bentham's distaste for judge-made law that accreted case by case grew out of his keen understanding of the logic of *stare decisis*. All courts, said Bentham, decide only the cases that they hear. A judge, basing a common law decision on an admirable policy that is generally approved by all right thinking people, cannot lay that policy down as *the* law. His holding is a precedent applicable only when the same facts recur. The reasons for a judge's decision stated in his written opinion may be useful, wise, and helpful to another judge deciding a different case; it is, however, his holding —and not his justification of that holding—which carries the political force of a precedent. Policies supported by a considerable body of case law are, in Bentham's view, constantly weakened by anomalies. He puts it this way:

[T]he anomalous decision . . . gives a shock . . . felt by the whole future of customary law. Nor is the mischief cured until a strong body of connected decisions, either in confirmation of the first anomalous one or in opposition to it, have repaired the broken thread of analogy and brought back the current of reputation to its old channel.[20]

In other words, Bentham believed that judicial decisions neither establish the law firmly nor readapt it smoothly; by their very nature the holdings of common law judges are *ad hoc*, and case law never quite transcends this characteristic. Enacted law, on the other hand, can establish general policies which have force until they are repealed or revised. When legislatures revise enacted law they firmly establish new policies; legislative change can be clear, quick, and certain. Bentham concluded, on these grounds, that we should be governed, insofar as possible, by the enacted laws of a systematic and comprehensive code.

Even though Bentham, the "Great Utilitarian," was committed to the greatest happiness of the greatest number, his case for codification did not spring from a dedication to either liberty or democracy. Bentham championed enacted law as a jurist concerned with the technical improvement of legal processes—a far cry from the political considerations that motivated Montesquieu and Rousseau. Though Bentham's case for codification embodied both his respect for formulated general principles of law and his realization of the weaknesses of *ad hoc* decisions, the legal clarity that would, he thought, flow from legislative formulation and reformulation of the law was unlike Kant's case for exercising free will divorced from happiness and emotion. Perhaps Bentham was closer to Hume than to the three others; both wanted a legal system more rigorously institutionalized than the common law in which judges relied on examples rather than principles. Hume saw law as a human invention needed for an orderly world in which the peaceful arts would thrive; Hume's position, it seems to me, implied his dedication to utilitarianism, that is, to advancing happiness. Hume, a nonlawyer, was naive about the power of enacted law to constrict the judicial process. Bentham understood that judges who apply the law inevitably participate to some extent in lawmaking.[21] Bentham, however, suffered from other naivetes; he believed that a one-volume code of moderate size could encompass virtually all the law a nation needed and would be increasingly clarified and amplified by the legislature as its ambiguities and gaps appeared in court cases. Such a code would near perfection and leave to judges only a few shreds of lawmaking.

Here ends the description and comparison of the great and, perhaps, influential eighteenth-century champions of enacted law. It is by no means my thesis that they were the first proponents of preformulated general rules. Famous lawgivers promulgated rules for the decision of cases in antiquity. The eighteenth-century philosophers were neither unique nor first in calling for enacted law. They were, however, the thinkers who first spoke up for enacted law in modern national states. While they wrote, Western society was feeling the first twinges of the industrial revolution growing out of the technological applications of science. These five philosophers were, of course, speaking for themselves; each was an artist whose singular creative talents and personality were stamped on his unique writings. Each, however, lived in society and, in his own peculiar way, formulated and interpreted public aspirations for enacted law which would promote civil peace, prevent tyranny, embody widely shared values, employ abstractions voicing both clear reason and the worth of mankind and its society, and, perhaps, improve the law's techniques. In any event enacted law bulked larger in the nineteenth-century than it ever had before in the Western world. There was the Napoleonic Code in the first decade of the century, followed by the great continental codes that came in its train. Toward the end of the century Anglo-American legislatures increasingly enacted regulatory and penal statutes and other laws that either regularized or revised various areas of the common law. It would be hard to trace the inspiration for this growth of legislation directly to the five philosophers discussed. Perhaps they influenced it little, if at all, though there is some evidence to the contrary. Yet even if the five did not influence it much, they nevertheless did voice and formulate various motivations that resulted in the growth of enactment and its willing acceptance by the public as one desired form of lawmaking.

PART TWO: TWENTIETH-CENTURY LEGISLATION

Civil codes were drafted and adopted in a few American states during the nineteenth century; by and large they were, however, stated in terms so general that they rarely made much difference. Serious consideration of complete and up-to-date codification of the law of any of the states of the U.S.A. in the immediate or remote future is unlikely. Hume's, Rousseau's, and Bentham's conviction that all legal rules and principles should be promulgated is not shared by the American public. The reasons behind the eighteenth-century philosophers' postures on enacted law, nonetheless, do have a lively bearing on widely shared American values.

Hume's case for wise preregulation of commercial transactions has its recent counterpart in the successful drive made for the adoption of the Uniform Commercial Code. The enactment of the Code by state legislatures got off to a slow start. In 1960, about a score of years after the drafting of the Code was finished, only six states had adopted it. The magnitude of so bulky a bill [22] tends to repel American state legislatures. The Congress of the United States, of course, often passes massive statutes, enacting them after they have been studied by generously staffed committees and are recommended in documented reports. The committees of most state legislatures have up to now been poorly staffed and are reluctant to spend the time needed to report out large chunks of systematic legislation. Many sections of the Commercial Code, however, tidied up muddy branches of the commercial law. With the growth of multistate businesses the lack of uniformity of state law became intolerable. Various sectors of the commercial community were eager supporters of some particular chapter of the Code, and became lobbyists amalgamating their influence into a powerful block of businessmen who favored the Code. Uninterested and reluctant legislators witnessed the Code's enactment in an ever-growing number of states, and were brought around by a combination of strong lobbies, their own committees, and the prestige of both the Commissioners on Uniform State Law and the American Law Institute who appointed the draftsmen and approved their product. The Code has now been enacted in fifty states.

Another well-nigh universal form of codification of state law is the penal code, restating and revising the common law of crimes. Legislators were rarely hesitant to enact comprehensive and systematic statutes defining the serious crimes and fixing the limits of punishment. They were actuated by a number of factors, not the least of which was the public demand for publicized and certain rules of criminal law that would circumscribe judicial discretion. This public aspiration was, at base (like Montesquieu's thesis on the need for separation of powers), a desire to check high-handedness. *The Spirit of the Law*, I believe, was a strong influence (direct or indirect) on the American desire to promulgate the criminal laws. In the trial of a criminal case a judge who is obliged to respect the exact wording of formulated and enacted statutes (which, in cases of doubt, he is enjoined to interpret in the accused's favor) is, we think, less likely to convict an unattractive man in the prisoner's dock because of his irrelevant unattractiveness. A legislature that defines and codifies criminal law without knowing to whom its definitions will be applied (and that is forbidden to pass criminal laws *ex post facto*) is, we think, unlikely to wreak its wrath on its political enemies—it seldom exercises its "particular will." Enacted criminal law can, nevertheless, be politically motivated and aimed at existing factions in political disagreement with the legislators. Congressional criminal legislation aimed at draft-card burners protesting American participation in the Vietnam war, even though it singles out no one culprit, tends to constrict liberty.

The length of the nineteenth- and the early twentieth-century penal codes did not hinder their enactment. Legislators did not doubt their competence to deal with crimes; they were, I suppose, as competent as courts whose looser definition of crimes, in any event, took a form not so desirable as that of enacted law. Legislators may have been emboldened to enact criminal law because prosecutors, juries, and judges retained power to deal leniently with the technically guilty whose legal misdeeds merit little or no punishment. These same safeguards may have allayed concern about obsolescence; an old blasphemy statute, for example, is not nowadays likely to put anyone behind bars—though an old "blue law," having economic as well as religious significance, is more likely to be enforced. All these comforting flexibilities—which could often be used in favor of the accused but rarely against him—probably mobilized legislative force for enactment of traffic, sanitation, and building codes, all of which are dotted with criminal sanctions.

Codes of civil procedure also have been adopted in virtually every state. These enactments reflect the influence of the organized bar on the legislatures, insofar as matters of legal procedure are involved; most legislatures are heavily laden with lawyers who usually can understand and champion the enactment of procedural reforms. Though common law judges can make minor changes in their procedure on a case-by-case basis, they are reluctant to do so for fear of unsettling their procedural system entirely—a real, not an imagined, danger. Here, especially, the ineptitude of the common law, as stressed by Bentham, is obvious to lawyers; once the bar developed a consensus on the need for procedural reform they were likely to turn to the legislature for immediate and sure technical improvement of the law. These codes of procedure, however, fall far short of the technical improvement of law Bentham envisioned when he urged the complete codification of all law. Bentham's discussion of the clumsiness of the common law way of dealing with its outmoded rules is, however, especially applicable to rules of procedure; since no lawyer would intentionally risk his client's fortunes merely to give the court an opportunity to make procedural reforms, courts are afforded opportunities to change rules of procedure only in cases in which lawyers have inadvertently departed from established procedure.

Procedural reform is beyond the ken of nonlawyer legislators. In some states, therefore, the legislature has been willing to delegate the power of procedural codification to the courts themselves by authorizing them to draft and adopt their own rules of procedure. Montesquieu would not disapprove; he would not see in this augmentation of judicial powers either a serious temptation to tyranny or a covert threat to liberty.

Legislative dissatisfaction with the common law often is not rooted in the courts' inability to make changes quickly and smoothly, but in the common law's failure to do justice. For example, courts refused to entertain tort actions for personal injuries after either the perpetrator of the injury or his victim had died. Judges, in my view, could and should have overruled this stupidity; they perpetuated it by favoring precedent over common sense. Rousseau's sovereign, the common people, determining the general will in meeting assembled, probably would not have tolerated such nonsense. Most American legislators had common sense views on this subject and were quick to follow the British Parliament's example of enacting law that countermanded this court-made injustice.[23]

Inequity entrenched in the common law of industrial accidents also led to reform by enactment. An injured workman who, before legislative reform, turned to the courts and sued his master for negligently failing to furnish him reasonably safe working conditions often went away empty handed. The master could raise three defenses that were likely to bar such claims; they were contributory negligence, voluntary assumption of risk, and the fellow servant rule. The Congress dealt simply with these unjust common law defenses in an act which revised the common law of on-the-job injuries for railroaders working in interstate commerce. The Congress abolished both the assumption of risk defense and the fellow servant rule; it also reduced contributory negligence from a complete defense to a partial one by providing that the workman's own negligence could be considered only in mitigation of damages.[24] The state legislatures, however, adopted more complicated Workmen's Compensation Laws based on European models. These statutes give all injured workmen covered by them substantial medical benefits and scheduled payments for various kinds of disablements.[25]

The impetus for other large-scale legislation differs greatly from the motivations that actuated the five eighteenth-century philosophers' calls for enacted law. The philosophers thought of law as a regularizing or rectifying force performing watchdog functions. The law, in their view, had the mission of discouraging wrongdoing and of requiring wrongdoers to honor their contracts, make restitutions, and so on. Hume gave to the state the function of preserving property rights and protecting commerce; he did not, however, call upon the state to develop new kinds of property or to reshape the ways of commerce.[26] The modern business corporation is not only regularized and rectified by enacted law; it is, as a legal entity, a creature of enacted law—a useful modern means of aggregating capital, dispersing the ownership of large properties to a myriad of investors, and, thereby, promoting commerce and industry. The early legislation that enacted corporate charters was simple; it dealt with one corporation at a time. All legislatures have by now dealt with all corporations chartered under their laws in lengthy Corporation Codes.[27]

Dynamic—as distinguished from regularizing—enactments have not, of course, been created only for private enterprise. Social security statutes, school law codes, and mental health laws are examples of systematic statutes dealing with other topics. Insofar as they create new institutions they are beyond the ken of the eighteenth-century philosophers. Perhaps Kant should be looked on as the exception; his admiration of free will made him, in an abstract way, an admirer of man's capacity for pure reason. Man, he thought, should therefore be treated as an end in himself; man so viewed deserved institutional public succor when needed.[28]

The bills introduced during one legislative session compete with each other for attention. No legislature could possibly give serious attention to all the bills that are dropped into the hopper. Each session must deal with appropriations and other current and pressing problems. A bill raising problems less urgent is acted on only when it is shepherded through the legislative process by a legislator willing to spend his energies pressing for its enactment. A bill to name the carnation as the state flower is not likely to be voted on unless the carnation growers' lobby can enlist legislators who actively work persistently for its passage.

The limit on legislative energies has a double importance: it not only restricts initial output but also hinders revision of enacted law. The legislature should move with caution on proposals likely to come to need, but not get, revision, for once a clear and constitutional statute has been passed and signed by the governor, no court has power to repeal or revise it. Sensible liberal interpretation, Bentham tells us, may limit the harm that an outmoded or badly drafted statute might otherwise do, but courts are not authorized to do or undo the legislature's jobs. The schedule of benefits adopted in a Workmen's Compensation Act can, for example, be reasonably generous at the time of enactment and become outmoded by inflation. Labor's political power, however, will eventually be felt by the legislature and induce reconsideration of the schedule in light of the changed conditions. Those who propose scheduled benefits for the victims of automobile accidents [29] may be overlooking the absence of forces that will keep this schedule up to date: motor accident victims have no lobby.

When legislatures enact very general rules they do not do so with Kant's categorical imperative in mind. Sometimes general statutes cover a political compromise arrived at when more specific proposals fragment legislative support. More often enactment of very general rules is calculated to save legislative energies and to prevent obsolescence; the courts administering these enacted imprecisions settle specific applications as the need arises. The

Uniform Commercial Code provides, for example, that in an action on a contract the legal effect of an unconscionable clause can be dealt with in three alternative ways: the court may hold that (1) the contract is a nullity and therefore has no legal force, or that (2) all of the clauses except the unconscionable one are binding, or that (3) the legal force of this unconscionable clause is limited in a way that avoids unconscionability.[30] The code contains no specific criteria of unconscionability. Changed conditions are not likely to outmode so flexible a statute. This enactment is unresponsive to Hume's, Montesquieu's, and Rousseau's reasons for circumscribing judges' powers. The enactment, even though it leaves to courts the function of making the law for specific cases, is flexible but not limp. It withholds authority from the courts to condone unconscionability and it requires courts to weigh the three alternative methods for dealing with it—one or more of which might otherwise go unconsidered.

Sometimes, however, the purpose of enacted law is to create inflexibility—to provide just the kind of certainty that Hume envisioned, certainty that eliminates results other than those stipulated. Courts are loath to draw hard and fast lines. Workable statutes of limitation, for example, produce results not likely to be reached by common law courts. The legislature entertains no compunctions that would turn it away from picking, say, a five-year period in a statute of limitations, when four or six years are arguably just as good. The traditions of the judicial process are, however, usually more functional and less rigid. Even those courts which, for example, channel "due care" by holding that violation of a criminal statute is negligence as a matter of law in an automobile accident case, are likely to retain an escape hatch for eluding their rigid rule by recognizing an exception for excusable violations.[31]

The most questionable aspect of the eighteenth-century arguments in favor of enacted law is the assumption that once rules are enacted their application becomes almost mechanical. Bentham was alternately knowing and naive on this point. After remarking that legislation must deal with *classes* of cases, he says:

[Each] class is composed of a certain number of individuals . . . [By] what means is it that they have come to be aggregated to this class? . . .

By whatever means . . . such event either depended or did not depend upon the will of a human being. . . . To juries, in most cases, belongs in conjunction with the regular Judges as also with prosecutors, witnesses and individual officers of justice . . . the power of aggregating persons . . . to the disadvantageous class of delinquents. . . . The power of legislating *de classibus* even though it be supreme, can never of itself be absolute and unlimited.[32]

After approving of liberal judicial interpretation of enactments ("that delicate and important branch of judiciary power, the concession of which is dangerous, the denial ruinous")[33] he says:

Laws that are hasty have often been cited in proof of the necessity of interpretation: but methinks it might also have been well at the same time to have observed that they are indications equally strong of imbecility and short sightedness on the part of the legislator: that they bespeak the infancy of the science; and that once it shall be brought to a state of tolerable maturity the demand for interpretation will have been in great measure if not altogether taken away.[34]

Bentham, then, after calling for care in the design and wording of enacted law, advances a view ("methinks") calculated to squelch judicial talent whenever well-drafted statutes happen to touch on problems either that had eluded direct legislative scrutiny or that fell within the inevitable soft auras that surround hard cores of statutory meaning. Laws carefully enacted are, of course, clearer than "hasty laws"; deliberateness and eloquence will not, however, result in statutes so crisp that no question of their interpretation will ever arise. On the contrary, the world is so rich that words used carefully on one day are often likely to be ambiguous on another. Lawyers seldom advance conflicting interpretations of an enacted law that yield to decisions reached by judges who merely consult a good dictionary. When a court pauses over the meaning of a statute it entertains a real doubt about legislative intention; when such a doubt is dismissed dogmatically the pontificating judge may thwart legislative purpose and impair the operation of enacted law.

The proper interpretation of statutes is, however, not fully accomplished by judges who only fathom and effectuate the intention of the legislature. The other side of the coin is also important; judges are obliged to recognize and respect the lack of meaning of legislative silence. Of course no one reads well who does not read between the lines; there are, however, inevitable gaps in enacted law—gaps that cannot be filled by careful consideration of both the express and implied meaning of the words used. We are sometimes told that a judge confronted with a gap in a statute should try to guess what the legislature would have done had it tried to fill the gap. Perhaps this advice tends to put the judge in a properly objective frame of mind and helps him to control his own irrelevant predilections. It seems to me, however, that this advice is always theoretically and sometimes practically unsound. It is like confusing the pianist's permitted improvised cadenza with the composer's written music. The gap-filling judge must proceed judicially and not legislatively; he should keep in mind that the problem before him has not been screened by legislative committees and their staffs, has not been a subject of publicized debate in legislative halls, and has not been adopted by widely elected legislators whose constituents' views may affect their votes. Judges should forego the sterile exercise of trying to guess what the legislature would have done and should turn, instead, to the real task at hand, that is, to render a judicial decision of a case raising a problem not considered by the legislature. Such judges should, it seems to me, bear in mind that they do not command legislative lawmaking resources. This does not mean that a gap-filling judge should spurn useful analogies found in enacted law; nor should he neglect his obligation to consider the systematic design of the enacted law surrounding the gap he fills. When neither of these last two considerations adequately supplies answers, he is obliged to conform to common law traditions that guide judges in making and refusing to make new case law. Such a judge advances Hume's case for stability by his thoroughgoing respect for enacted law; he gives statutes all the genuine meaning they have; when faced with problems not covered by enacted law he usually should maintain the social values promoted by the processes of the common law. Such a judge effectuates Montesquieu's separation of powers by honoring the intent of all constitutional enactments and proceeding to dispose properly of the problems presented to him that fall outside of the ambit of enacted laws. He will not, of course, be guided by the general will determined in accordance with the procedures required by Rousseau. By honoring the legislative intent of enacted law when it speaks and by using the traditionally objective techniques of applying or revising the common law when enacted law is silent, he does, however, suppress the biases that influence the particular will. This objectivity may fall short of Kant's ideal on two scores: (1) the enacted law which he is bound to honor may not be sufficiently reasoned, and (2) the common law traditions sometimes fall short of recognizing the worth of each man as an end in himself. Kant's universal principle of right, after all, calls for a greater sublimity than the rule of law which Kant himself was willing to call sublime. Though no court can bindingly decide more than the case before it, as Bentham noted, Bentham's case for enacted law underestimates the ability of the common law to develop some principles in some of its sectors that are clear, clearly applicable to the core center of a class of cases, and clearly just. The American common law has demonstrated some ability to deal both firmly and reasonably well with some new topics —like, for example, the right to privacy—and to revise some old case law when change is in order—as, for example, in the law of products liability. A judge who, without exceeding traditional bounds of the judicial process, wisely enlarges or revises the common law relieves, at least in some small measure, the legislature from expending its limited energies. He corrects injustices to which the legislature may never advert.

Of course all law, whether enacted or traditionary, can be, and sometimes is, unjust. Perhaps the greatest injustices persist in those sectors of social structure that are untouched by legal prohibitions or by legal constructive innovations. The law as governmental intervention—enactments, plus judicial decisions, plus administrative law —can never add up to complete justice. Some public aspirations must be implemented by the private elites that affect the structure of the administration of business, science, education, and the like. Private actions affected with a public interest can be the subject of enacted law, but no legislature can possibly occupy the field completely and forever.

Chapter 6

Law, Reason, and Sociology*

Sociology is a latter day social science.[1] Max Weber, thought by some to be the father of modern sociology, was originally a student of the law. One of his famous works is *Wirtschaft und Gesellschaft* (1925);[2] in it Weber classified the legal processes that have been used in a wide variety of societies. His classification categorizes methods of litigation according to the reasoning processes they exhibit. This heavily textured book displays Weber's ranging familiarity with many cultures and their legal practices.

This chapter is divided into three parts: (1) a summary of Weber's classification of legal processes, (2) a comparison of Weber's system with Cardozo's classification of the kinds of thought used in deciding issues at common law, and (3) a statement of some of my views growing out of the comparison.

I WEBER'S FOUR CLASSES OF LEGAL PROCESSES

1. Formal irrationality.   Most Western philosophers of law from Aristotle to Roscoe Pound expressly or impliedly portray litigation

* An earlier version of this chapter appeared in 107 *U. of Pennsylvania Law Review* 147 (1958).

as a process of applying rules of law to the facts of cases and, therefore, as "rational," in the sense that decisions are made in conformity
to patterns of thought that are logically valid.

   In the nineteenth century, a few legal philosophers dignified parts
of litigation at the expense of the syllogistic whole; Austin, for
example, said that law was the sovereign's general commands and
that, therefore, decisions of cases were merely applications of law; [3]
Holmes said that prophecies of what courts will do was law and that
high-sounding abstract talk about legal obligations often resulted in
an unprofessional and misleading overidentification of law with
morality.[4] Both of these jurists, nevertheless, assumed that at least
some rules of law prescribe legal consequences to a class of facts
and that, when the facts of a litigated case are covered by such a
rule, a dose of the rule's prescription is likely to be administered.

   Weber wrote that this syllogistic model has, in law's primitive
beginnings, no resemblance to what happens; he said that primitive
law is not rationally applied to cases. He rejected a widely held
nineteenth-century view that the customs and usages of primitive
societies become, by promulgation, explicit and official rules of law.
When a primitive lawmaker sets forth law, said Weber, he intends
to alter usages, he does not intend to reinforce them.[5] Primitive
customs are rigid, but nevertheless changed, rather than buttressed,
when a headman makes legal pronouncements from time to time.[6]

   Weber defined law as a rule of conduct backed by a coercive
apparatus; he defined a coercive apparatus as a group of persons
poised to inflict punishment on those who break the law.[7] All
polities, including primitive societies, have law and coercive ap-
paratuses. From time to time occasions are bound to occur on which
a suspicion of violation of the law is entertained; then the coercive
apparatus must decide whether or not the suspect should be
punished. It is a mistake, wrote Weber, to think that primitive
peoples conduct rational criminal trials; their trials are magical
ordeals in which occult rites reveal either the guilt or innocence of
the accused. In these oracular proceedings no sensible inquiry need
be made into the details of the suspected misconduct, and no
thoughtful consideration need be given to the meaning of the pronounced law; ordeals can proceed without either rational investiga-

tion of the facts or rational cogitation on the law. The oracular spirits who are asked about the accused's guilt always give a monolithic, unambiguous answer. If anyone were to question the spirits' knowledge about what the accused did, and whether or not that conduct was wrong, he would, himself, be guilty of criminal profanation.[8] According to Weber, when proclaimed, aboriginal law happens to be framed so clearly that it could be a rational guide to, and test of, conduct; nevertheless aborigines did not use it rationally; they believed that since all law is god-given [9] and only wizards and priests can communicate with the gods, these adepts alone can find out whether or not a case is covered by the law's interdictions.[10] Because the law's source is supernatural, reason is of no use in the process of applying the law; in a trial by ordeal, reason can throw no light either on the scope of a ban or on the significance of the facts.

When decisions result from magic, the *form* of the legal process is irrational; this kind of legal process Weber classified as falling in his category of "formal irrationality." [11]

Weber accounted for the transitions from magical to rational trials in various ways. Three of his examples follow. In the first, sometimes a number of primitive kinship groups banded together in an alliance. The headmen of each of these allied groups, from time to time, convened in council. At one of these meetings the alliance's accredited magician disclosed a new divine law that had been revealed to him. Each headman, on returning to his own clan, proclaimed the new law, and commanded that it be obeyed. Weber continued:

However, the boundaries between technical decree, interpretation by individual decision, and revelation of new rules were vague and the magicians' prestige was unstable. Hence the creation of law could be . . . increasingly secularized and revelation could be either completely excluded or applied as an *ex post facto* legalization of the compacts. As a result, wide areas in which [magical] law making was once possible became subject to regulation by the simple consensus of the assembled authorities.[12]

In the second example, military commanders issued orders, which were rationally understood and reasonably applied. The organizing force of reason was, in this manner, brought to bear on getting ready for war, directing troop movements, carrying out strategies, and so on. Victors had spoils to divide; these apportionments sometimes might be governed by orders from headquarters, that is, orders which governed the allotment of the prisoners taken, the booty seized, and the territory won. Military orders for allocating the booty of war, wrote Weber, "created new individual rights and, under certain circumstances, new law." [13]

Third, "In early medieval Europe . . . the Christian Church, by its example of episcopal power, everywhere strongly encouraged the interference of the princes in the administration and enactment of the law. Indeed the Church often instigated this intervention for its own interests as well as the interests of the ethics it taught." [14]

2. Substantial irrationality. Several of the great legal philosophers over the centuries, have advocated that law be laid down as statutory rules which, when specific cases arise, would govern the decisions of judges. Most of the great philosophers who espoused such theories were activated by political motives, such as the prevention of tyranny, the protection of liberty, and the promotion of the peaceful arts.[15] St. Thomas Aquinas' proposal is relatively nonpolitical and is put forward primarily to advance the rationality of the law. St. Thomas gave three reasons for preferring law enacted by one arm of government and applied by another. They are: (1) A statutory rule may neutralize the irrelevant and evocative aspects of the facts of a case that otherwise might deflect the reasoning of a judge who is adjudicating such a case without legislative guidance. (2) Legislators have an opportunity to give systematic attention to a whole area of the law; judicial *ad hoc* reasoning, focused as it is on the facts of a single case, may be too narrow and must be concluded with dispatch; statutory law, therefore, is often conceived more thoughtfully than is case law. (3) The number of men needed to staff a far-flung system of courts greatly exceeds the number of men required to staff a legislative body; the legislature, therefore, can consist of a few men of great capability, while the judiciary's large need for manpower perforce results in the employment of some men of lesser wisdom.[16]

Weber, too, said that a characteristic of substantive legal rationality is a constitutional separation of powers, which limits the courts to the application of general rules enacted by the legislature. He may have been influenced in reaching this conclusion by some of the great legal philosophers.[17] But Weber gave a cultural, rather than a jurisprudential, argument to support his conclusion. In the Western world almost all of the countries, he said, place their lawmaking authority entirely in a legislative branch of their government, and restrict the authority of the judicial branch to the application of statutory law; therefore the legal processes in which judges are authorized to make their own law must be classified as substantively irrational. Since "free" adjudication is not substantive legal rationality, only the Roman legal system and those derived from it, said Weber, can be characterized as substantively rational.[18] The Common Law, of course, is not modeled on the Roman system.

3. **Substantive rationality.** Weber's substantive legal rationality obviously cannot include the two categories of legal irrationality already described, namely, formal legal irrationality—in which category Weber put all magical ordeals [19]—and substantive legal irrationality—in which category Weber included those systems allowing judges to evaluate concrete facts on an emotional, political, or ethical basis, rather than by applying legislated "general norms." [20]

Substantive legal rationality in Weber's system has in addition a positive characteristic, going beyond the exclusion of the two classes of legal irrationality; that is, the statutes applied to cases are themselves rational. When a statute embodies only legal abstraction, application of that statute can not produce substantive rationality. An enactment intended to further "ethical imperatives, expediential rules, and political maxims" is rational; [21] judicial application of such an enactment to a case falling within its ambit constitutes substantive legal rationality.

4. **Formal rationality.** This fourth and last of Weber's categories includes those legal processes in which judges apply abstract, technical statutes,—statutes not grounded on "ethical imperatives, expediential rules, and political maxims." These statutes are professional, legal products, derived from juristic reasoning—a kind of professionalism that is unconcerned with social policy. Formal legal rationality is likely to seem arcane to most laymen much of

the time; to Weber, however, it was, nevertheless, importantly rational.

Weber subdivided formal legal rationality into two species. The first subclass involves the proper use of ceremonials or legal forms, exemplified by (1) the words of art in a promissory note that make it negotiable, (2) the binding force of the seal on a sealed instrument, (3) the ritual delivery of a clod of earth that conveys land by livery of seisin. The other subclass of formal legal rationality "is found where the legally relevant characteristics of the facts are disclosed through the logical analysis of meaning and where, accordingly, definite fixed legal concepts in the form of . . . abstract rules are formulated and applied." [22]

II CARDOZO'S FOURFOLD CLASSIFICATION OF THE REASONING USED IN DECIDING COMMON LAW ISSUES COMPARED WITH WEBER'S SYSTEM

Cardozo, one of America's judicial idols, published his best known jurisprudential book, *The Nature of the Judicial Process,* in 1921, four years before the appearance of Weber's book on legal sociology. Cardozo dealt with the reasoning processes of American judges when confronted with issues of common law. Most of these issues, wrote Cardozo, are hardly problematic; experienced judges make quick work of them, easily applying well-established, but non-statutory, common law rules; in many cases these rules are clear, clearly just, and clearly applicable. When a judicial decision on a common law issue is not a foregone conclusion, judges, said Cardozo, use one of four alternative methods of reasoning to adapt the common law to the case at hand. In these problem cases, a pre-existing common law rule is neither completely apt nor clearly inapplicable, and the judge, therefore, has the problem of deciding the direction in which the common law should develop. At the heart of the decision of a problem case is the judge's choice of a method of adaptive reasoning.

Cardozo called his first-mentioned form of judicial reasoning "the rule of analogy, or the method of philosophy." This method differs from and yet resembles Weber's "formal rationality"; both involve abstract professional legal reasoning. A judge who produces an instance of Weber's formal legal rationality applies to the case at hand an abstract, legalistic rule enacted by the legislature; a judge who uses Cardozo's method of philosophy uses abstract, legalistic thought to reformulate the common law so that the law speaks about the case at hand; [23] each of these processes involves a rule based on conceptual juridics. In Weber's formal legal rationality the legislature promulgates the abstract rule applied by the judiciary; in the use of Cardozo's method of philosophy, a judge himself formulates the abstract rule which he then applies.

Cardozo's second form of judicial reasoning is "the method of history." A judge using this method studies the history of a rule and then continues the rule's development further along the path it has taken until the law so developed can dispose of the case at hand. His third form is "the method of custom or tradition"; it is a process of developing the meaning of a rule in light of custom so that the decision of the case at hand conforms to prevailing usage.

Cardozo's darling is his fourth method of developing common law rules, "the method of sociology." A judge using this method turns to social welfare for clues to the direction in which the common law develops so that it will dispose of the case at bar. Cardozo's use of the term "social welfare" is broad; he meant expedient or prudent decisions intended to advance the good of the collective body, or to result in social gain by carrying out the community's ideals— ideals which are based on the demands of religion, ethics, or the social sense of justice.[24]

Common law judges, said Cardozo, variously use each of these four methods from time to time, but Cardozo was most interested in two of the four; he discussed at length the interaction between the method of philosophy and the method of sociology, that is, between professional, abstract logic and rational concern with public policy, as competing forces in the development of the common law.

Weber, the sociologist, took a value-free scientific stand; he described and classified legal processes; he did not pass judgment on them. He believed, as a matter of fact, that social control through law will inevitably produce, in any society, a predominance of formal legal rationality. He put it this way:

> Only that abstract which employs the logical interpretation of meaning allows the execution of the specifically systematic task, i.e., the collection and [logical] rationalization . . . of all the several rules recognized as legally valid into an internally consistent complex of abstract legal principles.[25]

Cardozo, the jurist, made no effort to avoid evaluations. He approved of the persistence of the method of philosophy (resulting in abstract, logical development of the common law) because that method, he said, promoted both orderliness and impartiality—two qualities to be prized.[26] "I am not," Cardozo wrote, "to mar the symmetry of the legal structure by the introduction of inconsistencies and irrelevancies and artificial exceptions except for some sufficient reason, which will commonly be some consideration of history, or custom, or policy, or justice." [27] Even though Cardozo's book was written after he had become a seasoned lawyer and judge—and, therefore, held legal systematics in high regard—he was not an inveterate conceptualist. Cardozo believed, with St. Thomas Aquinas, that the factual world changes and, therefore, that the words of some resolutions that deal clearly with the problems of the day may, on the morrow, become imprecise and need recasting; sometimes the reduction of the common law's imprecisions, thought Cardozo, should be made with social welfare in mind. Cardozo also, however, came close to Weber's conclusion that formal legal rationality is bound to bulk large; Cardozo believed that formal, conceptual development, carved out with little concern for policy, has been, and inevitably will be, the chief part of the judicial development of the common law.

Cardozo assumed throughout his book that the common law system was rational.[28] Weber, in contrast, described the common law system as incorporating fluid and shifting doctrines and unsteady procedural devices, which were likely to result in discrepancies.

Weber described the interaction between private business practice and the development of the common law; he characterized the legal fluidity resulting from this interaction as outside of "the rational character of legal propositions as evolved by modern legal science." Cases, he wrote, are "distinguished from each other in a thoroughly empirical way in accordance with their objective characteristics rather than in accordance with their meanings as disclosed by formal legal logic." [29]

American jurists have esteemed Cardozo as an enlightening legal philosopher, one who understood the common law's potential for rationality and whose influence has, they believe, made the common law more rational. Our comparison of his and Weber's contrasting theories of the rationality of the common law judicial processes raises this question: is Cardozo apologizing for less rationality than Americans deserve? This question is made more pointed by a further specification of Weber's factual portrayal of forces that, in all societies, accelerate or retard the development of rational legal processes.

Weber wrote that in ancient times men who were politically dominant, with a view to increasing their own power, did not voluntarily relinquish legal magic. The bourgeoisie of Rome and of the middle ages became powerful allies of their rulers; the bourgeoisie looked on rationality in substantive law and procedure as an advance, and pushed their rulers into setting up rational legal processes. Legal irrationality, said Weber, tends to persist in the legal processes of those societies whose rulers are not allied with traders. High priests and potentates are likely to have temperaments and ambitions that are not compatible with codified rules of law.[30] Powerful political champions of democracy also disrelish enacted, statutory law; they are seldom willing to tie themselves down by rules, even rules of their own making.[31] Democrats, Weber continued, are inevitably put to the choice between enacted law's certainty and impartiality on the one hand, and other democratic ideals on the other; [32] codified law tends not only to ensure impartiality, but also to stabilize enonomic inequalities; it affords protection to the affluent in economic systems that are undemocratic.

Formal justice is . . . repugnant to all authoritarian powers . . . because it diminishes the dependence of the individual upon the grace and power of the authorities. To democracy, however, it has been repugnant because it decreases the dependency of . . . individuals upon the decisions of their fellow citizens.[33]

Both authoritarians and leading democrats prefer, according to Weber, "khadi justice"—that is, *ad hoc* decisions, made by magistrates who react to the facts of each concrete case in accordance with the way that case happens to evoke their ethical, political, and social predilections. In "khadi decisions," considerations of ethics, polity, and sociality are directly applied without the intermediation of formulated rules of statutory law.[34]

Laymen, Weber said, are likely to see economic or utilitarian meanings in formal legal rationalities; these images are, however, disappointing mirages; judges applying formally rational statutes proceed without concern for laymen's private expectations. (Weber's next several paragraphs are about "lawyers"; they seem, however, to deal mainly with legally trained magistrates.) Lawyers, said Weber, are not likely to renounce formalism; lawyers' law, therefore, is not calculated to protect lay expectations. English lawyers are as prone to formalism as are continental lawyers; therefore formalism will doggedly persist both in England and on the continent.[35]

Some few lawyers are irked, said Weber, by the doctrinaire simplicity of formalism; their discontent leads them to believe that the judicial process should be creative—at least whenever statutory law is "silent." The advocates of "free law" are extreme examples of lawyers who try to justify judicial creativity; statutes are inarticulate, these free lawyers say, because life's facts are legally unorderly; each judicial decision, therefore, should be made as a concrete resolution of a unique problem, rather than as a set of facts whose legal significance is determined by reference to a formal legal rule.[36] The jurists who stress the existence of gaps in every code of laws, Weber said, then move one step further by saying that the judicial process

never consisted, or at any rate never should consist, in the "application" of general norms to a concrete case. . . . [In these jurists'] view "legal propositions" are regarded as secondary.[37] . . . [T]he preference for a case law that remains in contact with legal reality—which means the reality of the lawyers—to statute law is in turn subverted by the argument that no precedent should be regarded as binding beyond its concrete facts. The way is thus left open to the free balancing of values in each individual case.[38]

Weber says that most lawyers, nevertheless, recoil from theories of judicial creativity so transient that it leaves law unchanneled; they, therefore, try "to reestablish an objective standard of values." [39] The sum total of British statutes, Weber prophesied (in 1925), is bound to increase enormously. The enlarged bulk of statutory law will profoundly change the work done by British judges; they will become, for the most part, engaged in applying statutory law, and they will rarely be confronted with issues of common law. Weber adds that even if continental judges were coronated with "creators' crowns" they would not become self-assertive. "In any case," said Weber, "the juristic precision of judicial opinions will be seriously impaired if sociological, economic, or ethical argument were to take the place of legal concepts." [40] With the inevitable growth of technology, lawyers will, he believed, be forced to specialize increasingly, to cope with the legal problems that are bound to grow out of technological advance; the resulting new law will be complicated and formal. Consequently laymen will become increasingly ignorant of the law. Weber did not say, however, that esoteric law always escapes revision; "inevitably the notion must expand that the law is a rational technical apparatus, which is continually transformable in the light of expediential considerations and devoid of all sacredness of content." [41] This, however, is no forecast that judges will increasingly adopt Cardozo's method of sociology; since, in Weber's classification, substantive legal rationality can exist only when judges apply previously enacted statutes, he was predicting that, in the long run, an enlightened and mobile legislature will continuously revise statutory law.

III HOW IRRATIONAL IS THE COMMON LAW?

The common law, since it was nonstatutory, was categorized by Weber as a kind of substantive legal irrationality. The accuracy of

Weber's value-free, but uncomplimentary, description is, of course, a matter of concern to Americans.

We have Cardozo's—more or less offhand—testimony that most appellate cases that turn on common law issues are foregone conclusions; they are, Cardozo wrote, decided by applying clear and clearly applicable rules in a routine way. Against his view we must weigh several of Weber's delineations: namely (1) since common law decisions are free adjudications, they are not applications of general norms, (2) the fluid and shifting substantive law and procedure in the common law system make it unsteady, (3) common law judges distinguish between similar cases on insignificant differences, (4) even though the tendency of legally trained men is to prize and use formal, professional thought, some lawyers, nevertheless, yearn for creativity and argue for various dodges, which cut down the force of rules and precedents.

There are, of course, in Weber's sociological descriptions, other forces pushing in the opposite direction. Weber portrays political pressures that, from time to time, may inspire the enactment of statutes for the purpose of producing either impartiality or stability, and he foresees that the growth of technology will inevitably increase legislation. These developments will reduce the importance of the common law. He also believes that most lawyers and judges are fundamentally disposed to favor formalized law, applied with little concern for economics or social utility.

Weber's descriptions, taken one by one, all have something in them; most observers of the common law have at least glimpsed a few manifestations of each of his specifications. His statements are not backed up with statistical studies showing the extent of the common law's fluidities. Accurate knowledge of some social facts can be ascertained, however, without quantification.

We know without statistical inquiry, for example, that if judges presiding over criminal trials were allowed extemporaneously to define the crime with which the accused is charged, the judges' definitions would tend to disfavor unattractive defendants and to exonerate appealing ones. Criminal trials, then, fall into a class of litigation in which Cardozo's method of sociology is particularly inappropriate. In many states this evil is expressly recognized and the common law of crimes is abolished by statute.[42] Most state legislatures have not expressly abolished the common law of crimes; in all fifty states, however, the legislatures have enacted systematic and exhaustive penal codes. As a result of the codification of the criminal law, practically no accused is nowadays convicted of a serious crime by a trial court that does not invoke a statute defining the crime and dealing with its punishment.[43]

We can say with assurance that few American judges yearn for the formalizing force of law completely codified in the continental style. Many lawyers and judges, as knowledgeable American citizens, favor various legislative reforms of some parts of the common law. Most of these professionals, however, are rarely troubled by the fluidity of case law; their concern is usually with injustice or lack of national uniformity. More substantive legal rationality (not more abstract formality) is their goal.

Especially in the last several decades, American judges have deferred meticulously to the legislature's judgments whenever constitutional statutes come up for application; a reader of contemporary American case reports is likely to come away with the impression that the judges conscientiously try to interpret statutes so as to effectuate the legislature's purposes. A few judges, no doubt, cunningly substitute their own views for those of the legislature. In earlier times such subversion was more common. For example, the New York legislature in 1852 revised the state's civil procedure by adopting the Field Code. Many other state legislatures also provided for "code pleading" modeled on the New York statutes. The reforms of the code were uncongenial to many sitting judges who were habituated to the technical intricacies of common law pleading. Early judicial "interpretations" of the code often were calculated to salvage the very common law technicalities which the legislatures had tried to sweep away. Other instances of judicially mangled statutes were relatively common during the late nineteenth and early twentieth centuries.[44] In those days, therefore, some statutory law did not produce the rationality that Weber ascribed to the application of enacted law. Our American experience in those times was, perhaps, unique and escaped Weber's notice.

The legislatures of our day certainly have, as Weber foresaw, greatly ramified the statutory law. Statute books have grown from single volumes to large sets. Since our courts have become more respectful toward legislation, and since new statutes tend to be substantively rational, larger fractions of the total systems of state law tend to fall into Weber's categories of rationality.

There remains to be considered, however, the rationality of the common law decisions that still are made; they may be occupying a smaller range, but they will, no doubt, not disappear from our legal systems in our time.

One of Weber's comments on the irrationality of the common law involves jury trial. Our juries are not allowed to interpret statutes, but they are sometimes asked to apply abstract, common law concepts; for example a jury in a tort case may be told to determine whether or not the defendant "acted with due care." Weber said:

The popular view which assumes that questions of fact are decided by the jury and questions of law by the judge is clearly wrong. Lawyers esteem the jury system, and particularly the civil jury, precisely because it decides concrete issues of "law" without creating "precedents" which might be binding in the future, in other words because of the very "irrationality" in which the jury decides questions of law.[45]

The tone of Weber's description of the jury seems a little sharp. If juries are used to "avoid creating precedents that might be binding," perhaps a system that, much of the time, follows other precedents is not so fluid and shifting after all. Moreover, jury verdicts are theoretically reached by applying settled rules of the common law to the facts of cases, and, therefore, are not far removed from the Weberian category of formal legal rationality. Some respected American jurists think that the practice of submitting issues to the jury is, in some instances, preferable to freezing a doctrine by fragmenting it into a set of formal rules; rigid and structured criteria of standards like "due care," they think, may result in outmoded and unjust decisions.[46] My limited knowledge of the Romanistic systems may be insufficient to justify my impression that "bona fides" on the continent is no crisper than "good faith" in the United States, though no doubt judges apply such standards more professionally than do jurymen.

Though the common law regularizes routine cases, fluidity there is when a judge faced with a perplexing issue of common law arbitrarily selects any one of Cardozo's four methods of reaching decisions. Cardozo's picture of judicial thought used in nonroutine cases depicts the temperament and predilections of judges as turning them to either the method of philosophy or the method of history or the method of custom or the method of sociology; each of these four courses is ingrained in the history of the permissible techniques of decision by common law judges. Primacy, said Cardozo, usually goes to the method of abstract legal reasoning, but it can properly be superseded whenever a court sees its way clear to proceed along the lines of history, custom, or social welfare; a judge deciding a problem case, therefore, can choose one method out of this wide range of methods of thought and, as a result, enjoys options leading to varying and inconsistent structuring of the common law. The fresh and forceful aspect of Cardozo's book lies in his legitimation and sponsorship of the method of sociology. He is content to argue for judicial authority to revise the common law so as to enhance social welfare on those occasions when judicial conservatism does not inhibit such revisions. Hereby a "khadi" element lies embedded in our judicial process. Our courts have revised the common law in service of the common good, but over the centuries these revisions occur sporadically, and only on those rare occasions when the courts have felt judicial revisions were appropriate.

Such too has been the way of our legislatures. Their wide *authority* to update the common law and advance social welfare harks back to their beginnings. Their *obligation* to keep our common law system up-to-date is more of a preachment than a duty.

The courts are, however, in recent years beginning to recognize that they have not only the *authority* to use the method of sociology to revise the judge-made common law, but they also have the *obligation* to do so. If the courts' *obligation* coincides with their *authority*, then the element of fluidity in Cardozo's system is, at least in theory, drying up. A proper understanding of the limits on the courts' authority to revise the common law also implies that the courts have an obligation to use their authority; the next succeeding paragraphs are calculated to demonstrate this conclusion.

Judges are not authorized to revise the common law whenever they suspect that an established common law rule calls for a decision in the case at bar which may be inimical to social welfare. Bentham pointed out in the eighteenth century that a common law judge deciding a case in a novel way may or may not be originating a new common law rule.[47] A maverick decision is not at all unlikely to be viewed as a mistake the next time that the court is faced with a similar case.[48] When a court disavows its own innovation the decision denounced becomes an admitted instance of irrationality. There are, in my view, two kinds of novel decisions that are likely to be repudiated, and which, therefore, are rarely made in the first place.

Cardozo himself recognized that a judge, since he is a public servant, is not authorized to make decisions that humor his own idiosyncracies.[49] The occasions on which judges have authority to revise the common law occur only when common law rules are out of joint with the public's aspirations. A novel holding that implements widely shared values—and is unwelcome or vexatious to, at most, a few selfish or unbalanced people—is almost sure to command the respect of the court in the ensuing indefinite future. If, however, an innovation overrides the unselfish aspirations of a substantial fraction of the public, it is likely to lack the feel of rectitude which an innovation should have. In other words, a change in the common law not underpinned by public morality is not and should not be made because the revision lacks sufficient patent probity to compete with sureness with the old law that it replaces. The legislature sometimes can properly venture to pass statutes uncongenial to a substantial minority of the citizenry; their statute will stand as law until revised or repealed; a single decision, however, becomes embedded in the common law system only when it honors a principle that will also be honored in sequent similar cases. A well-meaning, innovating judge who varies the common law in an area of fragmented values, may seem, at a later time, to have become lost on his search for social welfare. When the public's values are conflicting or inchoate, steady reform comes only from the legislature.[50]

The second limitation on judicial authority to change the common law involves the courts' knowledge of the factual impact of their revision. If a judicial attempt to implement a public aspiration by revisions of the common law were likely to produce side effects inimical to social welfare, it would obviously be beyond the courts' authority. When a court's knowledge of the relevant social facts is slim and uncertain, an impulsive change in the common law would be irrational. Suppose, for example, that a claimant asked a court to increase the traditional liability of a public accountant for an error in one of his audits to liability without fault (by analogy to recent extensions of manufacturers' liability for defective products). Suppose further that the accountant's counsel suggests to the court that such an increase in accountants' liability might drive most responsible accountants away from that branch of accountancy. If the court entertained serious doubts about its ability to know whether or not such an untoward effect might result from a change in the common law, revision should be left to the legislature, which is better equipped to inquire into the probable results of change.[51] Even though the court has no assurance that the legislature will consider the matter, judges are not authorized to make a revision that may, in fact, involve great risks of impairing the common good. If they move rashly forward in this single case, the likelihood that their holding will become a respected precedent is reduced. The court may have to retreat from its holding after prejudicing both the business world and respect for the judicial process. A likelihood of such a retreat should and does inhibit change.

Another factor limiting the courts' authority to revise the common law is an inhibition against attempting novel specific justice in the case at hand to the prejudice of wider justice that may be seriously weakened by exceptions. Some courts, for example, have persistently observed a rule providing that the owner of a life insurance policy can name a new payee only by doing everything within his power to comply with the procedure for beneficiary-change stipulated in the policy.[52] These courts say that nearly all beneficiaries of life insurance are dependents of the insured,—widows, orphans, aged parents, and so on. The strict-performance rule usually prevents anyone but the named beneficiary from making an arguable claim to the avails of a policy. The rule, therefore, reduces litigation, some of the costs of which would otherwise come out of the benefits of the policy. The social value of this rigid rule lies, then, in its power to avert wastage of life insurance benefits. Note, however, that the rigid rule will also control the disbursal of life insurance benefits when neither claimant is a dependent of the buyer of the life insurance policy. An art museum, we shall say, can clearly prove that a dead millionaire clearly intended that his life insurance should be paid to the museum, instead of to the exclusive country club originally named as the payee. If the millionaire's attempt to change beneficiaries falls short of complying with the rigid rule, the museum's claim will fail; the rule operates with the same rigidity as it does in a dispute between a grocery clerk's wife and his mother. Were the court to make an exception and break the shell of rigidity, the yolk of justice might spill out. The public aspiration for more adequate support of art education and the public indifference to the fortunes of exclusive clubs would not, as a matter of policy, be advanced significantly by excluding this case from the operation of the rule. The likelihood that a judgment against the club will stimulate litigation contesting the rights of dependents named as beneficiaries should keep the court from making an exception that will endanger the rule. If the rule itself does not have the merit claimed for it, of course, its destruction may in fact start erratically and on naive grounds. If, however, the rule is sound, its destruction reduces public welfare, and the method of sociology has, in that case, misfired.

In the last three paragraphs I have tried to outline a little more clearly than Cardozo did the limits on courts' authority to use the method of sociology. Each of the three factors explicated, limiting the courts' authority to revise the common law, is an aspect of the character of our judicial process. The likelihood that a novel holding made in the face of fragmented public values will become a repudiated disturbance of the common law, rather than a sound revision, should and does warn courts away from such a change. Judges recognize their limited ability to prevision the factual impact of revision and, therefore, are wary of changes in the common law whenever they suspect the change involves a palpable risk of an untoward side effect. A danger of structural damage to the common law, when a proposed insignificant exception threatens the value of a socially significant rule, should and does deter courts from making such exceptions.

All of these limitations on the authority of courts to use the method of sociology are limitations that hold the courts to occasions when the judicial process can be used safely to update our legal system. The courts, as public servants, are authorized only within these confines to better implement the public's aspirations by use of the method of sociology; their authorization to use the method of sociology is implied from the nature of the office entrusted to them. Are the courts equally authorized, as Cardozo put it, to use other methods of developing the common law that ignore social welfare? Given a clear possibility of bettering social welfare, are the courts, as public servants, impliedly authorized to turn away from consideration of that opportunity to indulge in professional abstract thought, historical analysis, or the ways of common usage? Courts themselves seem to be coming around to the negative answer to the question just put; in my view it is none too soon to recognize that whenever courts are authorized to use the method of sociology they are obliged to use it. The obligation is rational and is, from time to time, becoming better rationalized. A judge who revises the common law should exercise cool and demanding reason while exploring the public's aspirations, the social facts, and the social value of the particular segment of structured common law.

In some cases of judicial revision of our common law the legislature, if it had had a mind to, could have done a better job. The revising court, however, has no assurance that the legislature will do a timely job. When he is authorized to revise he is also obliged to do so, and if he neglects his obligation, justice suffers.[53] The legislature always has the last word, and can always add further improvements when it wants to. Because of the necessarily confined authority of judicial law reform, most of our hopes for a more just society will be realized, if at all, through legislation. Nevertheless the obligation of our judges to revise the common law so that it speaks more justice promises a substantial increment of justice; that obligation does not call for judicial irrationality.

Chapter 7

The Board of Punishments' Interpretation of the Chinese Imperial Code*

When magistrates apply statutes to cases they usually find that the meaning of the enacted words is clear. In most trials of defendants accused of bank holdups, for example, the presiding judge readily understands the statutory definition of "armed robbery" and easily imparts that understanding to jurors. Nevertheless, no legislature can anticipate and provide clearly for all contingencies; in any system of statutory law, therefore, cases that raise doubts about the pertinence and meaning of a statute are bound to occur.

The purport of foreign statutes is usually not difficult for lawyers to understand when they share the lawmaker's cultural environment; comprehending the gist of a New York statute usually presents no special difficulties to California lawyers or judges. Outlanders, however, are likely to find that legal rules developed in an alien culture are often cryptic. Even when the words in an article of the seventeenth-century Ch'ing code seem clear, a twentieth-century Pennsylvania lawyer may, nevertheless, misunderstand them. One

* This chapter is a shortened, amended and somewhat simplified version of Part III, *Law in Imperial China,* Bodde and Morris (Cambridge, Mass.: Harvard University Press, 1967) and is published with the permission of Harvard University Press.

of the roots of such a Pennsylvanian's misconceptions may lie deep in his assumptions about the proper use and nature of statutory law—assumptions that are almost entirely at odds with the attitudes of Ch'ing legislative draftsmen and judges.

Legislation is an old institution in the West; modern legislation, however, did not bulk large much before the nineteenth century. We saw in Chapter V that the attitudes vivifying the nineteenth-century eruptions of legislative activity developed several decades earlier. Three eighteenth-century political theorists seemed to be especially influential in both expressing and formulating some of our American attitudes toward legislative promulgation of general rules of law in a predominantly common law system. They were Hume, Montesquieu, and Rousseau. Each of these three spoke for himself, and each spoke in his own unique way. They were, however, born into their times and were influenced by, and talked about, their Western society and its problems. Two of the main features of eighteenth-century Western society were the emergence of modern industrialization and the beginnings of modern democracy. The force of these two developments is not yet spent, and the values espoused by the three philosophers not only were influential in their time but still are operative in ours.

David Hume (1711–1776) favored promulgated laws to promote three social needs: (1) the stabilization of property rights, (2) the furtherance of voluntary transfers of ownership of lands and chattels, (3) the obligation to perform contractual promises. These three legal developments, he believed, were prerequisites for widespread commerce and industry; these three legal developments were, therefore, in Hume's view, at the base of good order and prosperity.[1] Promulgated rules of law, he thought, would stand firm and thwart prejudicial sympathies that might otherwise exert unstabilizing force in some particular instances. Hume foresaw, as a result of the system of promulgated law, a further division of labor and greater economic growth.

The forces that produced and nurtured the Chinese dynastic codes were not rooted in economic concerns. The codes were largely penal, and seldom were used to regulate commercial transactions. Business disputes between traders were thought of as private matters, often settled within guilds. The stimuli to legislate that emanated from the appearance of Western mercantilism and capitalism had no counterparts in those forces that produced the codes of imperial China.

The motivation behind Montesquieu's advocacy of a system of legislated rules of law was quite different from Hume's. Montesquieu focused not on economics but on politics, not on prosperity but on liberty. Great power, Montesquieu wrote, is subject to great abuse. If one branch of the government must lay down general principles of law with no particular case in mind, and if another must apply those neutral principles once a case arises, the threat of abuse of power is diminished. Central to Montesquieu's design for government was the separation of governmental powers, which could not occur without legislation. Statutes, then, could promote civil liberty.[2]

The codes of imperial China did, of course, promulgate principles in advance, but the codifiers were not concerned with invasions of civil liberties resulting from extemporaneous prosecutions for crimes. The emperor enjoyed unlimited power, and his code was proclaimed to effectuate his policies; his laws were not designed to check his whims. Civil liberty had nothing to do with the Ch'ing code or any other proclamation of the emperors of China.

Rousseau's motivation, like Montesquieu's, was political; he shared Montesquieu's distaste for imposed and unchecked political power, but he added a new dimension. Legislation that set forth general rules of law in advance of disputes could be and ought to be the product of the entire citizenry, expressing its "general will" and thus ruling itself. Law formulated *ad hoc* during the course of dealing with a particular case was, in Rousseau's opinion, at the dangerous mercy of the "particular will." A judge's particular will was not only likely to favor both the judge himself and his friends, but was also likely to be uninformed and unwise. Only the general will formulated by the whole corporate citizenry tapped the composite judgment of the whole people; their judgment was both fair and wise because it was composite. The wisdom of the corporate citizenry was fragmented or thrown off balance by partisanship once a particular case arose; the general will, therefore, could be expressed only in abstract legislated rules promulgated in advance of disputes.[3]

In imperial China the idea that the rude peasantry was fairer and wiser than the emperor and his ministers was unthinkable. Occasionally a well-thought-of Chinese publicist suggested that some wisdom lay in the natural inclinations of the masses. The Chinese authority who properly spoke on propriety was not, however, the consensus of a village meeting; Chinese norms were formulated by sages, and, in imperial times, some of these norms were the basis of laws promulgated by the emperor. No imperial Chinese code was a distillation of the folk spirit of justice. The Ch'ing code and its forerunners were never challenged on the ground that their framers were elite scholars who looked to history for their models.

The main incentive of Chinese emperors to promulgate codes was to extend their rule throughout the empire. No emperor's code was, however, intended to stimulate economic growth, protect civil liberty, or further popular government. What values, then, did underlie and shape the codes of imperial China? The most important influence on most of the oldest imperial codes, in my view, was the value placed on a system of assigned punishments adjusted so that each crime carried the exactly correct penalty.

Even before China was unified, criminal law was more likely to be called "punishments" (*hsing*) rather than "laws" (*fa*). One of the earliest disquisitions on law was the *Lü hsing*; its date is uncertain, but it was unquestionably written no later than the fourth century B.C. Its author-king said, "Now when you tranquilize the people . . . what should you attend to if not punishments." He then discusses in detail some instances in which wrongdoers were either punished too severely or let off too lightly. He concluded by urging "reverent carefulness" in assessing the right punishment in every case.[4] More than two thousand years later, imperial Chinese jurists were still caught up in fitting each punishment to each crime. The highest judicial organ of several dynasties, including the Ch'ing, was called the Board of Punishments (*Hsing pu*). The Board's deliberations, in each case they reviewed, centered almost exclusively on whether or not the sentence recommended by the governor of a province called for exactly the right punishment. The

Board seldom concerned themselves with the accused's guilt or innocence.

Only for the fourteen years between 221 B.C. and 207 B.C. was the jurisprudence of imperial China differently oriented. During the short Ch'in dynasty, which unified the empire for the first time, the Legalists over-shadowed the Confucianists. One of the Legalists' principles called for a system of criminal punishments so drastic that no one would dare commit any crime. This principle may have cut much of the ground from under the earlier preoccupation with exactly befitting punishments, a preoccupation which had not theretofore centered on deterring crime by punishment.

The unifying Ch'in dynasty may have been the first Chinese regime to adopt a uniform criminal law for all of the empire. An emperor threatening unendurable punishment for all crimes, with little regard for who committed them, had small need for a finely wrought, wide spectrum of punishments; his penal edicts would suit his purposes if they warned against specified misbehaviors and threatened drastic consequences.[5] The ruthlessness of Ch'in punishments was one of the roots of the popular disaffection that doomed the dynasty to a short reign.

The Han dynasty (206 B.C.–220 A.D.) succeeded the Ch'in. During the Han there was a turn toward Confucianism which affected the development of law. Han legal processes were destined to become archetypes for the many centuries of imperial rule.

One earlier Confucianism, however, was ignored during the Han dynasty. Some of the Master's followers deplored preformulated rules of criminal law on the ground that when the people know formulated statutory texts they become contentious and appeal to technicalities; these theorists favored judicial *ad hoc* sentencing of each wrongdoer to a punishment improvised at each trial. Unformulated criminal law applied extemporaneously by local authorities did not appeal to the Han emperors of a unified China; they preferred to promulgate criminal law from the capital whence it could be uniformly applied throughout the empire. In this respect their law probably resembled Ch'in's Legalistic System.

The jurisprudence of the Han dynasty rejected some of the radical Legalistic notion of the equality of most men before the criminal law. Confucian proprieties were reasserted, and a complicated system of family rank and status, affecting—among other things—criminal responsibility, was reestablished.

In Han times Confucianists adopted an idea held by the "naturalists" who looked on human order as an integral part of natural order. The naturalists thought that human disorder reverberated throughout nature, that human misconduct disrupted natural harmony. Serious crimes might, they thought, jangle the cosmos and bring on floods and other natural catastrophes. Criminal disturbances of nature could be offset by proper punishments. Punishments of befitting severity reattuned disordered nature. Punishments that were either too severe or not severe enough for the crime committed would not re-establish natural harmony, but would instead disrupt it still more. This kind of reasoning was back of the *Lü hsing*, written two or more centuries earlier; it was probably not, however, until the Han dynasty that a highly organized sweeping system of befitting punishments was first promulgated.

The theory of the imperial franchise in Han and some of the succeeding dynasties tended to reinforce the importance of a codified spectrum of befitting punishments. An emperor ruled as heaven's mandatory. If he failed to preserve natural harmony, heaven would withdraw its mandate and his dynasty would fall. Since unsuitable punishments threatened the dynasty itself, the emperor was obliged either to promulgate and enforce a system of befitting punishments or suffer dire consequences.

These archaic beliefs about nature and heaven were not, of course, an article of faith for the jurists who served imperial China for twenty-three centuries. Pragmatically disposed members of the Board of Punishments wrote easily and without apology, from time to time in the Ch'ing dynasty, about the need for making an example of a culprit; they probably never even noticed their departure from earlier naturalist theory. An unexpressed policy of using punishment to discourage wrongdoing no doubt affected penal thought and practice during the span of imperial times. We would be mistaken, however, if we were to equate the importance of deterrence in Western penal theory with its place in imperial Chinese criminal jurisprudence. The Chinese of imperial times were predisposed to cherish antiquity; whenever they departed from ancient ways, they were likely to adopt archaistic modifications embodying a stylistic reference to the past. Anciently there were "the five punishments"; the seventeenth-century Ch'ing code, drafted millennia later, still used "the five punishments." [6] The age-old five and the Ch'ing five are in substance different, but both fives were designed to be available systems of severities matched against the gravity of the crimes punished. Each rule in the Ch'ing code was calculated to link a narrow category of misconducts to a single specified punishment in such a way that every infraction of a single provision will be equal in gravity to every other infraction and merit exactly the same punishment.

The intention of the seventeenth-century draftsmen of the Ch'ing code, then, was to requite each kind of misdeed with the appropriately severe retaliation. They did not mention natural harmony in the code itself, and I have read no Ch'ing Board of Punishments' report that even alludes to the order of nature. When the code was drafted its authors in all probability would not have seriously entertained the primitivism that miscarriages of criminal justice would bring on either natural catastrophes or the dynasty's downfall. From Han times onward, nevertheless, every imperial code followed the Han archetype; for centuries and centuries imperial jurists took it for granted that every punishment should be carefully calculated to fit a culprit's crime; they did not even advert to any alternative theory. The codifiers of the Ch'ing law were not subjected to arguments for departure from the style of the Ming code or the codes of earlier dynasties; no one challenged their intellectual and political allegiance to age-old tradition. The Board of Punishments, who applied the Ch'ing code, did not have their traditional views challenged either. Ch'ing statutory law was drafted and applied by jurists who were "employing a received and so authoritative technique by the light of received and so authoritative ideals." [7]

WHAT DO THE STATUTORY WORDS MEAN?

Many Ch'ing statutes spoke clearly to the judges to whom they were addressed. Some cases involved statutes whose clarity was routinely obvious to the accultured members of the Board of Punishments, but which, nevertheless, may bewilder outlanders. In Wang Ssu's case,[8] for example, the culprit had participated in an affray with other ruffians. Two men were killed. Wang had struck one of the mortal blows. The statute dealing with homicidal affrays sets the punishment of mortal-blow-strikers at strangulation after the assizes. In this case, however, the ringleader who first plotted the affray had since died. A substatute provided:

If several persons have planned a joint assault resulting in the death of two persons . . . , and if the original planner of the assault should die of illness while awaiting sentence in prison, his death will be acceptable as requital for the deaths of the victims, the result being that any of the other assailants guilty of having actually inflicted fatal blows, and therefore punishable by strangulation, shall have this penalty reduced by one degree to life exile.

The Board's opinion says, "Inasmuch as the original planner, Tseng Li-fang has subsequently died of illness while in prison, the governor of Hunan has . . . sentenced Wang to . . . life exile instead of strangulation." The Board of Punishments approves.

An outlander might suspect that the whole statute is a typographical error. Why be lenient to a murderer because his confederate has died in prison of illness? Dr. Derk Bodde's researches establish that, even though the statute quoted was not promulgated until 1801, it "embodies a cosmological conception of very early origin." The key Chinese term in the statute is *ti ming* (requiting a life). Bodde says:

To the ancient Chinese, with their insistence on the basic harmony existing between man and nature, a human crime—particularly a homicide—was regarded as disruption of the total cosmic order. This disruption could be repaired only by offering or sacrificing adequate requital . . . Thus, in the sub-statute the death of the original planner . . . is reckoned as cancelling out the death of the victim . . .[9]

Those at home in the Chinese imperial intellectual climate can, then, sometimes understand literal sense that may perturb a stranger.

THE UNRELIABILITY OF LITERAL INTERPRETATION

Wooden-headed insistence on the literal meaning of statutory words is an unacceptable and rejected method of statutory interpretation in nearly all legal systems. A hundred years ago the Supreme Court of the United States had an occasion to interpret the statute which provided, "If a person shall knowingly and wilfully obstruct or retard the passage of the mail" he shall be guilty of a crime. Federal authorities prosecuted a Kentucky sheriff for executing a warrant and arresting a mail-delivering-postman on a murder charge. The Supreme Court held the statute inapplicable. The court said, "All laws should receive a sensible construction . . . The reason of the law should prevail over its letter . . . The act of Congress which punishes the obstruction . . . of . . . the mail does not apply to a case of temporary detention caused by the arrest of the carrier . . . for murder." [10] This reasonable interpretation of the mail obstruction statute accords with Congressional intention. The Supreme Court held the statute inapplicable even though the dictionary meaning of "retarding the passage of the mail" arguably covers the case. The Congress did not intend to shield working postmen from warranted arrests for murder. Americans put a high value on rapid delivery of the mail, but are not so passionate about it that our legislators are likely to prefer punctilious mail delivery over prompt detention of postmen indicted for murder. The general presumption is, of course, that lawgivers intend the ordinary meanings of the words they use. Judicial departures from common meanings of statutory words are not and should not be everyday occurrences. Sometimes, however, only by making such a departure can the judges act with fidelity to the lawgivers' intended meaning.

The design of several statutory provisions enacted together sometimes indicates a legislative intention contrary to the literal meaning of a fractional part of the legislation. In Ts'ai Ssu-ching's and Mai Shu-hsin's case [11] the two culprits banded together with others in a planned affray. Each of the two defendants killed one of eleven men slain by their party. While they awaited trial, another two members of their band, each of whom had also killed one of the eleven, died of illness while in jail awaiting trial. A substatute on joint assaults provided that death from illness before trial *either of the original planner* of an assault *or of any confederate who struck a fatal blow* shall entitle surviving killers to punishment reduced from strangulation to exile. Taken alone, these words in this statute seem to call for decreased punishment in this case. Another substatute, however, provided that when the *original planner* dies of illness while in jail awaiting trial, his confederates should not receive commuted punishment if their joint assault took three or more lives. This second substatute, taken literally and in isolation, says nothing about this case—since neither of Ts'ai and Mai's confederates who had died of illness were *original planners*. However, the first substatute equated death by illness of *original planners and fatal-blow-strikers*. The Board of Punishments, seeing no reason for not honoring this equation in their interpretation of the second substatute, said that consistency required them to conclude that the second substatute forbade commutation in such cases as this. The literal wording of neither substatute, taken alone, would justify the Board's holding. Viewed in isolation, the words of the first substatute are literally applicable but not applied, and the words of the second substatute are literally inapplicable but are determinative. When the Board read each statute with the meaning of the other in mind, the Board's ruling comported with the intention of the statutes.

The combination of the meaning of these two substatutes is not an exercise in pure formal reasoning. If a Kentucky legislature should enact a statute granting and limiting clemency for murders committed by feuding mountaineers when their confederates die of illness while in jail awaiting trial, the Kentucky courts would, in all likelihood, find the statute too unreasonable to be constitutional.

The Board of Punishments' willingness to discover the legislative intention in Ts'ai's and Mai's case by honoring the unexpressed implication drawn from both of the two substatutes would be uncongenial to Americans on another ground. We, in the style of Montesquieu, tend to believe that, for the protection of the accused, crimes should be clearly defined and criminal law should be expressly promulgated before the misdeed is committed. The requirement of advance promulgation of criminal statutes for the protection of the accused had no standing in imperial Chinese legal thought. An interesting case illustrates this point. The eminent Ch'ien Lung emperor (1736–1795) was on the throne when the case of Mrs. Ch'en née Chang [12] was decided. When she committed her crime, an article of the code provided that a *married* woman whose adultery shames her father into committing suicide incurs a death sentence to be executed *after the autumn assizes.* At the assizes commutations could be and often were granted.[13] Another statute provided that when a father commits suicide as a result of his *unmarried* daughter's illicit sexual relations, she incurs a death sentence to be executed *immediately*—a sentence not subject, at the assizes, to review with a view toward clemency.[14] The emperor was dissatisfied with the statutory distinction in favor of married daughters. Contrary to custom, he sentenced the culprit to immediate strangulation and ordered the code changed accordingly. Since statutes were imperial edicts, the judicial official had no power to change them; judicial officials were obliged to act in accordance with the statutes in force when a crime was committed, out of respect for the emperor but not, however, out of concern for those accused of crime.

In Mrs. Chiao's case,[15] proof showed that the culprit's daughter-in-law caught her committing adultery; a quarrel ensued and Mrs. Chiao set about beating the girl with a poker. While the girl was trying to grab the sharp-pointed poker to protect herself, she was accidentally stabbed to death. A statute punished by three years' penal servitude a mother-in-law guilty of "unreasonably beating a daughter-in-law and thereby causing her death." Two other inapplicable statutes dealt with mothers-in-law who intentionally slew their daughters-in-law; one of these punished by death a mother-in-law's premeditated killing to seal the mouth of a daughter-in-law who knew of her adultery; the other punished by exile a mother-in-law who with premeditation unjustifiably beat her daughter-in-law to death. Since Mrs. Chiao did not plan to kill her daughter-in-law, neither of these statutes applied. But the problem that remained was whether or not the "unreasonable beating" statute with its punishment of three years of penal servitude was applicable. It was held not directly applicable, and the culprit was given the more drastic punishment of exile.

The relationship between Chinese mothers-in-law and daughters-in-law was often contentious; frictions are generated in this relationship all the world over, but resentment was intensified in imperial China by the iron-handed discipline to which the younger women were subjected. Unmerited nonfatal beatings of daughters-in-law were not uncommon, and they seldom occasioned criminal punishment. Adultery was, however, a gravely reprehensible offense. The statute punishing deaths resulting from "unreasonable beating" was intended to deal with severe abuse of power indulged in by women whose chastity was, almost invariably, not in question. If the Board were to say that Mrs. Chiao's beating was "unreasonable," they would have laughably and shockingly understated the case. This inappositeness of the "unreasonable beating" statute is borne out by the fact that adulterous mothers-in-law who killed their daughters-in-law with premeditation to seal their mouths were punished much more drastically than mothers-in-law who killed their daughters-in-law with premeditation for other unjustifiable reasons. The provincial governor said that, in his view, Mrs. Chiao's adultery made the unreasonable beating statute—with its three-year-servitude penalty—inapplicable, and sentenced her to exile; he also recommended that the money redemption usually accorded to women sentenced to exile be disallowed in this case. The Board's report says, "Since [the governor's recommendations] constitute the heaviest suitable punishment, it would seem that approval may be given." The opinion is tinged with regret that, in the absence of premeditation, a capital penalty would have been out of line with the established system of severities. The governor and the Board did not substitute their predilections for the statutory law on unreasonable beating; they believed, instead, that the unreasonable beating statute was not intended to apply directly to a crime so serious as the one committed.

Mrs. Chiao's case illustrates the point that the importance of suitable punishment affected not only the drafting of statutes, it also affected the interpretation of statutes. When, during a trial, the meaning of words used to describe a crime became doubtful, the size of the penalty might negate or confirm the applicability of the statute. Predicates mean something about subjects; therefore the magnitude of the punishment that a lawgiver assigned to a particular crime tended to establish the gravity of the crime he intended to cover. Single Ch'ing enactments were intended to deal only with one kind of crime; when, therefore, a statute arguably covered two kinds of crimes of unequal gravity, the severity of the single punishment stipulated tended to show which alternative was meant. In the Ch'ing system, then, suitability of punishments affected not only the style of the code, but also the style of its application to particular cases.

A knottier problem is raised by two prosecutions for wielding dangerous weapons. The statutory punishment for a fighter who uses a *weapon* (a sword) is more drastic than that for a fighter who uses a tool (a plow-share)—even though they each inflict identical wounds.

In Liu Tien-cheng's case [16] several men launched an affray. Liu went into combat unarmed. During the melee someone dropped a small war club. Liu picked it up and used it to wound an adversary. The statutory punishment for inflicting a wound with a dangerous *weapon* is military exile. A provincial court, however, held this statute inapplicable to Liu and imposed a less drastic penalty. The Board of Punishments reversed and held that Liu's acts fell within the statute. The Board said, "Inasmuch as the culprit did . . . use a dangerous weapon . . . the mere fact that he picked up the weapon on the spot cannot differentiate him from any other handler of such dangerous weapons."

A year later the Board read the statute differently. In Chang Ssu-wa's case [17] the culprit had, during an affray, wrested a mace from a foe and used it against him. The Board this time ruled that the dangerous weapon statutes were inapplicable. The Board said:

Anyone *possessing* such a dangerous weapon is . . . not a law-abiding citizen, so that even though his use of the weapon . . . may lead to injury no greater than that caused by an ordinary knife . . . his offense . . . is nevertheless more serious . . . Any injury whatever, when caused by the use of a dangerous weapon . . . is to be punished by military exile; even if no injury at all results, the penalty is still to be one hundred blows. . . . When, however, a dangerous weapon is used in an affray by one who does not himself initially possess the weapon but who seizes it during the fray from the hand of his opponent, it is evident that his act should not be punished by 100 blows . . . Nor, if it results in any kind of injury, should it therefore be punished by military exile.

The good sense of the second opinion appeals to Western readers; this occidental praise, however, gives little assurance of the Board's fidelity to the meaning of the oriental statute. The earlier literal interpretation recognizes the unmitigated evil of intended, even though unplanned, use of dangerous weapons. The later nonliteral interpretation does, however, probably better respect the statute's meaning. Usually, in the Manchu Ch'ing dynasty, arms were properly carried only by soldiers. The dangerous weapon statute was a device for fixing the punishment of men who intentionally bore arms; it was not enacted to set the befitting punishment for fighters who by chance became armed in the course of an affray. The Board did, not, however, hold that Chang's use of a dangerous weapon was irrelevant; they gave him a lesser punishment than that called for by the dangerous weapon statute, but a greater punishment than that called for by the statute on wounding with an everyday implement. The extensive authority of imperial judicial officers to punish for an evil deed not covered by the code will be discussed at length later on. At this juncture, however, it is especially appropriate to point out that the judicial franchise to fix apt punishments for misdeeds not dealt with by the code precludes the temptation, which American judges sometimes experience, to stretch the ambit of a statute to deal with an evildoer who would otherwise escape punishment.[18] The Chinese judicial extemporizing, of course, involves other disadvantages.

INSTANCES OF INFIDELITY TO STATUTE

The general impression given to the casual reader by much of the Western writing on traditional Chinese law is that judicial officers did not consider themselves bound by the code, but viewed the code merely as laying down guidelines to be modified whenever circumstances, in their estimation, warranted departure from statutory provisions. I look on this thesis with skepticism. It may stem, in part, both from Western failure to see, because of cultural bias, some fidelities to statute and from misidentification of legitimate uses of analogy. Judicial officers usually stood in awe of the code, and most of the time tried to understand and give effect to the statutes' genuine meanings. From what I know about the histories of statutory interpretation by both the American and the Chinese imperial judicial officers, I find it hard to say at this writing that the Chinese showed less fidelity to legislation than our judges.[19]

Nevertheless, there are Ch'ing cases in which the Board of Punishments did, it seems, substitute its views for the statute's provisions. The most difficult to analyze are borderline cases involving greatly extenuating or seriously aggravating circumstances which the code did not take into account.

An example of extenuating circumstances is Chang Hsiao-hsü's case.[20] The culprit confessed to a homicide committed not by him, but by his brother. The statutory penalty for such perjury was one degree less than the punishment for the crime to which the perjurer had confessed. This culprit's mother had ordered him to confess to committing his brother's crime and he had obeyed her. The Board, impressed by his filial piety, did not follow the statutory formula which would have resulted in exile, but instead sentenced him to three years of penal servitude. The Board said, "He was acting under the pressure of his mother's orders. Hence his deed differs from that of an ordinary man who is bribed to assume another's guilt." The statement implies that befitting punishment for the case before the Board was not considered by the codifiers, and hence there was, in effect, no legislation on the point. Certainly filial piety was greatly valued by Confucian imperial lawgivers. Silence on its force as an extenuating circumstance can be seen as a gap in a code that was, by design, full of gaps which the judiciary were authorized to fill.[21]

Liu Wen-huan's case,[22] involving aggravating circumstances, is harder to square with fidelity to statute. The culprit, while making an official investigation, discovered that a district magistrate had padded his budget. He tried covertly to solicit hush money from the magistrate. The magistrate spurned his proposal. A statute provided two different punishments for attempts at extortion: (1) 100 bamboo blows for an unsuccessful attempt to extort "in which *no precisely stipulated sum of money* is involved"; (2) three years' penal servitude when an attempt "does involve a *precisely stipulated sum of money* and is connected with a proposed evasion of the law." Since the culprit put no price on his perfidy, his wrong was outside of the ambit of the second clause. The wording of the first clause seems to cover all attempts at extortion not covered by the second. Because of their inadequate salaries, many officials in imperial China were slow to perform their official duties until they got a little squeeze. These extortions were not exacted by raising expectations of illegal official action; they were exacted only to overcome an official's inertia and move him to perform an otherwise legal act. The reprehensibility of this culprit's act transcended the gravity of routine squeezes; he proposed, by not reporting a crime which he should have exposed, to compound the magistrate's felony. His proposal, however, *named no price* for his complicity. The Board of Punishment held the 100-blow clause inapplicable and gave him, "by analogy," the very penalty provided in the second clause—i.e., three years of penal servitude. In this case the two statutes seem very carefully to have provided for only two kinds of extortion attempts. The more serious kind involved both a demand of a stipulated sum and a proposal to evade the law. The less serious kind covered all other attempts at extortion. The draftsmanship is poor from the point of view of the value system implemented by the imperial code; draftsmen, we know, usually tried to define crimes so narrowly that all violations of a particular clause would be of equal gravity. The Board, nevertheless, seemed to ignore an applicable statute. In the Board's defense we can say, however, that they did not substitute their personal predilection for the code's provision; instead they adhered to a traditional policy—usually honored by the code—of giving the culprit a punishment befitting his crime.

Infidelity to statute has a different explanation in Mrs. Chang's case.[23] The culprit was prosecuted for forcing women into prostitution. She had once before been prosecuted for a similar offense and was sentenced, in accordance with the code, to life exile. She was allowed, however, to pay a redeeming fine, under a statute giving judicial officers discretion to grant this clemency to women. Thereafter she again forced women into prostitution and this is the offense with which we are now concerned. The statute that was applied to convict her the first time was literally applicable to the proof made in her second prosecution; if the statutory punishment fitted the crime—viewed abstractly—the first time, it fitted it the second time. In her second prosecution the code had authorized alternative sentences: (1) another sentence to exile, coupled with the privilege of avoiding exile by paying a monetary redemption; (2) a sentence to exile with a proviso—like that in the adulterous Mrs. Chiao's case—denying the privilege of monetary redemption. The Board of Punishments rejected both of these statutory alternatives. Mrs. Chang was sentenced to three years' imprisonment. Without breathing a word about their authority to *exile* her by not allowing monetary redemption of the statutory punishment, the Board said, "Such a wicked woman should not, this time, be allowed to redeem her crime and should be made to suffer what she deserves." The sentence, from our point of view, is a defensible one; the penalty is severe. We can say that the statute punishing coerced prostitution did not deal, one way or another, with recidivism, and therefore—in a sense—was inapplicable. But saying that silence on recidivism makes the statute inapplicable proves too much from the point of view of traditional Chinese jurisprudence; it impliedly argues that punishment ought to fit the criminal, when the scheme of traditional Chinese jurisprudence is to impose punishments befitting to the crime.[24] In most cases, statutory punishments calculated by the codifiers to fit crimes do fit the criminal well enough— at least in the opinion of Ch'ing judicial officers—to raise no problems. The law of monetary redemption involved the aged, the young, women, officials, and some others.[25] In a sense, the clemency permissible for these classes of wrongdoers was simply an extension of the notion that status had a bearing on befitting punishments for crimes. Since, however, the clemency was within the discretion of judicial officers, they were, indeed, empowered to fit the punishment to these classes of criminals. This power, however, was a limited authorization to vary statutory penalties; the judicial officers were officially empowered only to reach one of two alternatives, that is, either the statutory penalty in full or complete redemption. Here the board exceeded their powers and, without statutory authority, adopted a third course—reduction of the statutory penalty.

Infidelity to statute is still more flagrant in some wife-selling cases. In Wang Pao's case [26] a husband "because of poverty" prevailed upon his father-in-law to report his death and sell his wife. The husband, wife, and buyer were each sentenced to a hundred blows in conformity to a section of the code. Four years later, in Wang Hei-Kou's case [27] another husband sold his wife. The sale, said the Board, "was prompted by poverty and illness which gave him no other alternative." The Board displayed a warmheartedness which it had not evidenced four years earlier, by categorizing this husband's transaction as "differ[ing] from the selling of a wife done without due cause." This compassion seems to come from a judicial, not a legislative source; it flows from the predilections of the Board and not from the intention of the statute. This lapse from fidelity to statute must have been prompted by a feeling that to inflict punishment for wife-selling in desperation was intolerable. Perhaps the code's unrealistic inflexibilty on this topic grew out of an unwillingness to recognize the power of famine to destroy the bonds of peasant families. The Board's infidelity to this statute is at least as understandable as the American judicial accommodation to unrealistic divorce laws.

The bulk of the Board of Punishments infidelities to the Ch'ing Code is not large and such infidelities as there are can seldom be classified as self-willed disrespect for the system. When Staunton translated the statutes of the code in 1810, the following was included:

Section 415. In all tribunals of justice, sentence should be pronounced against offenders according to all the existing laws, statutes, and precedents applicable to the case, considered together, the omission of which in any respect shall be punished at least with 30 blows; when, however, any article of law is found to comprise and relate to other circumstances besides those that have occurred in the case under consideration, so much of the law shall be acted upon as is really applicable.[28]

This statute is calculated to call for liberal interpretation but, nevertheless, respectful fidelity to the intention of the code. The Board of Punishments, writing in 1870,[29] said, "It is essential to examine the exact facts . . . , as well as to impose sentence in strict accord with the relevant statutes or sub-statutes." The prosecuting witness whose complaint had resulted in the trial under the Board's review had been sentenced by a provincial governor to 100 blows for making an accusation that turned out to be unfounded. The Board continued:

The statute cited above, under which the presenting of an accusation which proves to be false, is punishable by 100 blows of the heavy bamboo, has reference to such an act *only* when effected by stopping the imperial chariot or beating the complaint drum. . . . It commonly happens that cases which a judge deems to be baseless are conveniently settled by him through sentencing the [accuser] to a maximum bambooing under the statute on accusations which prove to be false. In so doing, no mention is made of that part of the statute limiting such incorrect accusations to those presented by persons who stop the imperial chariot or beat the complaint drum. . . . Not only is this detrimental to law in general, but more particularly it makes empty words out of the statute[s] . . . When . . . citation is made of the statute . . . the habitual omission . . . cannot possibly be permitted.

The emperor responded, "Let it be as has been deliberated."

THE ROLE OF ANALOGY

In the United States, conviction for committing a felony is usually predicated on conduct done in violation of a statute. Only after a breach of a promulgated statute that has both defined the ambit of the crime committed and provided a penalty for breach are our courts likely to entertain a prosecution for a serious crime. The jurisdiction of the federal courts does not, under the United States Constitution, extend to prosecutions of "common law crimes." In some of the states, common law crimes have been abolished.

In the other states the courts are still authorized, in theory, to declare conduct criminal even though it violates no statute, but judges are reluctant, in fact, either to invent new crimes or to recognize ancient ones not covered by their state's statutory penal code. In these states the courts occasionally convict some petty offender of a common law crime and his resulting punishment is generally a small fine.[30] An extreme example of the American aversion to criminal punishment not clearly authorized by statute is found in United States v. Evans.[31] A federal statute forbade either landing *or* harboring an immigrant who unlawfully entered the United States. The statute's penalty clause, however, defectively provided that those convicted "shall be punished by a fine not exceeding $2000 and be imprisoned for a term not exceeding five years for each and every alien *so landed*." No express penalty for *harboring* was set forth. The United States Supreme Court reversed a conviction of a harborer on the ground that, even though the Congress clearly intended to make his conduct criminal, the Congress had not expressly addressed itself to the penalty incurred. Even though American statutes, including this one, often allow judges some latitude in sentencing the guilty, we treasure the idea that legislative determination of maximum punishments protects personal liberty against bias that might actuate some judges to give outrageous sentences some of the time.

No desire to protect personal liberty is evident in imperial Chinese law. There were, nevertheless, some prosecutions which, for other reasons, failed when punishment was not authorized by the code. In Wang Tuan-ch'ing's case [32] the governor reported that the culprit was a convict entitled to pardon for his original crime because the emperor had proclaimed an imperial amnesty which covered that crime. The culprit had escaped from jail, however, before the amnesty took effect. The amnesty did not cover jailbreaks, which were, according to statute, to be penalized by increasing by two degrees the punishment incurred for the original crime. The Board of Punishments held that since the amnesty nullified Wang's original crime he incurred no punishment for the jailbreak, on the theory that "there is no article in the code punishing a guiltless prisoner who escapes." The Board did not mean, of course, that they pun-

ished only crimes expressly covered by the code; *if* they had
thought that punishment for this jailbreak was suitable and fitting,
they would, no doubt, have levied it, even though no statute expressly required it. Wan T'ing-hsuan's case,[33] decided three years
later, illustrates the reverse side of the coin. Wan refined a small
quantity of salt for his own consumption. The code did not forbid
this conduct, and it was apparently legal. A salt examiner, nevertheless, improperly tried to arrest Wang for what he mistakenly
supposed was a violation of the salt laws; Wang resisted and
injured the official. Resisting arrest was a statutory crime and was,
like jailbreak, to be penalized by increasing by two degrees the
punishment of the original crime. The Board, however, did not
rely, as they did in the jailbreak case, on the absence in the code
of an article punishing a guiltless person who resists arrest. Instead
Wang was sentenced to penal servitude for a year and a half.
No doubt the Board was unwilling to overlook the wrong of an
ordinary man who inflicted an injury on an official—gross impropriety in their eyes as compared to the impersonal wrong of a
jailbreak.

Some statutory definitions of crime have, in context, an unstated
negative meaning as well as an expressed affirmative intention.
The case of Mrs. Cheng [34] involved the extent to which the innocent
relatives of a convicted traitor incurred criminal punishment. An
article of the code set out a schedule of punishment for a sizable
list of relatives of traitors, including spouses, children, and siblings.
Mrs. Cheng was the traitor's brother's wife. The Board's opinion
said, "The statute says nothing about implicating the sister-in-law of
a principal offender, and it is presumably for this reason that the
governor . . . has not taken her into account in his deliberations."
The governor's holding was affirmed. A statute listing those blame-
less relatives of a traitor who are implicated in his crime is not
likely to be incomplete; it, therefore, tells who does not incur this
awful liability as well as who does.

These instances of acquittal of accused persons who contravened
no section of the code exemplify practices of very limited scope.

Although the Ch'ing code dealt expressly with thousands of
crimes, the circumscribed coverage of each article of the code

resulted in the total omission of punishments for many serious misdeeds. The codifiers suspected they had left many gaps in the code. One way in which they tried to plug these gaps was to authorize and require punishment of misdeeds analogous to those penalized by the code.

The statutory basis for analogy is translated by Staunton this way:

Section 44. *Determination of Cases Not Provided for by Any Existing Law.* From the impracticality of providing for every possible contingency, there may be cases to which no laws or statutes are precisely applicable; such cases may be determined by an accurate comparison with others which are already provided for, and which approach most nearly to those under investigation, in order to ascertain afterwards to what extent an aggravation or mitigation of punishment would be equitable.[35]

The statute provided for review of such punishments by "the superior magistrates" *and by the emperor.* The statute also imposed punishment on judicial officers who did not search the code for analogies throwing light on the proper punishments for cases not covered directly.

Sometimes the Board of Punishments made an analogical use of a statute that appears to Western lawyers to apply directly to the facts before the Board. In Wu Pao-wa's case [36] the culprit was advancing along a narrow path, urging on a laden mule in front of him. He met head-on traffic and was summarily ordered to give way, but churlishly whipped up his pack mule. The mule kicked and killed a member of the oncoming party. A statute punished by life exile the owner of a domestic animal who deliberately releases the beast and thereby causes a human's death. The Board sentenced the defendant to life exile "by analogy to this statute." [37]

Compare the mule case with the 1961 case of State v. Provenzano.[38] The State of New Jersey indicted the defendant for breach of a criminal statute that imposed punishment on "any duly *appointed* representative" of a labor union who accepts a bribe. The bribe-taker contended in vain that the statute did not apply to him because he was not "appointed" but "elected." The court said:

[T]o accept the defendant's argument would be to find that the Legislature intended the application of the statute to depend upon the mode of selection which each union may choose to adopt. . . . So to hold would be to attribute sheer inanity to the Legislature. . . . In providing that the representative be "duly appointed" the Legislature meant only that the representative be in fact designated as such by the labor organization.

If the New Jersey practice permitted its courts to hold that a criminal statute not quite applicable to a misdeed could, nevertheless, be used by analogy, the judges probably would not have held that the elected official was an appointed one. Even though elected and appointed union officials who accept bribes are equally guilty of wrongdoing, judges allowed to punish miscreants whose misdeeds are analogous to statutory crimes could, nevertheless, placidly accede to the narrow literalism of holding that the New Jersey statute was not precisely applicable to this bribe-taker, since they could still hold that he had committed an analogous and functionally indistinguishable wrong and, therefore, should suffer the statutory punishment. Accordingly, the imperial Chinese analogy system provided for a style of decision that could pay respect to both the words used in the code and the principles behind those words.

The meaning of any command—including directions to a judge by the provisions of a statute—often so unmistakably includes the intention of the commander that purblind literalism never occurs to a faithful servant while he is executing that command. Sometimes the Board of Punishments did not advert to the possibility of applying a statute by analogy, but applied it directly, even though it was not formulated so as to be literally applicable to the case at hand. For example, in Mrs. Lo née P'eng's case,[39] Mrs. Lo's son abused her. The head of the Lo clan beat the son for mistreating his mother; he used such excessive force that he killed the boy. The clan head faced punishment for this homicide. Had Mrs. Lo killed the boy, her punishment would have been much milder than the clan head's. He bribed Mrs. Lo to go to the authorities and falsely confess that she had killed her son. All of these facts were established in her prosecution for violating the statute imposing punishment on a parent who "hushes up" the killing of his or her son. She was found guilty of violating that statute; the confession in which she *spoke out* was held to be a *hushing up*—as sensible as, and probably even less forced than, the New Jersey court's holding that an "elected" official is an "appointed" one.

Use of analogy is not always appropriate for reaching results that judicial officers want to reach. In Chang Ch'ing's case [40] the culprit killed two men who were "fourth-degree" cousins—first cousins once removed. The victims were taking a business trip together. The culprit was their porter. The victims' baggage and funds were, for the time being, intermingled. The code provides that a murderer of two members of the same family shall be decapitated, after which his head shall be displayed. The statute defines a single family as "those who live together [and] share their resources." A less grisly punishment is imposed by a second statute on murderers of two people not members of the same family. The Board did not have the alternative of using the single family statute by analogy; if the case were only analogous to, rather than covered by, the single family statute, the second statute applied. The Board's categorization of these traveling cousins as members of a single family is forced. They said:

Wu Teng-chü arranged with his fourth degree younger cousin . . . to go on a business trip together, during which time they traveled together and stayed overnight together. Between this and living together there is no essential difference.[!] The load carried [by the culprit] . . . was baggage belonging to both of them, and what he stole from them was likewise money belonging to both of them. They may thus be regarded as men who jointly shared their resources.

The impermanence of these travelers' consociation is suppressed in this analysis. Extraordinary punishment, no doubt, was suitable in the eyes of the Board and actuated their use of the term "single family." [41]

There are, of course, many straightforward analogies used in cases of misconduct clearly not covered by the code, but which closely resemble statutory crimes. Wen-yüan's case [42] is a simple example in which the Board of Punishments treated theft from a Buddhist monk by his disciple as analogous to theft committed by a junior member of a family who steals from a senior member of that same family. In Chang K'ai-p'eng's case [43] the homicide committed by a man who starved his concubine to death was held to be analogous to a homicide effected with force. The sentences in both of these analogy cases were the same as the punishments imposed by the code on those who commit analogous statutory crimes. The thieving disciple's misconduct was held to be no more serious than that of a son who steals from his father. Killing by starvation was held to be as reprehensible as killing by force. Sometimes, however, an analogous wrong is more or less wicked than a similar statutory crime. In Ch'ien Yün's case [44] a petty military officer was the culprit. He had, with an eye to advancement, arrogated to himself the construction of a lotus pond. The empounding dike collapsed and rushing floodwaters inundated government warehouses and private property. In the Board's opinion, Ch'ien's crime resembled the crime of those officials who, while executing public works put under their supervision, deviate from the governmentally approved plans. Ch'ien, however, had no authority to build the lotus pond; since he officiously undertook the project of his own accord, his botchery was graver than the statutory crimes committed while executing an authorized project. The punishment set for the statutory crime was penal servitude for three years, but Ch'ien was sentenced to military exile.

The crime not covered by the code in Chang Fu-lu's case [45] was less grave than its statutory analogy. The culprit, a jailor, guarded a petty offender in his custody as though he were charged with a dire offense, to the point of keeping him in shackles. Even after the jailor received notice that his prisoner would be released on bail the following morning, he handcuffed and chained the prisoner for the night. This rigorous restraint induced the prisoner to believe that he was held on very grave charges, with the result that the prisoner committed suicide during the night, hanging himself with his chain. A statute provided that a jailor whose unreasonable beating inflicted fatal injuries on his prisoner incurred a death sentence. The Board held that the culprit's crime was not so flagrant as the analogous statutory crime and reduced Chang's sentence to exile.

One preconception tended to constrict judicial discretion in the sentencing of convicts befittingly in analogy cases. When articles of the code imposing death penalties or exile were used by analogy, and when the culprit's offense was less grave than the analogous statutory offense, the Board proceeded to reduce the statutory penalty by "one degree." When the statutory penalty was softened, it was reduced to the next lower punishment of the five major kinds; that is, a capital sentence—whether decapitation or strangulation—was reduced to exile at a distance of 3000 li, and exile—whether at a distance of 3000, 2000, or 1000 li—was reduced to penal servitude for three years. These reductions were, of course, considerable; as a result, when a little leniency was appropriate, the Board, nevertheless, imposed the statutory penalty in order to avoid an unbefittingly overgenerous reduction. In T'eng Ch'üan-ching's case,[46] for example, the father standing trial was prosecuted for having made "wild accusations" to save his son from conviction on a murder charge. The father's accusations had to be looked into, the coroner thought, by exhuming and steaming a corpse. The ensuing post mortem "disproved" the defendant's wild accusations. A statute imposed life exile at a distance of 3000 li on those who *destroyed* the corpse of a person outside of the destroyer's family by burning it or throwing it in water. This culprit was not guilty of violating that statute; the Board, however, held that his misconduct was an analogous crime and approved a sentence of a 3000 li life exile. If the Board had reduced the punishment "by one degree," the defendant would have been sentenced to only three years of penal servitude. Perhaps the Board thought both that this father's parental motive was not an extenuating circumstance and that steaming a corpse was tantamount to destruction by burning or liquefaction. In fact, the Board said approvingly, "The Provincial Court of Shantung has taken the viewpoint that to cause a corpse to be needlessly steamed is as grievous an act as to mutilate or destroy it." Even so, an effort to shield a son is an act of Confucian virtue. The Board may have abstained from reducing the father's punishment because the usual one-degree commutation would have resulted, in their view, in inadequate punishment.

The Board sometimes also mechanically gave a large reduction of penalty on the basis of some slight mitigating circumstance. In, for example, Ni Tao-yüan's case [47] the culprit *copied* and propagated noncanonical magical writings. "Fabricating" magical writings and spells was a statutory crime punishable by life exile. Since the words were not composed by the culprit in the first place, his punishment was reduced to three years of penal servitude, even though he surely knew he was copying and disseminating intellectual contraband.[48]

Some analogies used may look farfetched to Westerners and yet be apposite. Five people in Hsü Hsüeh-ch'uan's case [49] made use of legal documents drafted for them by Hsü. The statute against practicing law provided military exile for "habitual litigation tricksters who conspire with government clerks, trick ignorant country folk, or practice intimidation or fraud." This statute did not address itself specifically to condemning the practice of law; it seems to impose punishment only on cases of flagrant pettifogging. Since Hsü had not committed any of the three kinds of malpractices covered by the statute, he could not, of course, be convicted of violating it. The statute, moreover, does not appear to us to implement any principle violated by Hsü. Private intermeddling in legal affairs, however, had been reprobated in China since early Ming times. The statute provided punishment for extremely evil forms of practicing law; any private practice of law, however, was a kind of conduct not tolerated by the Ming and Ch'ing Chinese governments. The statute, then, was in fact an exemplification of a principle disapproving of the practice of law. Hsü's misdeed was not so evil as the crime covered by the statute; his misdeed was, however, in its cultural context, an analogous wrong. The Board so held and reduced the statutory punishment by one degree to three years of penal servitude.

All of the analogy cases discussed up to this point are instances of genuine analogical reasoning; the judicial officers in these cases showed respect for principles that in fact underlay articles of the code and extrapolated from a statute in accordance with an underlying principle to decide a case not covered by the article of the code. Sometimes, however, the Board of Punishments' citation of a statute as analogous to the problem before them was a display of good form rather than a reliance in fact on a principle underlying the statute cited. I do not mean that none of these strained analogies should have been drawn; after all, an article of the code required that gaps be filled by using the closest analogy that the code afforded. When the closest analogy was a long way off, analogical reasoning was bound to be far fetched.[50]

Consider P'eng Lo-wan's case [51] in which P'eng, a gambler, dunned a loser so tenaciously that the latter undressed and gave P'eng his clothes as collateral security for payment of his gambling debt. Cold drove the naked man to suicide. The statutory crime of causing death by depriving a person of his clothes called for the strangulation of violators. This prohibition appears in the same article of the code as that punishing those who force foreign objects into a victim's eyes, nose, and so forth. The article is directed at violence, and its underlying principles seem to have little bearing on high-pressure debt-collection tactics; the gambler's misdeed is not much like the crime of a robbing ruffian who disrobes a victim and steals his clothes. The strained analogy, however, may have been better than none at all; a drop of wisdom may have trickled from the statute and stained P'eng's conduct so that its criminality stood out more clearly. The statutory punishment, strangulation, seemed to the Board to be too severe, and they sentenced P'eng to life exile. If the Board had drawn no analogy at all they might have been able to do as well in placing P'eng's wrongdoing on the scale of the five punishments; if, however, the Board took a statutory crime as a point of departure, even though that crime resembled the wrong before them only superficially, the court endowed with palpability the problem of equal, or greater, or lesser evil. Analogies, even when farfetched, often did sharpen the focus of Chinese judicial officers on their most important problem—the fixing of a befitting punishment.

When the facts of a case resembled a statutory crime carrying a penalty extremely unsuitable for that case—by being either much too lenient or much too severe—the superficiality of the resemblance was usually obvious and an analogy was not drawn. The game of analogies, however, could be played so that descriptive configuration overpowered judicial sensitivity. When this happened, use of an overly technical analogy could produce baneful decisions. In Wei Yü-chen's case [52] the defendant, a shallow scholar, wrote a boastful biography about his dead father, referring to him in terms used properly only in connection with members of the imperial family. He should have known better. The governor of his province recommended that he be stripped of his rank and—absent any statute directly applicable—be given a hundred blows under a catch-all statute. The Board, however, analogized the crime to "contumacious use of the dragon or the phoenix." Use of silk raiments bearing the figure of the dragon was proper for only the emperor; those bearing the figure of the phoenix for only the empress. The statutory crime does superficially resemble Wei's impropriety. The case arose during the Ch'ien-lung emperor's reign and at the height of an imperial drive against seditious writing. If the Board was trying to please the strong-minded emperor by borrowing and imposing on Wei the statutory punishment of penal servitude for three years, they probably succeeded. Even though Wei's vain or foolish use of phraseology that abstractly and by innuendo tinged his ancestor with a little royal color is somewhat like intentionally sporting regal raiment, it seems less public and less presumptuous. If the Board thought their analogy pointed the way to a suitable penalty, they may have been in error.

There are some opinions in which the Board draws an analogy merely to discharge their statutory duty of citing the closest statute. The culprit in Te-t'ai's case [53] had a job in the imperial park. He negligently allowed a caged tiger to escape, "causing loss of life." An arguably analogous statute punished by strangulation the crime of faulty tethering of animals who escaped and caused death; this seemingly drastic statute, however, contained a proviso allowing those convicted under it a moderate monetary redemption of the punishment of strangulation. The lower tribunal said, "It would be overly lenient were the offender to be punished merely under [that] statute which, just as for accidental homicide permits monetary redemption . . ." This implies a sound theory of interpretation of the improper hitching statute; that statute was intended to apply to the unsure tethering of domestic animals and not to the graver negligence of improperly caging a ferocious beast. The statutory crime was, of course, closely analogous to Te-t'ai's wrong, but if the Board recognized this analogy and then raised the inadequate punishment, the smallest increase available was denial of the right to make monetary redemption. Such an increase, in effect, would jump the punishment from a trivial fine to a death sentence—an unpalatably severe punishment. Another statute was forced into the mold of an analogy; that statute imposed punishment on any custodian of government animals who allowed them to perish, and set out a scale of punishments that varied with the number of animals lost up to a maximum of penal servitude for three years. The Board did not think this maximum was severe enough and raised the defendant's punishment to life exile. Their reasoning by analogy was only a formal exercise; it played no genuine part either in establishing the defendant's criminality or in quantifying his punishment.

The statute that required judicial officers to use analogical reasoning for cases not covered by the code also provided that all punishments based on analogies must be submitted to the emperor for review. In analogy cases the Board itself does a job of judicial lawmaking and hence cannot urge the emperor to honor the codified statutory definitions of crime which the emperor himself has promulgated.[54] It is not surprising, then, that the emperor felt especially free to reduce or increase punishments assessed by the Board in analogy cases. As a matter of fact, the emperor reduced the Board's punishment of Te-t'ai in the tiger case.[55]

CATCH-ALL STATUTES

Criminal statutes in the United States usually authorize judges who hear criminal cases to exercise a large measure of discretion in sentencing convicted defendants. The statutory punishment for, say, illegal sale of firearms could be a fine of not less than $50 nor more than $5000, or imprisonment for not less than thirty days nor more than two years, or both. Since statutory penalties for American crimes vary within such wide limits, the crimes punished by a single statute can cover a gamut of offenses much broader than the grasp of a Ch'ing criminal statute carrying a single penalty. As a result the relatively short penal codes of American states usually are more comprehensive than the detailed and longer codes of imperial China.

The American penal codes, therefore, stand less in need of catch-all statutes than did the Chinese imperial codes.

Even so, nearly all American states do have on their books what amount to catch-all criminal statutes. The special broadness of these statutes is effected by defining a crime so vaguely that enforcement officers and petty magistrates can selectively jail or fine seedy individuals on small pretext. The vagrancy statutes come to mind. In Virginia, for example, vagrancy is defined, in part, like this: "[A]ll persons who have no visible income lawfully acquired and who consort with [either] idlers and gamblers . . . or persons engaged in illegal enterprise of any kind" are deemed vagrants and their vagrancy may be punished as a misdemeanor. The constitutionality of statutes of this type was seldom, until recently, challenged. The Virginia statute quoted above passed muster in the Virginia court of last resort in 1937.[56] Some recent decisions, however, seem prophetic of the unconstitutionality of all of the vagrancy statutes.[57] State statutes imposing drastic penalties for vaguely defined crimes have already been held unconstitutional in the Supreme Court of the United States.[58]

The Ch'ing Board of Punishments would not have agreed with United States Supreme Court Justice Butler when, in commenting on a vague statute, he said, "All are entitled to be informed as to what the state commands or forbids." The Board reviewed a conviction in Ch'i Ch'eng-ê's case.[59] He was a grateful scholar who contemplated suicide to join his dear, dead, revered teacher. He notified the authorities of his intentions to save them the bother of investigating his death. Thereafter he changed his mind, and incurred prosecution for so stupidly wasting the time of officialdom. The Board of Punishments held he had violated the article of the code that forbids anyone "to do what ought not to be done." This article is one of the few that provides for judicial choice of punishments, that is, forty blows for lesser violations and eighty blows for greater ones. The culprit got the heavier penalty, but since he had passed examinations which gave him the status of an official, he escaped corporal punishment by making a monetary redemption.

Other catch-all statutes carry more drastic punishment. The army officer who pledged his certificate of commission as security for repayment of a loan was, in Wang Hsün's case,[60] dismissed from office. This dismissal made corporal punishment possible. He was sentenced to one hundred blows—the statutory punishment for violating imperial decrees. This article of the code was held applicable not only to acts contravening some imperial promulgation, but also to acts that the emperor would have interdicted had they attracted his attention.

Military exile was the statutory punishment for being a "vicious scoundrel who repeatedly creates disturbances and molests decent people." In Li Wei-t'ang's case [61] the culprit was sentenced under this article for a series of misdeeds including a seduction, using the seduced woman as a prostitute, and several extortions.

The Board of Punishments also used the catch-all statutes analogically in order to mete out punishment more drastic or more lenient than that imposed by the catch-all statute cited.[62] In this way the Board often fleshed out the omissions of the code when no analogies seemed apt and developed flexibility to make their discretionary punishments fit the crimes punished.

CLEMENCY

Procedures for considering clemency were built into most convictions for *capital crimes* by sentencing the culprit to strangulation or decapitation "after the assizes." Many of these sentences were reduced to exile when they were further reviewed at the autumn assizes in the highly structured administrative proceedings described in Chapter IV of Bodde and Morris, *Law in Imperial China.* Clemency was, however, also granted, on occasion, during the judicial process and played a part in some of the cases.

In Lu Ch'üan-hai's case [63] the defendant's father was slain in a battle between two families; the prosecuted son, who was also participating in the fight, immediately thereafter killed two foes who were brothers. The statutory punishment for slaying two members of the same family in an affray is "immediate" strangulation. Sentences calling for immediate capital punishment were reviewed, but could not be considered at the autumn assizes. Both the provincial court and the Board of Punishments thought an avenger of his father's death deserved clemency. They did not, however, think themselves authorized to grant this clemency for so unquestionable a violation of the two-family-member statute. The provincial court and the Board, therefore, both recommended to the emperor that he reduce punishment. The emperor commuted the punishment so that the sentence could be reviewed by the assizes.[64]

Contrast Sun Shou-chih's case,[65] in which the emperor proposed to disregard the statutory increase of punishment for batteries committed by junior relatives on senior relatives. The victim, a distant senior relative of Sun, had stolen a trifle from Sun and had thus provoked Sun's attack on him. The emperor opined that this theft was an extenuating circumstance justifying clemency. The Board disagreed; they pointed out to the emperor that the statutory penalty for theft from a relative is less than the statutory penalty for theft from a stranger, and therefore that in this case the victim's theft was not, in the eyes of the law, much of a provocation. On the other hand, the Board continued, directing an attack against a senior relative, in the eyes of the law, is a seriously aggravating circumstance not to be minimized. The emperor was convinced and came round; Confucian family theory won out; an article of the code prevailed over the emperor's impulse to extend clemency.

When, however, an offender commits a crime affecting the emperor's personal interests, his impulsive desire to extend grace to the culprit is less likely to be questioned. In the case in which the death-dealing tiger escaped in the imperial park because of the offender's negligence, the emperor "as an act of imperial grace" rescinded an exile order without explaining his leniency. This commutation went unchallenged.[66] The emperor, of course, did not always extend his grace to those who criminally invaded his interests. In Chi Erh's case,[67] for example, the emperor extended no grace to a thief who stole yellow satins from an imperial temple and, as a result, was sentenced to immediate decapitation.

Statutes authorized judicial clemency for children, old people, and women; they could be allowed to redeem corporal punishments by making money payments. This clemency lay within the discretion of the judicial officers. The Board of Punishments often refused to soften corporal punishment in cases in which they thought full severity of corporal punishment was a befitting penalty for the crime of a youth, an oldster, or a woman.[68]

When, however, the code provided for clemency because of mitigating circumstances—rather than because of status—clemency was due to the defendant as a matter of right. In Wu Ch'i-li's case [69] Wu's fireworks accidentally set a grass fire which engulfed and killed four people. The statutory punishment for accidentally causing death was, nominally, strangulation—probably out of respect for the life requital principle. The statute, however, also provided for monetary redemption in the form of payment to the family of the deceased of 12.42 ounces of silver for funeral expenses. Both the governor and the Board of Punishments ruled that Wu's punishment was redeemable. When the planner of an affray dies of illness while awaiting trial, his co-defendant who struck a mortal blow is entitled, according to the terms of an article of the code, to a one-degree reduction in penalty. Wang Ssu's case [70] was such a one; the governor held Wang was entitled to the one-degree reduction and the Board affirmed without question. Another article of the code entitles certain homicides to a one-degree reduction of punishment if the death did not occur within the ten days following the time that injury was inflicted. Fang Hsiao-liu's case [71] fell under this statute; accordingly the governor reduced his punishment by one degree and the Board affirmed. In none of these cases in which mitigating circumstances were recognized by the code as grounds for reduction of punishment did either the governor or the Board ask for leave to grant clemency.

Sometimes a case appears to be an instance of judicial clemency when in fact it did not involve the reduction of a statutory penalty but was, instead, a tacit holding that the code did not cover the crime. In these cases a statute was used only by analogy; the offense committed was somewhat like the statutory offense, but was less reprehensible; the statutory penalty, therefore, was both inapplicable and unduly harsh. Ho-chi'-erh-pu-ni's case [72] is a good example. Ho was a forest warder, who captured a man caught cutting and stealing wood. To keep the prisoner from escaping, he bound the prisoner and staked the prisoner's robe to the ground. The prisoner wriggled out of his robe and escaped. Lacking his robe, he died of exposure. The Board of Punishments said that the warder should be sentenced "under the statute" punishing those who cause death by disrobing; his punishment, however, was put at exile, rather than the statutory punishment of strangulation. The Board did not think that he committed the statutory crime; they said that the prisoner's exposure "was of his own choosing." Obviously they used the statute analogically, and their failure to say so was at most a slip of the brush. This pattern was repeated so often that one is led to suspect that the analogical use of the code was clearly understood by all concerned, and the lack of express statement that a statute was used by analogy was of no real consequence.[73]

The Board of Punishments did, however, occasionally take the position that statutory punishments should be softened judicially whenever mitigating circumstances of some real weight were established. In one general circular, for example, the Board said:

We beg Your Majesty to issue an order to . . . governors . . . instructing them that hereafter whenever a case initially submitted to Peking is then transmitted to them for trial, they are to handle it with justice. If its charges are found accurate, the grievances must be redressed. . . . *Should there be extenuating circumstances, no obstacle should be placed upon possible mitigation of punishment.*[74]

The imperial rescript was, "Let it be as has been deliberated." This circular, then, argued for varying the punishments fixed by the code and encouraged judicial officers to depart, in cases of extenuating circumstances, from applicable statutory law. The circular approved of judges designing punishments to fit those crimes that came before them, even though different punishments had been promulgated in legislation. This 1870 circular was issued late in the period covered by the Conspectus of Penal Cases (1738–1883); it came too late to influence any case discussed in this chapter. (In fact, it came too late to have any considerable influence on the law of imperial China, since the last dynasty fell in 1911.) On the other hand, we must recognize that a program suggested by the Board of Punishments for imperial proclamation was not likely to be newly hatched, undried, and untried theory. The climate of legal thought that made the 1870 circular possible must have existed for some time before the circular was published. Nevertheless, very few cases are, it seems to me, instances in which a culprit whose crime was covered by a statute was sentenced to some punishment other than that specified by the statute. I found, however, three decisions, next to be discussed, that tend to bear out the theory of the general circular.

Tsou San's case [75] (1825) involved a boat tracker for the lighters of the grain transport administration who incited his associates to press for higher pay. They voiced their demands to the representative of the grain transport administration in charge of their work. A lieutenant ordered them to stop their clamor. The defendant, nevertheless, started a fracas, struck the lieutenant, and tore his clothes. The code provided, "If rowdies among grain boat trackers form a group to press for money, and this group attacks someone, . . . their ringleader will be sent into military exile at a nearby frontier." The Board set about describing the facts of Tsou's case so that he was put in a favorable light: "Finding that food prices were rising to a point where his wages no longer met the cost of living, Tsou San got the idea of assembling a group of fellow trackers . . ." The Board then pointed out that the tumult broke out after the lighters had reached their terminus and that the trackers' clamor, therefore, did not slow down grain shipments. Since Tsou's misconduct was not, says the Board, "in the nature of an obstructionist act done in order to extort money . . . he is . . . deserving of leniency." The Board was not using the article of the code merely by analogy. They sentenced Tsou "under the sub-statute," but, nevertheless, reduced his punishment from life exile to penal servitude for three years—a clear case of judicial recasting of an applicable statutory punishment because of circumstances that are only slightly—if at all—extenuating.

In Chan Chin's case [76] (1819) the culprit's clan was at odds with the Yeh clan. A Yeh woman was passing through Chan's village. He ordered that she be forced into his house. This was done. Thereafter Chan raped her. The code provided capital punishment for "abducting and having sexual relations with a woman." At the time when Chan ordered the woman seized he had no thought of raping her; this idea occurred to him a little later. The Board looked on this sequence of his animosities as an extenuating circumstance and said, "Chan Chin is to be sentenced *under* [emphasis added] the statute . . . with, however, the penalty therein stipulated reduced by one degree to maximum exile." The statute is silent on whether or not an intention to rape before the abduction is an element of the crime. Once the problem is raised, the answer cannot be taken out of the meaning of the words promulgated. To my contemporary Western mind the problem is almost senseless; the reprehensibility of the kind of act condemned by the statute and that of the kind of act Chan committed seem to be a close match; the circumstances seem to have no mitigating force; the argument for inapplicability of the statute seems inane. This case, too, seems to be a judicial reworking of an applicable statutory penalty.

In Chou Heng-yü's case [77] (1823) the defendants dredged goods and wares out of the hold of a sunken ship that went down in a storm. The owner discovered the salvage activities and protested the expropriation of his property but the defendants calmly proceeded to help themselves to the cargo. Because this depredation, said the Board,

was done only after the vessel had already sunk, it does not, strictly speaking, constitute plundering which is carried out at the moment of, and takes advantage of a crisis. . . . [Their exploit, however, gives] their acts the characteristic of plundering. . . . Therefore, Chou Heng-yü and his associates in accordance with the sub-statute on taking advantage of a crisis to plunder property, . . . are all sentenced to maximum penal servitude, a punishment one degree less than that prescribed by the substatute.

Why should the Board have punished this reprehensible looting any less severely than an equally reprehensible expropriation done earlier in the disaster? This sentence, too, appears to be a judicial refitting of a statutory punishment.

Technical defenses for these last two cases might be built on verbalistic manipulations of the abduction-rape and the crisis-plundering statutes. Once, however, the statutes are made verbally inapplicable, the statutory crimes remain so closely analogous to the cases that the statutes would have to be applied—in the absence of some other applicable statute—by analogy. And once they are applied by analogy, since the misconduct of the defendants is as reprehensible as that condemned by the statutes, the Board has no basis for reducing the statutory penalty other than by arrogating to itself the function of remaking statutory punishments. There is an interesting inconsistency of theory in these two doctorings of statutory punishments: The abductor's hotheadedness after the abduction is looked on as an extenuating circumstance; the looters' cold-bloodedness after the ship had bottomed is looked on as an extenuating circumstance.[78]

The few decisions that seem to be instances of judicial infidelity to the code are not surprising. In nearly any legal system some judges some of the time prize their own judgment more highly than the established rules of law. Chinese judicial officers were expected to decide their cases in accordance with the code's genuine—which was not always its literal—meaning. They were expected to fill the many gaps in the code by drawing analogies between the crimes dealt with by statute and misconduct for which no specific provision had been made. In a system demanding a good deal of judicial creativity, occasionally judicial officers exceeded the system's demand and substituted their own judgment for a clearly applicable statutory provision. When they did so it seemed rarely done on personal caprice; in most instances they appear to have been trying to sentence a culprit to a punishment that fits his crime better than the codified punishment.

The invention of the law of imperial China was originally a constituent part of a powerful central government's creation of a unified Chinese empire. Pre-Ch'in China was feudal in the sense that nobles had autonomy in the local governance of the people. The first unifiers broke away from centuries of tradition when they imposed centralized Ch'in rule on the Chinese people. Their new, harsh government was powerful enough to control and direct the people's conduct for a time, but its militaristic, hard-driving regimentation was inspired by the writings of a handful of Legalist theorists; it did not grow out of the mores of the people and did not inspire popular loyalty. Terrifying punishments of Ch'in law were typical of the kinds of governmental measures used in furthering all of the dynasty's projects—measures that were to lead to the mass disaffection which doomed the short-lived dynasty.

The Han dynasty which followed lasted for four hundred years— with one close call after the first two hundred. Its durability may not attest to an increase of popular loyalty, but is some evidence that it manged to avoid alienating the people. There is probably a connection between Han law's implementation of Confucian values —such as filial piety and family loyalty—and the dynasty's long rule. The "naturalization" of the law, the law's attempt to restore and preserve natural harmony, must have seemed just to a nation of farmers who lived in dread of drouth and flood. Punishments that were hailed as befitting were not likely to arouse popular antagonism. The ideals of Han law were, then, reflective of the aspirations of most thoughtful members of Han society, and not likely to disturb less reflective common people. It is not strange that a legal system designed to organize, regularize, and administer the criminal law so that punishment should fit each crime should become the archetype for legal systems in all the durable dynasties that followed the Han. Befitting punishment had become a part of habitual jural thought by the time the Ch'ing code was drafted; it was no longer either a way of preventing natural catastrophe or of preserving the heavenly mandate of the emperor. Befitting punishment, nevertheless, continued to be thought of as just punishment. As a result, decisions made in accordance with, or by analogy to, the code did not arouse popular disaffection. The Ch'ing judicial officers, therefore, may have served the dynasty well by their fidelity to the code in the eighteenth and early nineteenth centuries.

Chapter 8

The Rights and Duties of Beasts and Trees*

At Basel, Switzerland, in 1474, a cock laid an egg. The civil authorities indicted "him" for violating the natural law; he was tried, found guilty, and sentenced to burn until dead. To the ancient Chinese, Dr. Joseph Needham tells us, legal punishment of animals would have been unthinkable. They believed that men, but not animals, could be guilty of violating nature's dictates; their emperor, for instance, could disrupt natural harmony by misrule; this kind of misconduct would cause cocks to lay eggs, and these aberrations, trivial in themselves, were portents of disastrous floods or droughts soon to come.[1]

From time out of mind most of the Chinese tilled the soil. Seldom do simple farmers think of themselves as nature's masters. They do, of course, break the sod, manure the soil, plant in rows, and tend the sprouts. Nature, however, tucks the germ inside the seed, and shines the sun that warms the stalks, and pours the rain that wets the roots. Before grain heads full for harvest, spring gives way to summer and summer turns to autumn. Prudent, artful husbandry often swells the yield, but in the bad years diligent and proper tillage ends in only meager harvest.

* I first wrote on this topic in 17 *Journal of Legal Education* 185 (1964).

191

Some say that Chinese farmers were fatalists. No doubt many were; most of them, however, were not; they believed that their best efforts would tend, at least sometimes, to meliorate their hardships, even though, at other times, fate might deal them disastrous blows. Fate, they thought, sometimes gives ground. Men who become wise are able to sense the cosmic order; one who comes to know the Way can stay attuned to natural harmony, and enhance his well-being.

Knowledge of the Way is hard to come by, because each of the specific contents of the world is unique; looked at one at a time all things are *sui generis;* at each moment man-and-the-world-about-him is a novel concatenation. Nature, however, flows; the cosmos is ever-changing, but, nevertheless, a continuum. Chinese sages looked on singular happenings and specific things appreciatively; that is, they were like sensitive critics who bring their trained and cultivated intuitions to bear on, say, a beautiful painting. The sages' knowledge, then, was a form of intimacy; it was not a kind of cleverness; they merged experience with their inner feelings so that they attuned themselves to the on-going world. The cosmos, so conceived, is not malleable, but benign to those who stay in consonance with its rhythm. The world view of Westerners is radically different from that of the Chinese; Western cosmology promises regularity, predictability, and some docility on the part of nature once her secrets are scientifically known.

In China an egg-laying cock, says Dr. Needham, would not have been liable to prosecution because the Chinese "were not so presumptuous as to suppose that they knew sufficiently well the laws laid down by God for non-human things to obey, to enable them to indict an animal." [2] Since this quotation is out of context, it might mislead; the Chinese did not suppose that any laws were enacted in heaven. They opined, instead, that heaven constantly intones a cosmic harmony; this intonation vibrantly orders the animate and inanimate world. One of the elements of heaven's harmony is natural morality to which men are obliged to conform. This morality is not a compendium of stern commands, but a part of the on-going, flowing, natural order. Beasts are unable to jangle cosmic harmony; only men can disrupt it, and when they do, order can be re-established only when they are properly punished. No doubt the Chinese punished murderers and thieves to make an example of them. Deterrence was, however, not the only, and in early times not the principal, reason for the punishment of wrong-doers. Dr. Hulsewé says that Chinese writings which refer to befitting punishments for particular crimes "reflect the archaic idea that punishment is to redress the harmony of nature which was disturbed by the crime." [3]

The Chinese, of course, were not the only farmers in antiquity; few other ancient peoples, however, were so proud of, and so dedicated to, tilling the soil. The forebears of many Europeans were flock-raisers, who, like the Texas cowboys, may have looked on farming with disdain.

A shepherd's rapport with nature differs from a farmer's. When nature threatened the crops of an ancient farmer, he had few defenses; he stood helpless when floodwaters covered his field with mud, when drought sucked the juice from his stalks, or when locusts devoured his every leaf and shoot. A drover, on the other hand, often could herd his beasts away from high waters and out of brown pastures. An old Chinese joke makes fun of a slow-witted planter whose young sprouts shriveled and died after he had pulled at them to help them grow. A herdsman, however, often makes his beasts do his bidding; he manages matings, he takes their milk, he forces fattening, and so on. The shepherd, with so much control, rarely thinks of his own husbandry as only one single ingredient in a natural cycle; he is likely to personate himself as an outside user of nature.

When the fifteenth-century Swiss judge sentenced the egg-laying cock, he acted as God's surrogate. A more virile rooster could rule the roost; only a man, however, could punish an errant animal and thereby vindicate God's natural law. In the medieval West, then, God imposed legal duties on nature, and obliged man to enforce them.

Man's chore of policing the physical world as God's monitor was, however, only a sideline. God, they believed, had made the Earth and all that was on it for the use and comfort of men, his favorite kind of creature. No seventeenth-century Chinese could have writ-

ten, as Locke did, "God who hath given the world to men in common, hath also given them reason to make use of it to the best advantage of life and convenience. The earth and all therein is given
to man for the support and comfort of their being." [4]   Men so
favored are obliged to punish, not only brutes' sex reversals, obscene
in the sight of God, but also they must avenge any injury inflicted
by beasts and trees. "If," according to Exodus, "an ox gore a man or
woman that they die: then the ox shall surely be stoned." [5] And in
Plato's *Laws* it is said, "If an inanimate thing cause death it shall be
cast beyond the borders." [6] So, in the eyes of Westerners, the Lord's
natural law confers rights on man which run against nature, but no
rights on nature against man.

The earliest Chinese writings on law deal with "the five punishments," but they do not catalogue or itemize crimes. Before China
was unified in 221 B.C., some of the Confucians said that rulers
should not classify misconduct and promulgate appropriate penalties
for each species of wrong; [7] they believed that each misdeed could
be penalized correctly only when it was judged in context; a wrongdoer, they believed, does not offend against formulated policy that
can be vitrified into the abstract words of an inelastic canon; he
upsets the unique, tangible, natural order, subsisting at the time of
his misconduct, and should be punished accordingly. The wise
ruler, they said, will not promulgate a code of rigid laws. Such
statutes are, perforce, abstractly conceptual; their lack of concrete
meaning gives rise to argumentative dissension. A good overlord is
himself attuned to nature and knows, therefore, the magnitude
of punishment needed at the time and place of a misdeed. When,
however, China was unified, the central government, for the first
time, ruled the far-flung empire without the intermediation of local
overlords. One aspect of the then-new imperial rule was the promulgation of criminal laws binding throughout the empire. The first
short-lived dynasty repudiated Confucius; when the next dynasty
returned to Confucianism, the emperors, nevertheless, continued to
promulgate statutory penal law. Not many Chinese scholars prized
law in general or the imperial codes in particular; most of them held
that proper conduct is consonant with cosmic order and, therefore,
is determined not by law but by natural, traditional propriety.

Rulers, they believed, should inspire their subjects by leading spotless lives and, by so doing, emanating an atmosphere of virtue; promulgated criminal laws, they believed, served to control only the dregs of society, who were too churlish to respond to loftier influences. Law, as such, therefore, was not cherished as an ornament of Chinese culture.

In the West, by contrast, we have held law in high regard and looked on it as part of the very fabric of ongoing society. Our respect for law, as an institution, persisted even after we had come to look on everyday legal rules as written by men, rather than pronounced by God. We came to know that a man's rights against his fellows were not fully and clearly covered by God's natural law; God, we believe, has left to men the governance not only of their beasts, but also of their own society; men properly order society by developing and enforcing legal systems; we look with pride on our man-made legal regimes.

In the West this humanization of the law began more than two millennia ago. Aristotle, for example, said, "A [legal] rule is conventional that in the first instance may be settled in one way or another indifferently, though having once been settled it is not indifferent." [8] I cannot point to a citation which will show that for Aristotle conventional justice overshadowed natural justice; nevertheless, that it does is exuded in Book V (the book on justice) in his *Nichomachean Ethics*. In the Middle Ages St. Thomas Aquinas—whose writings are the fountainhead of both medieval and modern Roman Catholic natural law theory—stressed man's need for human law to deal with the concrete facts of the times. [9] Hume, in the eighteenth century, denied any existence to natural law—"nature . . . has not placed in the mind any peculiar original principles to determine us to a set of actions"— [10] and concluded, perforce, that both law and justice are artificial ("nonnatural") human inventions without which men would, in apprehension, guard their property and refuse to repose the trust in other men necessary for commerce and industry.

The definitions of law found in contemporary Western jurisprudence usually follow one or more of these patterns: law is defined as (1) sovereign command, (2) legislative enactments and/or judicial decisions, (3) a form of adaptive cultural growth—or some combination of these alternatives. Definitions so constructed continue the trend of elevating God's natural law above the details of law in the everyday world; natural law is now either characterized as an omnipresent, but highly abstract, aspect of eternal justice, or as soaring so high in the sky that it disappears altogether. Whilst modern jurists were losing itemized natural laws, modern scientists were searching out itemized laws of nature. For the scientist, order, or its statistical equivalent, exists and can be discovered, whether God-given or not. The nature that scientists study is, they believe, neither right nor a clue to what is right; it simply *is*.

In this unsuperstitious world—in which enforceable legal obligations were human artifices, and the laws of nature, in themselves, did not indicate where earthly right lay—men inevitably gave up their primitive practice of prosecuting brutes and things. So beasts and trees no longer had any legal duties. Westerners who gave up the conceit that nature had legal duties also became convinced more than ever that nature had no legal rights.

For Westerners, then, legal relations are a special kind of human relations; as such they oblige and entitle only human beings; only a man—or an aggregate of men, such as a corporation or the state—can have legal rights or duties. Our modern legal sociologists and other students of law in society agree that, for a variety of reasons, legal obligations are usually performed without the intervention of the courts of law. When, however, it happens that an obligor fails or refuses to carry out his legal duty, those whom he wrongs acquire a new right, that is, a right to a court's judgment giving them legal redress; judges are obliged to recognize neglects of legal duties by affording a remedy to those wronged. So when a legal right running against a private individual is not honored, that primary right is augmented by a remedial right which runs against a court. Lawyers have a quick way of pointing out that a failure to satisfy a substantive right occasions the rise of a procedural right; lawyers say, "no right without a remedy." This maxim not only means that courts are obliged to vindicate all breaches of genuine legal rights; it also means that if courts are not obliged to support an unsatisfied claim, that claim is not a genuine legal right.

Years ago, one of my colleagues examined his law students on an aspect of the rights of a pet-owner. He and I chuckled, in a superior way, over the first sentence in one student's essay. The student began by saying, "Dogs have very few rights." We were amused by what we tacitly thought a gaucherie, because we were sure that dogs had no rights at all. We would have been as disdainful of a loose-thinker's suggestion that legal rights are conferred on horses by a cruelty-to-animals statute, or that a cat can acquire rights under a clause of a will which provides for her care. We would have said that the cruelty statute conferred a right on the human public, represented by the state, to have a kind of culprit punished and that the bequest conferred the right on a human trustee to expend funds for the cat's support.

The conceit that characterizes every legal relation as a special form of relation between men, you will remember, is not God-given; this homocentric conceit was ordained by men, and, on a proper showing, it can be disdained by men. Dobbin and Kitty, we can say, were, respectively, the intended beneficiaries of substantive rights conferred by the cruelty statute and by the law of inheritance; the human plaintiffs who ask judges to enforce these rights, we can say, have only the right to demand that the courts supply a remedy that will vindicate the rights of the animals; the human plaintiffs are like guardians who assert the rights of their young wards. This proposal scorns the Lockean *ipse dixit* of those savants who postulate that legal relations can run only between men. Our contrary axiom is clearly truer to the facts; patently the purpose of the law of these cases is to afford legal protection to Dobbin and Kitty. Whatever satisfactions men may feel in acting as attorneys or agents for these animals are purely incidental; the animals themselves are the real parties in interest.

We can enlarge on our proposal and adopt an attitude not unlike that of the ancient Chinese. We can insist that conservation laws confer primary legal rights on nature and correlative duties on men. Nature's primary rights, we can say, can be enforced in courts in suits brought by nature's next friends, enlarged in legislatures by enactments responding to nature's lobbyists, expounded and furthered in forums of public opinion by nature's vicars.

My legal schooling does not, of course, fit me to draw up a sound bill of rights for beasts and trees; forensic thought, however, does have one special bearing on the protection of nature. In legal proceedings when a trial judge must enter a final judgment without knowing which side is right, he disfavors that side which has the burden of proof. Nature's integrity will be favored if a presumption in favor of the natural casts a burden of proof on those who propose to disturb nature—a burden to establish affirmatively that the change should not be prohibited. Nature should no longer be dislocated on whim or without forethought about the harm that may ensue; he who proposes dislocation should justify it before he starts.

The legalism, the presumption in favor of the natural, is, for instance, akin to the presumption of innocence, which also allots a burden of proof. Miscarriages of criminal justice come in two models—convicting the innocent and acquitting the guilty. The first of these is, in our view, more regrettable than the second. We guard against punishing the guiltless by resolving in advance not to convict an accused man unless his guilt is properly established. The presumption of innocence is not a proposition of fact; it is a program of procedure. We would keep it even in the face of proof that nearly all men who are indicted are guilty. The presumption is calculated to channel the decisions of criminal courts to the more acceptable result when a judgment must be entered in the absence of adequate knowledge of the facts of a case.

Where lies the sounder alternative when a proposal is put forward to disrupt nature, absent reasonable foreknowledge of what is likely to ensue? Whoever contemplates dumping tons of waste, killing myriads of pests, or uprooting expanses of natural growth should customarily have to make the case that sound reason warrants his plan to dislocate the natural order. He is not justified in deranging nature merely because no one, offhand, thinks of drawbacks; the proponent should have to bear the onus of showing that the change is not for the worse.

The presumption in favor of the natural should not be only a password, admitting well-meaning conservationists to their annual meetings; it should quicken the enactment of legislation creating nature's substantive legal rights—in the form of game and forest laws, green space and park protection statutes, and antipollution codes. These enactments should designate rangers and inspectors as nature's guardians, with the authority and obligation to represent nature's interests in the enforcement of these laws.

Proof of the value of laws that will implement the presumption can be made by expert witnesses, who can recount the ugliness, irreversible imbalances, and ill health resulting from past tamperings with the natural order. Man's enhanced ability to wreak havoc on nature is likely, unless brakes are applied, to increase the future costs of disruptions of the natural order. The presumption is not a spoke in the wheel, senselessly halting needed forward motion that would otherwise advance the public good; it is a warning to slow down when high speed is dangerous.

Payment of part of the costs of unwise interventions in nature is exacted from people; these people are usually not the same ones as those who enjoy the fruits of disruptive enterprise. The victims, known and unknown, should be safeguarded by recognition of their vested interests in the natural order. Other costs are borne by brutes and things which merit protection, not only because of their worth to men, but also in their own right. Surrogates of nature, then, not only have the office of protecting man because he is nature's creature; they also are the agents of birds, flowers, and ponds. Once the public generally aspires to preserve the natural order in all cases except those in which an adequate case can be made for human intervention, enactment of laws needed to protect the natural will become more likely, and the enforcement of these laws will become more certain. When legal rights are, by statute, conferred on feral beasts, green forests, outcroppings of stone, and sweet air, and when these legal rights are taken more seriously, men will respect these duties in much the same way as they respect their other legal obligations. A camper who thinks of his legal duty to clear up his mess as an obligation, not to the government, but to the campsite itself, is less likely to neglect his duty.

Of course the presumption in favor of the natural is not a presumption against the common good. Those who extend legal rights to nature may not deny them to men. If mosquitoes are an element in a balanced system of carp, lotuses and men, anopheles ought to be replaced by a variety that neither spreads malaria nor stings. When natural conditions cannot be reconciled with mankind's well-being, men, women, and children ought to be preferred over toads, weeds, and swamps.

Supplements are needed to protect both people and nature against nature's shortcomings. People deserve dental health promoted by fluoridation of water. The nurseries in which seedling pines are grown and the hatcheries where quail are raised counteract nature's inadequacies.

Appreciation of the world around us is often enriched by poetry; men's attempts to reduce nature to words may, however, misfire. The Chinese decapitated and strangled criminals only in autumn or winter. They delayed executing those convicts who were sentenced to death during the spring and the summer. In the vernal seasons executions, they thought, were inappropriate. Perhaps postponements of capital punishment on any ground, however odd, should be welcomed; wry penology, however, results from irrelevant seasonal delays of executions; the inappropriateness of summertime abolition of capital punishment is bought at the dear price of establishing its wintertime propriety.

Language warped some Chinese conceptions of nature into still more curious misunderstandings. Their oral speech—in which a few hundred monosyllables represent thousands of written characters— abounds in occasions for associating words of unrelated meanings. Like the rest of the human race, the Chinese seem to enjoy the humor of "good" puns; they sometimes, however, looked on homonyms as clues to natural knowledge. Dr. Derk Bodde gives us this example:

The Shuo Wen Dictionary, in its definition of *ming* "insect grub," connects this word with another different *ming* meaning "dark, blind benighted, obtuse," etc. Thus we read: "Ming (insect grub) is an insect which eats the heart out of grain. When government functionaries benightedly (ming) violate the law, the grubs (ming) are born.[11]

This verbalization of nature is no boon to the art of pest control; it is fraught, furthermore, with an implication that when the crops are good the government also is good. The Chinese who respected the Shuo Wen Dictionary were not, of course, blind to clear cases of maladministration whenever they occurred; they were, however, for many centuries after the dictionary's publication, somewhat disposed to tolerate trivial bribery and minor corruption. Perhaps the pun on *ming*, which does not appear in modern dictionaries, may have been a minor contributing cause of that tolerance.

The presumption in favor of the natural should not relieve man from correcting his own errors. It should be no bar to the search for better knowledge about both nature and man. It should be no excuse for maintaining an artificial or natural status quo whenever sound reason recommends an attainable change.

The presumption in favor of the natural extends beyond my unconditional respect for the humanity of all men. In this chapter I posit—but not unconditionally—a similar respect for both the bestiality of brutes (if they are not too bestial) and the arboreality of trees (but not to the point of forbidding sound thinning and reasonable lumber harvests). The presumption in favor of the natural is calculated, in part, to preserve the human race, to check our contemporaries from making the earth untenable for their, and our, offspring; the presumption is also intended to give man—a carnivore and a social animal—the satisfactions flowing from concordance with the natural order. Congeniality with their environment develops men's sensitivities; it disposes them not only to become better gardeners, but also to participate in the redefinition of the legal and moral limits on the private use of land, sea, and air; a redefinition which will quicken the public aspiration for living on the earth without laying it waste. There should be feedback. A man who has learned to respect the gallantry of a gnarled, old tree may also come to respect the humanity of a maladjusted man.

Notes

Notes to Chapter 1

1. Aristotle, *Nichomachean Ethics* (Rackham trans.; Cambridge, Mass.: Harvard University Press, 1949), p. 295.

2. *Ibid.*, p. 259.

3. Thomas Hobbes, *Leviathan* (1651) (A. R. Waller ed.; Cambridge: Cambridge University Press, 1904), p. 122.

4. *Ibid.*, p. 252.

5. David Hume, *A Treatise of Human Nature* (1740) ("Everyman's Library," No. 549 [New York: E. P. Dutton & Co. Inc., 1911]) Vol. II, Book III, p. 226. "As the obligation of promises is an invention for the interest of society it is warped into as many different forms as that society requires . . ." If this is so, the technical job of formulating it may be done badly.

6. Cicero, *Laws* (Keyes trans.; Cambridge, Mass.: Harvard University Press, 1928), p. 317.

7. Baron de Montesquieu, *The Spirit of the Laws* (1748) (T. Nugent trans.; New York: Hafner Publishing Co., 1949), p. 2.

8. Shaw v. Director of Public Prosecutions, 2 All E. R. 448 (1961); discussed in 24 *Modern L. R.* 626. The punishment in that case was nine months' imprisonment for publishing a lurid directory of prostitutes. Common-law grounds for the holding were alternative with statutory ones.

9. T'ung-tsu Ch'u, *Law and Society in Traditional China* (Cambridge, Mass.: Harvard University Press, 1961), p. 170.

10. "Common Law of Crimes in the United States," Note in 47 *Col. L. R.* 1332 (1947).

11. *Ibid.*, p. 1334. See also Warren and Brandeis, "The Right to Privacy," 4 *Harv. L. R.* 193, 219 (1890), in which a new civil remedy for the invasion of

privacy is proposed, but the authors say that a criminal action would not lie without legislation.

12. "Common Law of Crimes in the United States," Note in 47 *Col. L. R.* 1332.

13. Commonwealth v. Smith, alias Quinter, 17 Berks 40 (Pa. 1924).

14. Witness, for example, Caminetti v. U.S., 242 U.S. 470 (1917), in which the Mann Act, passed to combat commercial vice, was turned against amateurs.

15. See Roscoe Pound, "Common Law and Legislation," 21 *Harv. L. R.* 383-385 (1908).

16. See, for example, Union Pacific v. Cappier, 66 Kan. 649, 72 Pac. 281 (1903), a wrongful death action in which the plaintiff alleged that, after the defendant railroad ran over the decedent, railroad employes failed to come to his aid promptly and, as a result, he bled to death. Held: the railroad had no duty to come to his aid.

The judicial deaf ear of justice has also sometimes failed to hear just defenses to claims. This was so in the common law courts in the period immediately before the adoption of equitable defenses. See William F. Walsh, *Treatise on Equity* (Chicago: Callaghan and Company, 1930), p. 99.

17. See, for example, Roberson v. Rochester Folding Box Co., 171 N.Y. 538 (1902), in which the court refused to recognize that an advertiser who without permission put a pretty girl's picture in his ads violated her rights, and said that the problem was for the legislature.

18. See John Chipman Gray, *The Rule against Perpetuities* (4th ed.; Boston: Little, Brown and Company, 1942), especially pp. 169-170.

19. See, for example, Hubbard v. Halliday, 58 Okla. 244, 158 Pac. 1158 (1916).

20. "*Lawyers* saw an opportunity to secure the trial of title to realty without the expense and delay of the old real action . . . ," says Edmund Morgan in *Introduction to the Study of Law* (Chicago, New York: Callaghan and Company, 1926), p. 82 (italics mine).

21. *Ibid.,* pp. 81 *et seq.*

22. Mast v. Goodson, 3 Wilson 348, 351 (Pa. Common Pleas, 1772).

23. See Morgan, *op. cit.,* pp. 80 *et seq.*

24. R. H. van Gulik trans., *T'ang-yin-pi-shih, "Parallel Cases from under the Pear-tree"* (Leiden: E. J. Brill, 1956), p. 176.

25. A court interpreting a statute or a written constitution has a somewhat different function; analysis of this function is not treated here.

26. Learned Hand, "The Speech of Justice," 29 *Harv. L. R.* 617, 619 (1916).

27. *Ibid.*

28. Winterbottom v. Wright, 10 M. & W. 109 (Eng. 1842).

29. MacPherson v. Buick Motor Co., 217 N.Y. 382, 111 N.E. 1050 (1916).

30. Warren and Brandeis, "The Right to Privacy," 4 *Harv. L. R.* 193 (1890).

31. Benjamin N. Cardozo, *The Nature of the Judicial Process* (New Haven: Yale University Press, 1921), p. 22.

32. Monrad G. Paulsen, ed., *Legal Institutions Today and Tomorrow* (New York: Columbia University Press, 1959), pp. 48, 50.

33. Frederick Charles von Savigny, *Of the Vocation of Our Age for Legislation and Jurisprudence* (1814) (Abraham Hayward, trans.; London: printed by Littlewood & Co., Old Bailey, 1831), especially chaps. II and III.

34. I borrow this phrase and the idea from Bertram Morris' brilliant *Philosophical Aspects of Culture* (Yellow Springs, Ohio: The Antioch Press, 1961).

35. Eugen Ehrlich, *Fundamental Principles of the Sociology of Law* (Moll, trans.; Cambridge, Mass.: Harvard University Press, 1936), pp. 21-23.

36. Cf. John Austin, *Lectures on Jurisprudence* (3rd ed., London: John Murray, 1869), p. 162. "[Generally] every individual person is the best possible judge of his own interests: of what will affect himself with the greatest pleasures and pains. Compared with his intimate consciousness of his own peculiar interests, his knowledge of the interests of others is vague conjecture. Consequently, the principle of general utility imperiously demands that he commonly shall attend to his own rather than to the interests of others; that he shall not habitually neglect that which he knows accurately in order that he may habitually pursue that which he knows imperfectly."

37. See John Stuart Mill, *Utilitarianism, Liberty, and Representative Government* ("Everyman's Library," No. 482A [New York: E. P. Dutton & Co. Inc., 1951]), p. 28.

38. Wilmington General Hospital v. Manlove, 174 A.2d 135 (1961).

39. Mill, *op. cit.*, pp. 63-66.

40. Mill, *op. cit.*, p. 71. Italics added.

Notes to Chapter 2

1. *Summa Theologica* (Fathers of the English Dominican Province trans.; New York: Benziger Bros., 1947-48), QQ. 91, 3rd. art., first part.

2. In *My Philosophy of Law, Credos of Sixteen American Scholars* (Julius Rosenthal Foundation, Northwestern University [Boston: Boston Law Book Co., 1941]), pp. 52-53.

3. *Ibid.*, p. 57.

4. John Dewey, *Human Nature and Conduct* (New York: Henry Holt, 1922), Part III, chap. 6.

5. Jean Jacques Rousseau, *The Social Contract* (1762) ("Everyman's Library," No. 660A [G. D. H. Cole trans.; New York: E. P. Dutton & Co. Inc., 1950]), Book IV, chap. I, first par.

6. Frederick Charles von Savigny, *Of the Vocation of Our Age for Legislation and Jurisprudence* (1814) (Abraham Hayward trans.; London: printed by Littlewood & Co., Old Bailey, 1831), p. 30.

7. *Ibid.*, p. 39.

8. Thomas Hobbes, *Leviathan* (1651) (A. R. Waller ed.; Cambridge: Cambridge University Press, 1904), chap. 26.

9. Eugen Ehrlich, *Fundamental Principles of the Sociology of Law* (1913) (Moll trans.; Cambridge, Mass.: Harvard University Press, 1936), p. 181.

10. Clarence Morris, "Political Philosophy of Maritain," *Daedalus*, Fall, 1959, p. 706.

11. Jacques Maritain, *Man and the State* (Chicago: Chicago University Press, 1951), p. 76.

12. *Ibid.*, p. 80.

13. Aristotle, *Politics*, Book II (Jowett trans.; London: Clarendon Press, 1931), p. 80.

14. Hobbes, *op. cit.*, chap. 26.

15. Benjamin N. Cardozo, *The Nature of the Judicial Process* (New Haven: Yale University Press, 1921), p. 34.

16. *Ibid.*, p. 150.

17. *Ibid.*, pp. 31-34.

18. Ultramares Corp. v. Touche, 255 N.Y. 170, 174 N.E. 441 (1931).

19. Monrad G. Paulsen, ed., *Legal Institutions Today and Tomorrow* (New York: Columbia University Press, 1959), p. 50.

20. See Jefferson B. Fordham, *Local Government Law* (Brooklyn: Foundation Press, 1949), p. 632.

21. Maritain, *op. cit.*, pp. 126-130, 136-137.

22. *Ibid.*, pp. 139-141.

23. Donald G. MacRae, "The Culture of a Generation: Students and Others," *Jour. of Contemp. History*, 2, No. 3 (1967), 3. MacRae also suggests that liberalized views and practices have diminished the burden of romantic love and sex and hence released energies for viewing and attacking older social arrangements.

24. Learned Hand, "The Speech of Justice," 29 *Harv. L. R.* 617, 619 (1916).

25. See supra p. 2.

Notes to Chapter 3

1. Herbert Marcuse, *An Essay on Liberation* (Boston: Beacon Press, 1969).

2. *Ibid.*, p. 62.

3. *Ibid.*, p. 15.

4. *Ibid.*, p. 11.

5. *Ibid.*, pp. 87-88.

6. *Ibid.*, p. 88.

7. *Ibid.*, pp. 88-90.

8. *Ibid.*, pp. 90-91.

9. *Ibid.*, pp. 23-24.

10. *Ibid.*, pp. 45-46.

11. *Ibid.*, p. 91.

12. *Ibid.*, p. 63.

13. *Ibid.*, p. 65.

14. *Ibid.*, pp. 82-84.

15. *Ibid.*, p. 54.

16. *Ibid.*, pp. 51-52.

17. *Ibid.*, p. 59.

18. *Ibid.*, p. 60.

19. John Stuart Mill, "On Liberty," in *Utilitarianism, Liberty, and Representative Government* (1859) ("Everyman's Library," No. 482A [New York: E. P. Dutton Co. Inc., 1951]).

20. *Ibid.*, p. 86.

21. *Ibid.*, pp. 87-88.

22. *Ibid.*, pp. 88-89.

23. Ibid., p. 89.

24. *Ibid.*, p. 177.

25. *Ibid.*, p. 152.

26. *Ibid.*, p. 141.

27. *Ibid.*, p. 104.

28. *Ibid.*, p. 124.

29. *Ibid.*, p. 129.

30. *Ibid.*, p. 153.

31. *Ibid.*, pp. 185-186.

32. *Ibid.*, p. 91.

33. *Ibid.*, p. 154.

34. *Ibid.*, p. 159.

35. *Ibid.*, pp. 165-166.

36. *Ibid.*, p. 157.

37. *Ibid.*, p. 163.

38. Robert Waelder, "The Concept of Justice and the Quest for a Perfectly Just Society," 115 *U. Pa. L. R.* 1, 8-9 (1966).

39. *Ibid.*, pp. 10-11. I reacted in print against Waelder's views because he seems, once his whole article is read, to voice complacency with inequities that may be meliorated. My reply pointed out that slavery, child labor, *droit du seigneur*, imprisonment for debt and other aggressive outrages had been, in some societies, recognized as evils and downed, by and large, by outlawry and without loss of other important values. Clarence Morris, "A Dissent to Dr. Waelder's Theory of Justice," 115 *U. Pa. L. R.* 12, 13 (1966). My dissent ended in a rhetorical question to this effect: Shall we believe that because some men are so made that we cannot quench their aggressive desire for high status, others must inevitably be second-class members of the human race? *Ibid.*, p. 16.

40. Mill, *supra* note 19, at p. 108.

41. *Ibid.*, pp. 117-119.

42. Certainly the English theologic objections to the theory of evolution voiced in Mill's own day did not silence Darwin or his followers, and would fall within Mill's own protection of free speech.

Notes to Chapter 5

1. David Hume, *A Treatise of Human Nature* (1740) ("Everyman's Library" No. 549 [New York: E. P. Dutton & Co. Inc., 1911]) Vol. II. Hereinafter cited as Hume.

2. Hume, II:172-178.

3. Hume, II:166-168.

4. Hume, II:184.

5. Thomas Hobbes, *Leviathan* (1651) (A. R. Waller ed.; Cambridge: Cambridge University Press, 1904). See especially chap. 18.

6. Hume, II:231-232.

7. "As the obligation of promises is an invention for the interests of society, it is warped into as many different forms as that interest requires . . . " Hume, II:226.

8. Baron de Montesquieu, *The Spirit of the Laws* (1748) (Thomas Nugent trans.; New York: Hafner Publishing Co., 1949), I: 151-152.

9. Jean Jacques Rousseau, *The Social Contract* (1762) ("Everyman's Library," No. 660A [G. D. H. Cole trans., New York: E. P. Dutton & Co. Inc., 1950]), pp. 13-15.

10. *Ibid.*, pp. 26-27.

11. *Ibid.*, p. 102.

12. Immanuel Kant, *Philosophy of Law* (1791) (W. Hastie trans.; Edinburgh: T. & T. Clark, 1887), pp. 12-17.

13. *Ibid.*, p. 34.

14. *Ibid.*, p. 45.

15. *Ibid.*, p. 54.

16. *Ibid.*

17. *Ibid.*, p. 163.

18. *Ibid.*, pp. 230-231.

19. Jeremy Bentham, *The Limits of Jurisprudence Defined* (C. W. Everett ed.; New York: Columbia University Press, 1945), pp. 329-343.

20. *Ibid.*, p. 281.

21. *Ibid.*, pp. 167-176.

22. The 1957 official edition of the act ran to 223 pages of solid statutory material, i.e., without annotations or comment.

23. See William L. Prosser, *Handbook of the Law of Torts* (3rd ed.; St. Paul: West Publishing Co., 1964), pp. 923 *et seq.*

24. *Ibid.*, pp. 558 *et seq.*

25. *Ibid.*, pp. 554 *et seq.*

26. Hume, after making the point that our natural inclinations lead us to selfish disorder which we find we can avoid by organizing society, pictures that society in these words: "It is a convention entered into by all the members of society to bestow stability on the possession of . . . external goods, and leave everyone in peaceable enjoyment of what he may acquire by his fortune and industry. By this means everyone knows what he may safely possess; . . ." Hume, II:195.

27. See, for example, Purdon's Penna. Statutes, Vol. 5.

28. Kant, *Philosophy of Law*, pp. 186-187.

29. See, for example, Report by the Committee to Study Compensation for Automobile Accidents to the Columbia University Council for Research in Social Sciences (1932).

30. Uniform Commercial Code, sec. 2302.

31. See, for example, Phoenix Refining Co. v. Powell, 251 S.W. 2d 892 (Tex. Cv. A. 1952).

32. Bentham, *The Limits of Jurisprudence Defined*, chap. 11.

33. *Ibid.*, p. 336.

34. *Ibid.*, p. 342.

Notes to Chapter 6

1. Baron de Montesquieu, the eighteenth-century environmentalist, stressed the effects of climate, natural resources, geography, history, customs, morality, etc., on law and government. See Baron de Montesquieu, *The Spirit of the Laws* (1748) (T. Nugent trans.; New York: Hafner Publishing Co., 1949). His own acquaintance with differing cultures was, however, helter skelter, and obviously unreliable.

2. References to Weber in this article are to *Max Weber on Law and Economy in Society* (ed. and trans. from *Wirtschaft und Gesellschaft*, 2d ed. [1925] by Max Rheinstein and Edward Shils; Cambridge Mass.: Harvard University Press, 1954), hereinafter cited as *Law in Society*.

3. John Austin, *Lectures on Jurisprudence* (3rd ed.; London: John Murray, 1869).

4. O. W. Holmes, Jr., "The Path of the Law," 10 *Harv. L. R.* 457 (1897).

5. *Law in Society*, p. 34.

6. *Ibid.*, pp. 67-68.

7. *Ibid.*, p. 13. Weber goes on to say that the apparatus' power must be such that the rules will usually be respected because of deterrence resulting from the apparatus' existence (p. 14). Nevertheless, says Weber, most law-abiding people are motivated either by an unreflecting habituation to law or by fear of evoking adverse public opinion (p. 12).

8. *Ibid.*, 73.

9. *Ibid.*, 76. Cf. Rousseau's statement that in primitive times wise men controlled their societies by crediting God with their own wisdom and purporting to find a divinely authored law of nature. Jean Jacques Rousseau, *The Social Contract* (1762) ("Everyman's Library," No. 660A [G. D. H. Cole trans.; New York: E. P. Dutton & Co. Inc., 1950]), pp. 40-41.

10. *Law in Society*, p. 86.

11. *Ibid.*, p. 63.

12. *Ibid.*, pp. 83-84.

13. *Ibid.*, pp. 91-92.

14. *Ibid.*, p. 92. Trials were not the only legal magic in primitive times; the ways of undertaking some binding legal obligations also were magical. The invention of money, said Weber, tended to eliminate magic from legal transactions (p. 109).

15. Montesquieu, Rousseau, and Hume come to mind. See footnote 17, *infra*.

16. See, for example, Thomas Aquinas, *Summa Theologica* (Fathers of the English Dominican Province trans.; New York: Benziger Bros., 1947-1948), 1st pt. of 2d pt. QQ 95, art. 1, reply 2.

17. See, for example, David Hume, *A Treatise of Human Nature* (1740) ("Everyman's Library," No. 549 [New York: E. P. Dutton & Co. Inc., 1911]) II:231-233; Baron de Montesquieu, *The Spirit of the Laws* (1748), *supra* footnote 1., at pp. 151-152; Jean Jacques Rousseau, *The Social Contract, supra* footnote 9., at pp. 26-27.

18. *Law in Society*, p. 59. Cf. Jeremy Bentham, *The Limits of Jurisprudence Defined* (C. W. Everett ed.; New York: Columbia University Press, 1945), p. 244. Bentham says, "Written law is the law for civilized nations; traditionary law, for barbarians; customary law for brutes."

19. *Law in Society*, p. 63.

20. *Ibid.*

21. *Ibid.*, pp. 63-64.

22. *Ibid.*, p. 63.

23. Benjamin N. Cardozo, *The Nature of the Judicial Process* (New Haven: Yale University Press, 1921), pp. 31-32, hereinafter cited as *Judicial Process.*

24. *Ibid.*, pp. 66-72.

25. *Law in Society*, p. 64.

26. Weber, in passing, noted that one of judges' motives for respecting rules previously used was to escape charges of bias. *Ibid.*, p. 74.

27. *Judicial Process*, p. 33.

28. But see *ibid.* pp. 19-20 to the effect, "some judges' . . . notion of their duty is to match the case at hand against the colors of many sample cases spread out on their desks. The sample nearest in shade supplies the applicable rule."

29. *Law in Society*, p. 80.

30. *Ibid.*, p. 225.

31. Weber probably did not include constitutions; he excepted those norms that are regarded as religiously sacred and hence absolutely binding. *Ibid.*, p. 226.

32. *Ibid.*, pp. 226-227.

33. *Ibid.*, p. 228.

34. *Ibid.*, pp. 228-229.

35. *Ibid.*, pp. 307-308.

36. *Ibid.*, pp. 307-309.

37. *Ibid.,* p. 311.

38. *Ibid.,* p. 313.

39. *Ibid.*

40. *Ibid.,* p. 320.

41. *Ibid.,* p. 321.

42. See Note, 47 *Col. L. R.* 1332 (1947).

43. This is, of course, only a small help in preventing prejudice in criminal trials, a problem far from solved.

44. For a further example see the section on Mangled Statutes in my "Inadvertent Newspaper Libel and Retraction," 32 *Ill. L. R.* 36-49 (1937).

45. *Law in Society,* p. 79.

46. See F. H. Bohlen, "Mixed Questions of Law and Fact," 72 *U. Pa. L. R.* 111 (1924).

47. Bentham, *supra,* note 18, p. 281.

48. See Harris v. Lewiston Trust Co., 326 Pa. 145, 191 A.34 (1937) which immediately overruled a sudden departure from common law rule in Max v. Deutsch, 318 Pa. 450, 178 A.48 (1937).

49. *Judicial Process,* p. 108.

50. This paragraph has no application to federal constitutional law, an area in which the interpretation of very general constitutional doctrines sometimes requires the courts to make new law even though the values of the citizenry seem divided. "Given that enormous backing of inaction, it fell to the Supreme Court to break long-standing deadlocks on such highly inflamed issues as racial segregation, legislative apportionment and criminal justice. In all of these difficult matters, the court came down basically on the right side. It is very hard to imagine—indeed for me it is impossible—how any group of educated men could have endorsed manifest inequities for Negroes, urban voters and prisoners.

"Decisions on these vexed questions of public policy inevitably aroused hostility to the court among certain groups—notably Southerners, rural politicos and law-enforcement officials." Joseph Kraft in the *International Herald Tribune* (Paris) May 9, 1969, p. 6.

51. See Cardozo's own handling of a similar problem in Ultramares Corp. v. Touche, 225 N.Y. 170, 174 N.E. 441 (1931).

52. See Edwin W. Patterson, *Essentials of Insurance Law,* (2nd ed., New York: McGraw Hill, 1957), pp. 214-220.

53. See dissenting opinion of J. Ward, in Maki v. Frelk, 40 Ill. 2d 193, 239 N.E. 2d 445 (1968).

Notes to Chapter 7

1. David Hume, *A Treatise of Human Nature* (1740) ("Everyman's Library," No. 549 [New York: E. P. Dutton & Co. Inc., 1911]) Vol. II, Book III. See especially Part II, secs. III–IV.

2. Baron de Montesquieu, *The Spirit of the Laws* (1748) (T. Nugent trans.; New York: Hafner Publishing Co., 1949). See especially I: 151-162.

3. Jean Jacques Rousseau, *The Social Contract* (1762) ("Everyman's Library," No. 660A [G. D. H. Cole trans.; New York: E. P. Dutton & Co. Inc., 1950]). See especially Book II.

4. Bernhard Karlgren trans., "The Book of Documents," *Bulletin of the Museum of Far Eastern Antiquities,* 22 (Stockholm, 1950), 76.

5. On the severity of the Ch'in Law, and its Legalistic background, see Derk Bodde, *China's First Unifier* (Leiden: E. J. Brill, 1938), and see J. J. L. Duyvendak trans., *The Book of Lord Shang* (London: Arthur Probsthein, 1928), pp. 179-180, 278-280.

6. See Derk Bodde and Clarence Morris, *Law in Imperial China* (Cambridge, Mass.: Harvard University Press, 1967), pp. 76-78, hereinafter cited as B. & M. This work presents a hundred and ninety cases selected from some seventy-six hundred from the Ch'ing Dynasty (1736–1885) and translated so as to be available to English-speaking students of Chinese law.

7. The quoted words are Roscoe Pound's used as part of his definition of law. *My Philosophy of Law, Credos of Sixteen American Scholars* (Julius Rosenthal Foundation, Northwestern University [Boston: Boston Law Book Co., 1941]), p. 177.

8. No. 164.1 (1826), in B. & M., p. 330.

9. *Ibid.*, p. 331.

10. United States v. Kirby, 74 U.S. (7 Wall) 482, 486-487 (1868).

11. No. 164.2 (1818), in B. & M., p. 333.

12. No. 172.4 (1791), in B. & M., p. 359.

13. See B. & M., pp. 138-143.

14. See B. & M., p. 92.

15. No. 159.1 (1792), in B. & M., p. 315.

16. No. 178.8 (1816), in B. & M., p. 365.

17. No. 175.6 (1817), in B. & M., p. 362.

18. See the United States Supreme Court's dilemma in United States v. Hood, 343 U.S. 148, 72 Sup. Ct. 568 (1952), a case in which defendants were charged with disobeying a criminal statute forbidding solicitation of money "in consideration of the promise of support or use of influence in obtaining for any person any appointive office or place under the United States." The defendants promised their dupes appointments to nonexistent offices; authority to create those offices had been granted to the President, but he had not exercised that authority. Unless the court held the statute applicable, the defendants would escape punishment for their influence peddling. The court by a majority of five to four held the statute applicable.

19. For an example of American judicial infidelity to statutes see the section entitled Mangled Statutes in my "Inadvertent Newspaper Libel and Retraction," 32 *Ill. L. R.* 36 (1937).

20. No. 208.4 (1814), in B. & M., p. 420.

21. Cf. the U.S. Supreme Court case of Glus v. Brooklyn Eastern Terminal, 359 U.S. 231, 79 Sup. Ct. 760 (1959) in which the federal statute governing suits by operating railroad employees for on-the-job injuries required that action be brought within three years. This suit was not brought within the statutory period. The workman was allowed to excuse his tardiness by a showing that the railroad had represented to him that he had a longer time. The court said that the legislation was adopted in a system of law that had long recognized the principle that no one should profit from his own wrong, and therefore it was appropriate to apply that principle to this case. The principles of filial loyalty were extremely important in the system—and throughout the society—in which the Ch'ing perjury statute was passed.

22. No. 206.8 (1822), in B. & M., p. 417.

23. No. 12.2 (1830), in B. & M., p. 428.

24. But see Gui Boulais trans., *Manuel du code chinois* (Shanghai: Varietes sinologiques series, No. 55, 1924), Sec. 1122, dealing with enhanced penalties for recidivist thieves.

25. See B. & M., p. 79.

26. No. 223.4 (1814), in B. & M., p. 431.

27. No. 223.2 (1818), in B. & M., p. 428.

28. George Thomas Staunton, trans., *Ta Tsing Leu Lee, Being the Fundamental Laws . . . of the Penal Code of China* (London: Cadell & Davis, 1810), Sec. 415, p. 455.

29. No. 260.1 (1870), in B. & M., p. 461.

30. See Note, "Common Law of Crimes in the United States," 47 *Col. L. R.* 1332 (1947); but see Commonwealth v. Hochan, 177 Pa. Super. 454 (1955).

31. 333 U.S. 483, 68 Sup. Ct. 634 (1948).

32. No. 243.5 (1822), in B. & M., p. 449.

33. No. 80.23 (1825), in B. & M., p. 260.

34. No. 131.2 (1796), in B. & M., p. 287.

35. Staunton, *supra*, footnote 28, Sec. 44, pp. 43-44.

36. No. 126.2 (1822), in B. & M., p. 285.

37. Similarly in Mao Huo-hsia's case, No. 165.5 (1824), in B. & M., p. 337, the culprit spread ordure over the mouth and face of a victim who retched himself to death. A statute punished "Introducing foreign objects into someone's ears, nostrils, or other openings of the body. " The Board held the statute was not directly applicable, but the crime was held analogous to this statutory offense.

38. 34 N.J. 318, 169 A.2d 135 (1961).

39. No. 208.5 (1829), in B. & M., p. 421.

40. No. 161.3 (1832), in B. & M., p. 325.

41. I am assuming, of course, that these cousins, when not traveling, did not live together and share resources. If they had, the Board would in all probability have said so, and not relied on their travel arrangements.

42. No. 45.1 (1826), in B. & M., p. 247.

43. No. 167.11 (1819), in B. & M., p. 345.

44. No. 266.1 (1809), in B. & M., p. 480.

45. No. 248.3 (1819), in B. & M., p. 452.

46. No. 199.4 (1811), in B. & M., p. 402.

47. No. 133.2 (1815), in B. & M., p. 289.

48. Perhaps the Board was actuated by a sophistication that made this magic seem fairly harmless.

49. No. 203.5 (1820), in B. & M., p. 415.

50. See footnote 28, and the text to which it is appended.

51. No. 165.3 (1822), in B. & M., p. 335.

52. No. 267.2 (1779), in B. & M., p. 481.

53. No. 124.1 (1820), in B. & M., p. 282.

54. The Board successfully urged the Emperor not to depart from enacted law in Sun Shou-chih's case, No. 147.2 (1796), in B. & M., p. 298.

55. See also No. 134.1 (1875), in B. & M., p. 290.

56. Morgan v. Commonwealth, 168 Va. 731, 191 S.E. 791 (1937). See also on the crime of "disorderly conduct," Sanford H. Kadish, "The Crisis of Over-criminalization," 374 *Annals of the American Academy of Political and Social Science* (1967), pp. 167, 168.

57. Baker v. Binder, 274 F. Supp. 658 (W. D. Ky. 1967). See also Note, 3 *Harv. Civ. Rts.-Civ. Lib. L. R.* 439 (1968).

58. See, for example, Lanzetta v. New Jersey, 306 U.S. 451, 59 Sup. Ct. 618 (1938) in which the court struck down a statute providing "any person not engaged in any lawful occupation, known to be a member of a gang of two or more persons, who has been convicted at least three times of being a disorderly person or who has been convicted of any crime . . . is declared to be

a gangster" and may be fined not more than $10,000 or imprisoned for not more than twenty years, or both.

59. No. 237.1 (1819), in B. & M., p. 440.

60. No. 82.6 (1831), in B. & M., p. 261.

61. No. 8.1 (1803), in B. & M., p. 218.

62. In No. 263.1 (1826), in B. & M., p. 470, the statute on imperial decrees was used by analogy so that punishment could be raised from the statutory 100 blows to one year of penal servitude. The provincial court's sentence in No. 148.7 (1828), in B. & M. p. 304., reduced the punishment of the scoundrel statute by using it analogically.

63. No. 194.3 (1815), in B. & M., P. 394.

64. In No. 189.1 (1826), in B. & M., p. 385, the principal defendant discovered his younger brother was a robber. He "induced" his two nephews to join him in drowning the robber. These nephews were parties to the murder of their senior relative and under the code such a crime is punishable by decapitation after the assizes. Another article in the code, however, reduced this punishment to life exile when a junior relative's murder of a senior is coerced by another senior. The governor did not read this second statute as authorizing him to exercise clemency. He sentenced the juniors to decapitation but asked the Board of Punishments for permission to add his petition for clemency. The Board agreed that the petition for clemency, citing the second statute, should go forward.

65. No. 147.2 (1796), in B. & M., p. 298.

66. See footnote 53 and the text to which it is appended. Imperial commutation was also given to two robbers who stole from a state temple and were sentenced to immediate decapitation by analogy to the statute which punished stealing objects of imperial worship. No. 134.1 (1817), in B. & M., p. 290.

67. No. 134.2 (1813), in B. & M., p. 291.

68. See, for example, the case cited in footnote 15.

69. No. 166.3 (1813), in B. & M., p. 342.

70. See footnote 8, and the text to which it is appended.

71. No. 169.1 (1826), in B. & M., p. 348.

72. No. 165.2 (1816), in B. & M., p. 334.

73. See B. & M., p. 538, for eleven examples—more than six per cent of our hundred and ninety cases.

74. No. 260.1 (1870), in B. & M., p. 461 (italics mine).

75. No. 87.2 (1825), in B. & M., p. 263.

76. No. 60.5 (1819), in B. & M., p. 258.

77. No. 143.2 (1823), in B. & M., p. 293.

78. Perhaps this is an instance of what Max Weber would call "substantive irrationality," inevitable whenever any legal decision is influenced by concrete factors of a particular case as evaluated upon an ethical, emotional or political basis, rather than by general norms. See *Max Weber on Law and Economy in Society* (ed. and trans. from *Wirtschaft und Gesellschaft*, 2d ed. [1925] by Max Rheinstein and Edward Shils; Cambridge, Mass.: Harvard University Press, 1954), pp. 63-64.

Notes to Chapter 8

1. Joseph Needham, *Science and Civilization in China* (London and New York: Cambridge University Press, 1956) II, 574-575.

2. *Ibid.*

3. A. F. P. Hulsewé, *Remnants of Han Law* (Leiden: E. J. Brill, 1955) 8.1.

4. John Locke, *Two Treatises on Civil Government* (1690) (Peter Laslett, ed.; Cambridge University Press, 1960), Book II, chap. V, sec. 25.

5. Exodus 21: 28.

6. Plato, *Laws* (R. G. Bury ed. and trans.; Cambridge, Mass.: Harvard University Press, 1926), pp. 266-267.

7. T'ung-Tsu Ch'u, *Law and Society in Traditional China* (Cambridge, Mass.: Harvard University Press, 1961), p. 170.

8. Aristotle, *Nichomachean Ethics* (Rackham trans.; Cambridge, Mass.: Harvard University Press, 1949), p. 295.

9. Thomas Aquinas, *Summa Theologica* (Fathers of the English Dominican Province trans.; New York: Benziger Bros., 1947-1948), I, 1012.

10. David Hume, *A Treatise of Human Nature* (1740) ("Everyman's Library," No. 549 [New York: E. P. Dutton & Co. Inc., 1911]), p. 228.

11. Derk Bodde, "Sexual Sympathetic Magic in Han China," *History of Religions* (Eliade, Kitagaha and Long eds.; Chicago: University of Chicago Press, 1964), 3:296.

Pennsylvania Paperbacks

Pennsylvania Paperbacks continued